The 1960s

The 1960s

AN ANNOTATED BIBLIOGRAPHY OF SOCIAL AND POLITICAL MOVEMENTS IN THE UNITED STATES

Rebecca Jackson

Bibliographies and Indexes in American History, Number 24

GREENWOOD PRESS
Westport, Connecticut • London

Library of Congress Cataloging-in-Publication Data

Jackson, Rebecca.
  The 1960s : an annotated bibliography of social and political
movements in the United States / Rebecca Jackson.
    p. cm.—(Bibliographies and indexes in American history,
ISSN 0742-6828 ; no. 24)
  Includes bibliographical references and index.
  ISBN 0-313-27255-7 (alk. paper)
    1. Social movements—United States—History—20th century—
Bibliography. 2. United States—Politics and
government—1961-1963—Bibliography. 3. United States—Politics and
government—1963-1969—Bibliography. 4. United States—Social
conditions—1960-1980—Bibliography. I. Title. II. Series.
Z7164.S66J28   1992
[HN59]   # 26/30649
016.30348′4′0973—dc20   92-24261

British Library Cataloguing in Publication Data is available.

Library of Congress Catalog Card Number: 92-24261
ISBN: 0-313-27255-7
ISSN: 0742-6828

First published in 1992

Greenwood Press, 88 Post Road West, Westport, CT 06881
An imprint of Greenwood Publishing Group, Inc.

Printed in the United States of America

The paper used in this book complies with the
Permanent Paper Standard issued by the National
Information Standards Organization (Z39.48-1984).

10 9 8 7 6 5 4 3 2 1

110423

*In memory of William Van Horn,
who always said I could do it.*

Contents

Acknowledgments

A work of this nature is always completed with the support of many people and institutions. I would like to thank the Interlibrary Loan Departments of both the University of Maryland at College Park Libraries and the George Washington University's Gelman Library, who worked so hard to find the materials I needed. I would also like to thank those people who contributed to the work of locating books and carrying them thither and yon for me: S. Miranda and E. Doepke. Many friends listened to my unending conversations about this book and supported me with their encouragement. I especially appreciate everyone who believed I would complete this book, through all the delays and missed deadlines. Thanks to Greenwood Press for all the extended deadlines and for maintaining their faith in this unknown person who kept saying the book would be in the mail. And a special thanks to Carleton and Leah who gave up their time with me so that I could do this. All their love, support, and assistance made this book possible. However, any omissions or mistakes belong to me alone.

Introduction

The 1960s are considered by many to be the most important decade in the lives of the "baby boomers," that portion of the American population born from the late 1940s to the mid-1950s. For adolescents and young adults during that turbulent era, it was a time of personal upheaval greatly influenced by the political and social movements of the times. Most everyone looks back on the years from 13-25 as being either the best or worst years of one's life, but always the most stimulating. And because there were so many of us moving through these specific years together, our youth influenced the times as never before. This influence was characterized by a rich diversity of movements, activities, and spirits.

The time period covered by this bibliography is 1960 to 1974, an unusual "decade" to be sure. But precisely because the Civil Rights movement and the anti-Vietnam War protests were the defining elements of the era, it became impossible to compile a bibliography on the 1960s without entering the 1970s.

In order to cover a broader spectrum of the era, only books are included in this bibliography. Only by focusing on one particular aspect of the decade could one expect to do justice to the vast quantities of materials that are available on and from this era. Also, the sixties generation was the first to have its activities documented by television. There are a great many documentaries, art films, news footage, and programs available for research. I was unable to include these here, but suggest that this would be fertile ground for another bibliography. The Civil Rights movement has been covered adequately by others, so that only selected titles of books were included here as they related to or were crucial to the development of other movements. So, too, the enormous amount of information available on the Vietnam War and the United States's involvement in it necessitated limiting inclusion to those books which depicted the war at home, the anti-war movement. Also included are books that deal with the human face of the conflict, in addition to some that reflect United States policy and military strategy.

Having delineated certain limitations, mostly due to time and space considerations, it should be noted that only those editions of books that were examined personally by myself are included herein. In doing the research for this bibliography, I discovered that a great deal of material has been lost. If you have a copy of Abbie Hoffman's *Steal This Book* or William Powell's *The Anarchist Cookbook*, hold on to them; they may be the only ones left!

Perhaps the most appropriate descriptor for the era, *Strange Brew,* was coined by Cream, one of the most famous rock groups in the 1960s. Certainly the term "strange brew" reflects the diversity of ingredients that made up the 1960s. The emphasis for this book was to have been just movements of the 1960s: protest movements, religion, music, drugs, hippies and yippies and communes, the arts, and politics. However, I have taken the liberty to enlarge on this theme in some areas. For example, I have included a chapter on politics and economics with some titles I feel are important for understanding the cultural milieu which spawned all these movements.

For most of us, the decade of the sixties spanned more than the ten years of the actual decade. Kennedy's election in 1960 began the spirit of the 1960s. In 1963 Kennedy was shot; that same year saw the beginning of the popularity of the Beatles. Student protests began in 1964, with Berkeley's Free Speech Movement. In 1966-1967, the hippies attracted publicity with their colonies in New York and San Francisco. In 1968, so many things happened that I have devoted a whole chapter to this year. Starting with the Tet offensive in Vietnam, the year moved through riots and demonstrations, including the calamitous Democratic National Convention in Chicago. Woodstock Nation, a half-million youth who formed a peaceful communit for three days in upstate New York and were said to represent the spirit of 1960s youth was born in 1969, but in 1970 at Kent State and Jackson State Universities, youth were being shot during demonstrations, while hundreds of campuses all over the country were shut down because of protests. Even though 1972 saw the reelection of Richard Nixon, the Watergate scandal could not be contained and led directly to his resignation in August of 1974.

The Vietnam war did not end until 1975, which would seem a logical place to end the decade, driven as it was by protest against the war. However, Nixon's resignation sparked more interest and energy from 1960s youth than did the anti-climax of the end of the war. By that time, most of the antiwar activity had died, defused by Nixon's systematic de-escalation of the war over the previous four years. remember the night Nixon resigned: I was living in Albany, New York, downtown, in the midst of a large student population. During the news broadcast, when Nixon announced his resignation, there was a loud roar of cheering voices shouting from th windows of the buildings up and down the street; "Tricky Dick" had finally been unseated.   And after that, the sixties generation started looking forward to the rest of our lives, finishing our educations, getting jobs, becoming the responsible people our parents always wanted us to be.

In order to facilitate research, the book has been divided into eighteen chapters. An overview of each chapter is included in this Introduction.

The first chapter is a review of materials on "The Sixties in General." Many of the books cover the whole history of the sixties, with various cut-off dates. Most of these are very good--some are scholarly, some are personal reminiscences.   Some are collections of writings from authors published in magazines during the decade; these often cover a wide range of subjects.

"The Political, Social, and Economic Milieu" includes those books that are not about movements, but convey information that is necessary to help understand the movements. There are books about the CIA, the American working class, Cointelpro, cities, economics, the police, the upper class, the House Committee on Un-American Activities, U.S. foreign policy, liberalism, violence, the FBI, and crime.

The chapter on the presidencies has been divided into three major subdivisions: "The Charisma of Kennedy," "Johnson's Great Society," and "The Nixon Years." There are a few books that deal with more than one presidency in the decade, sometimes all three. Those books are included at the beginning of the chapter. There is a subdivision within the Kennedy section on "Kennedy's Assassination." Here are many books on the investigation of the assassination and the conspiracy theories that I have been able to include. Unfortunately, much is being published right now on this topic that could not be included. In the Nixon sections there is also a subdivision on "Watergate."

The next two chapters were the most difficult to divide. The first, "Youth," begins with general books about youth in the sixties: idealism, lower-class urban youth, alienation, high school experiences, the generation gap, and legal rights. A subdivision within this chapter is on "Education." In most cases, books about campus protests are not included, even though the titles of some of the books may seem to argue that point. The books in the "Education" section are primarily about the universities and education in general: problems, organizations, futures, and changes.

Campus protests are the subject of the next chapter, "Protest." The first part of this chapter is concerned with protest in general or different types of protest. The subdivision, "Youth," contains the books on campus protest and violence. A separate subdivision within this section deals with the violence on May 4, 1970, at Kent State University. Two other subsections of the chapter include works on other types of protest: "Economics" includes works on subjects such as the grape workers' strike and Spanish-American protests; the Weather Underground is explored in the books in the "Extremists" section.

The political radicals of the 1960s were often compared or contrasted with the counterculture, those whose rebellion was not necessarily reflected in political protest and violence. The chapter "Counterculture" is about this group. In it are books about the hippies, the yippies, the street people, and the flower people. The culture of Haight-Ashbury, a hippie mecca in San Francisco, has its own subsection. So do all the books about the drug culture, including books treating the informational as well as the cultural aspects. A third subsection in the chapter is on "Communal Living, the Concept of Family, and Sexual Freedom," all important aspects of being part of the counterculture, all newly defined by this generation.

Another distinct movement of the generation was the New Left. Although many of the members of the New Left were also part of the campus protesters, many campus protesters were not necessarily part of the New Left. For that reason, and because so many works have been written about the New Left, it was separated from the chapter on protest. At the same time the New Left was feeling its strength, there was reaction to all these movements from the re-emerging strength of the Far Right. Both the New Left and the Far Right are subsections within the chapter "Radicalism, the New Left and the Far Right."

The chapter "The Military and the Vietnam War" is next. Included in the first section are works on the military during the 1960s, books about the draft, some books that look at the Vietnam war from the perspective of U.S. policy, and the U.S. defense program in general. Books on the Vietnam war are included if they dealt mostly with American experiences of the war. These books are included in the subsection "Americans Fighting in Vietnam." The Pentagon Papers are in this section because they dealt with America in Vietnam. Many of the protests of the 1960s focused on the Vietnam war, but not all of them. The great majority of campus protests centered on other issues such as discrimination, free speech, recruitment on campus by the military and by companies producing war equipment, and student roles in campus governance. Therefore, a subsection within the "Military and Vietnam" chapter is entitled "Protest Against the War and the Draft."

Most writers about the decade agree that 1968 was the most critical year in the decade. Many books have been written about this year alone. The chapter "1968: The Pivotal Year" includes those books. Some are general books on all the events of the year: some focus on the election campaign, the Chicago Democratic National Convention, and the Conspiracy Trials that were the result of the Convention.

During the 1960s, there were several movements that were spawned as part of the new consciousness that was developing.   The two most important that are still of concern to us today, are the ecology movement and the Women's Liberation Movement. I have included chapters on each of these movements: "The Environment, Overpopulation, and Consumer Issues," and "The New Enlightenment of Women." The chapters include early writings that illuminate the thinking on these topics and what the important issues were in each of them.

"The Arts" and "Music" were part of the culture in a way that was unique to the decade. So many now famous names were part of this culture: Andy Warhol, the Beatles, the Rolling Stones, Tom Wolfe, Allen Ginsberg, Janis Joplin, Jimi Hendrix, the Doors, among others. The chapter on "The Arts" includes films, painting, happenings, fashion, literature, and theater. Books on censorship are also included in this section, because most censorship of the times seemed to be a backlash "movement" in itself, directed at these new and "dangerous" areas of the arts. The section on "Music" includes books about the diverse musical melange of rock, blues, jazz, and folk, as well as books on particular performers or groups of performers. The famous music festivals are also included in this chapter.

The chapter on "Media" reflects the new direction in communications apparent everywhere in the 1960s. The war in Vietnam and the war at home were covered by all types of media. Television became the primary means by which people got their news as well as their entertainment. The underground press developed to amazing proportions, mainly because counterculture youth did not believe the established press. New Journalism provided a way for creative journalists to diverge from the traditional type of news reporting and become a part of their reportage. And FM radio diverged from the top twenty standard of the AM stations to bring youth the music they wanted to hear.

All of these changes and the prevalent use of drugs forced traditional religions to take a closer look at their ability to serve the needs of youth. In the chapter "Religion and Its Alternatives," there are many books in which the authors reassess the activism of the church and propose means for making the church more relevant. At the same time, the use of psychedelic drugs spawned new interest in old and alternative types of religions. Eastern and native American religions attained some measure of popularity, and there were even some religions developed with the use of drugs as their primary canon. Fundamentalist religions and cults became attractive to many youth, looking for an anchor in a turbulent sea. All of these facets of religion are explored in this chapter.

Youth did a lot of reading during this time and there were certain books that could be found on any good hippie's "bricks and boards" bookcase. Many of these books are included in the chapter "Major Influential Literature." Although traditional education may have been scorned by the majority of protesting youth, their selection of reading material shows a literate background and an interest in learning about themselves and their world.

"The People Who Made the Times" includes biographies of the names on people's lips during and after the decade. It includes political figures, hippies, yippies, and political protesters, writers, comedians, rock stars, leftists, actors, and priests. Some biographies may appear in other chapters, especially the ones on the "Presidencies" and "The Music."

The bibliography concludes with books that were written after the decade and that look back to make some kind of assessment of this turbulent period of time in our nation's history. These retrospectives represent a wide range of attitudes toward this decade of idealism and activism. Some writers conclude that we have carried our commitments with us into our adult lives; others say that the whole spirit of the sixties was a figment of our collective imaginations. Some say we did have an impact on the Vietnam war; others that we did not. It appears that we are still diverse, and we are still having an impact on our society.

Finally, the I would like to mention another limitation of the book. Some people and events have been omitted, in most cases inadvertently, in some cases in the interest of time and space. I have tried to select what I believed was a representative sampling of the major works as well as books showing differing perspectives. Just as the decade was one of great change and exciting promise, the literature of the decade is also different and exciting.

The 1960s in General

1. Adler, Renata. *Toward a Radical Middle: Fourteen Pieces of Reporting and Criticism.* New York: Random House, 1970.
   Reflective articles written between 1964-1967. Adler touches on such subjects as civil rights, hippies around Los Angeles, Sartre and Genet, music, literary criticism, student radicalism, visual arts, and group therapy. Her generation was right before the 1960s youth, so she is usually sympathetic, but often critical.

2. Albert, Judith Clavir, and Stewart Albert. *The Sixties Papers: Documents of the Rebellious Decade.* New York: Praeger Publishers, 1985.
   Documents issued by people and organizations during the 1960s. Includes "Howl," the Port Huron Statement, SNCC Position Paper: Women in the Movement, the speeches of Martin Luther King, Weathermen papers, and others.

3. Atcheson, Richard. *What the Hell Are They Trying to Prove Martha? A Wary Convert's Report on the New Self-Expression in America Today.* New York: John Day, 1970.
   Articles on America in the 1960s. Includes pieces on Reston, Virginia; Old Town Chicago; Bennington College; Atlantic City; Esalen; Mendocino, California; nudist colonies; theater; nudity in the theater; *I Am Curious (Yellow)*; Yoko Ono; *Oh! Calcutta!*; San Francisco; and Monhegan Island. Written in New Journalistic style.

4. Ball, George. *The Past Has Another Pattern.* New York: W.W. Norton, 1982.
   Memoirs of a man who worked as an Undersecretary of State and acting Secretary. His work with the Department of State began in 1957 and he resigned in 1970. He gives an insider's point of view on the Kennedy years, the Johnson years, the Cuban Missile Crisis, Vietnam, and Nixon.

5. Berger, Arthur Asa. *Pop Culture.* Dayton, OH: Pflaum Press, 1973.
   Berger looks at a number of aspects of '60s and '70s popular culture--comics, sports, TV, advertising, newspapers, toys, appliances, food, cars, stereotypes--in an effort to see how they affected the psychology and social order of U.S. culture.

6. Boorstin, Daniel J. *The Americans: The Democratic Experience.* New York: Random House, 1973.
   From the end of the Civil War to 1961, Boorstin recounts the history of the U.S., giving insights into what may have led to the 1960s activism and strife.

7. Boyd, Malcolm. *My Fellow Americans.* New York: Holt, Rinehart & Winston, 1970.
   New Journalism essays on Hugh Hefner, Chicanos in Colorado. a west coast urban commune, and Vietnam veterans--all controversial at the time.

8. Braden, William.   *The Age of Aquarius.* Chicago: Quadrangle Books, 1970.
   Subtitled "Technology and the Cultural Revolution." This is a discussion of C.P Snow's Two Cultures (science and the humanities) in our country as factors in the civil rights movement, the New Left, the confusion of sexual roles, the drug culture, the interest in Eastern religions, the interest in astrology, the emphasis on the environment. All of these Braden relates to the questions of identity.

9. Buchwald, Art. *The Establishment Is Alive and Well in Washington.* Greenwich, CT: Fawcett-Crest, 1969.
   A collection of Buchwald's humorous columns on all types of subjects during the 1960s, e.g., protesters, the Russians, football, the U.S.S. Pueblo incident, the draft, the military, women's liberation, and Nixon's 1968 campaign.

10. Buckley, William F., Jr. *Execution Eve--And Other Contemporary Ballads.* New York: G.P. Putnam's, 1975.
    A series of articles from one of America's most famous conservatives written during the early 1970s, but touching on many 1960s issues-- Nixon, Watergate, college students, marijuana, sexism, and Russia.

11. ---. *The Jeweler's Eye.* New York: G.P. Putnam's, 1968.
    A collection of previously printed articles written since 1962 on the various aspects of the fifties and sixties.

12. Burner, David, Robert Marcus, and Thomas West. *A Giant's Strength: America in the Sixties.* New York: Holt, Rinehart & Winston, 1971.
    A short history of the 1960s which tries to include everything--music, drugs, philosophy, student unrest. Many photos included.

13. Center for the Study of Democratic Institutions. *The Establishment and All That: A Collection of Major Articles Selected from the "Center Magazine" Since Its Beginning in the Fall of 1967.* Santa Barbara, CA: The Center, 1970.
    A consideration of the major issues of the day--education, poverty, change, black and white revolutionaries. The Center existed to explore

democratic institutions and the writers of these essays explore the issues in the context of a democratic environment.

14. Chafe, William H. *The Unfinished Journey.* New York: Oxford UP, 1986.
    The author looks at post-WWII society as a new society--women, the family, workers, and minorities. He argues that American social reform had thrived until 1968 and that since 1968, America has been in an era of conservatism.

15. Chalmers, David. *And the Crooked Places Made Straight.* Baltimore: Johns Hopkins UP, 1991.
    Chalmers has constructed an excellent account of the 1960s. He also offers an assessment of the times.

16. Colby, Vineta, ed.. *American Culture in the Sixties.* New York: H.W. Wilson, 1964.
    American culture burgeoned in the 1960s mostly based on an economic boom. This book is a collection of essays by people such as Alvin Toffler, John F. Kennedy, Stanley Kunitz, and Alan Pryce-Jones, that examine and analyze some of the elements of this cultural boom, i.e., theater, music, dance, mass culture, and mass communications. A very early look at the phenomenon.

17. Colebrook, Joan. *Innocents of the West: Travels Through the Sixties.* New York: Basic Books, 1979.
    A journal of this writer that spans the time from November, 1964, to the end of 1969. International in scope.

18. Davis, Richard, and Jeff Stone. *Treasures of the Aquarians.* New York: Penguin Books, 1985.
    A spoof of an exhibit of artifacts from Berkeley in the 1960s uncovered at an archeological dig centuries later. Clever and humorous.

19. Dickstein, Morris. *Gates of Eden: American Culture in the Sixties.* New York: Basic Books, 1977. New York: Penguin Books, 1989.
    Dickstein has written a very important cultural history and criticism of the sixties. The author says that the book is not political, and yet it was hard to separate culture from politics at the time, and Dickstein also points to parallels. He uses the arts--music, poetry, fiction, and nonfiction--to make his history. This source is cited in almost every serious text on the sixties. The 1989 reprint includes a new preface by the author.

20. Didion, Joan. *Slouching Towards Bethlehem.* New York: Simon & Schuster, 1979.
    Pieces written 1965-1967 on a myriad of topics--a wife murdering her husband, John Wayne, a school for nonviolence run by Joan Baez, Communist Michael Laski, Howard Hughes, the Center for the Study of Democratic Institutions, Las Vegas weddings, the Haight, writing, self

respect, Hollywood, morality, families, East Coast/West Coast, Hawaii, Alcatraz, Newport, RI, Mexico, Los Angeles, and New York. Taken together, these pieces present a microcosm of American culture in the 1960s.

21. Drake, Nicholas, ed. *The Sixties: A Decade in Vogue.* New York: Prentice Hall, [n.d.].
    The sixties as seen in *Vogue* by some of the most important photographers of the time. Includes fashion, art, entertainment, politics, and society.

22. Ducovny, Amram M. *The Establishment Dictionary: From Agnew to Zsa Zsa.* New York: Ballantine Books, 1971.
    A humorous defining of 1960s personalities. Ducovny defines such names as Berrigan, Daley, Friedan, Johnson, Mailer, Reagan, Warhol, and Ziegler.

23. Dunne, John Gregory. *Quintana and Friends.* E.P. Dutton, 1978.
    A collection of New Journalism-type pieces written during the 1960s and 1970s on the stresses of the 1960s, Hollywood, and the differences between the East and the West.

24. Edelstein, Andrew J. *Pop Sixties: A Personal and Irreverent Guide.* New York: World Almanac Publications, 1985.
    A survey of popular culture in the 1960s--music, television, films, fads and fashions, and books and magazines.

25. Freeman, Jo, ed. *Social Movements of the Sixties and Seventies.* New York: Longman, 1983.
    A collection of essays which analyze social movements. Social movement is defined and the various specific movements analyzed include California farmworkers, the disabled, draft resistance, tenants, anti-nuclear activists, SDS and Weatherman, civil rights, and new religions.

26. Gardner, John W. *No Easy Victories.* New York: Harper & Row, Publishers, 1968.
    Excerpts from speeches and articles that speak about the state of American society. Good for getting glimpses of what was happening and reactions to events and ideas.

27. Gitlin, Todd. *The Sixties: Years of Hope, Days of Rage.* New York: Bantam Books, 1987.
    A comprehensive history of the era, centering on the political student movement. A later perspective than *Coming Apart* (O'Neill), with not as much scholarly research. However, told by one who was a part of the movement.

28. Gleeson, Patrick, ed. *America Changing* . . . . Columbus, OH: Merrill
    Publishing, 1968.
    Essays which interpret critical conditions of the 1960s, i.e., youth, the
    city, the new culture, students and politics, black power, and technology.
    Writers include Bruno Bettelheim, Marshall McLuhan, Paul Goodman,
    Mario Savio, Hannah Arendt, and many others.

29. Goldstein, Richard. *Reporting the Counterculture.* Boston: Unwin Hyman,
    1989.
    Collection of Goldstein's New Journalism pieces on the 1960s. Since he
    wrote quite a bit of music criticism, there is one large section on music,
    but he also covers such subjects as LSD, the Maharishi, the Haight,
    Canadian hippies, Hollywood, King in Chicago, Columbia, the
    Democratic convention in Chicago, and the trial of Angela Davis.

30. Golembiewski, Robert T., Charles S. Bullock III, and Harrell R. Rodgers, Jr.
    The New Politics: Polarization or Utopia? New York: McGraw-Hill,
    1970.
    An analysis of the challenges to the U.S. political institutions and
    traditions, including hippies, drugs, the draft protesters, education,
    poverty, blacks, and the police.

31. Goodman, Paul, ed. *Seeds of Liberation.* New York: George Braziller, 1964.
    Articles from *Liberation* magazine from 1956 - 1964. Issues of the 1960s
    were just beginning to be heard--nonviolence, education, technology,
    and others. Writers include Camus, A.J. Muste, Bertrand Russell, David
    Dellinger, Nelson Mandela, Martin Luther King, Jr., Theodore Roszak
    and others.

32. Goodwin, Richard N. *Remembering America: A Voice from the Sixties.*
    New York: Harper & Row, Publishers , 1988.
    Memoirs of the man who served under Kennedy as special council,
    under Johnson, and who worked for the campaigns of Robert Kennedy
    and Eugene McCarthy. He says this book is an exhortation to bring back
    the spirit of the 1960s.

33. Greenfield, Jeff. *No Peace, No Place: Excavations Along the Generational
    Fault.* Garden City, NY: Doubleday, 1973.
    An examination of the influences from the 1950s that made the 1960s
    explode. The author looks at rock music, television, and campus life.

34. Gross, Bertram M., ed. *A Great Society?* New York: Basic Books, 1968.
    A collection of essays which examine the idea of "the Great Society."
    Writers include Herbert Marcuse, Hans J. Morgenthau, Daniel Bell,
    Kenneth Boulding, Alvin Toffler, and several others.

35. Harris, David. *Dreams Die Hard.* New York: St. Martin's Press, 1982.
    A memoir of three activists' experiences of the sixties: Allard
    Lowenstein, Dennis Sweeney, and the author. Lowenstein began the

"dump Johnson" movement and was a fairly famous social change agent. Sweeney, one of Lowenstein's students and converts, shot Lowenstein to death in 1980.

36. Haskins, James, and Kathleen Benson. *The 60s Reader*. New York: Viking Press, 1988.
    A very readable history of the 1960s, touching on civil rights, music, the peace movement, religious movements, drugs, and the legacies of the 1960s.

37. Hayes, Harold, ed. *Smiling Through the Apocalypse: Esquire's History of the Sixties*. New York: Crown Publishers, 1987.
    A collection of essays from various famous and not-so-famous writers that were published in *Esquire* during the 1960s. Most of them reflect the New Journalistic style popular at the time.

38. Heath, Jim F. *Decade of Disillusionment: The Kennedy-Johnson Years*. Bloomington: Indiana UP, 1975.
    Heath interprets the 1960s as a time which seemed to offer a lot of promise, but was in reality a decade when Americans were struggling to escape from their own "Armageddon." He looks at interactions among the leaders of the period and notes the immense amount of government materials accumulated that were closed to society.

39. Hodgson, Godfrey. *America In Our Time*. New York: Doubleday, 1976.
    A history of the 1960s, from Kennedy through Nixon.

40. Horowitz, Irving Louis. *Ideology and Utopia in the United States, 1956-1976*. New York: Oxford UP, 1977.
    A collection of essays on the American scene during these two decades. Horowitz analyzes the Robert Kennedy assassination, Johnson's terms in office, Mao Tse-Tung's importance, Nixon and Watergate, liberalism, radicalism, the Pentagon Papers, war as a game, and the anti-war movement.

41. Howard, Gerald, ed. *The Sixties: The Art, Politics, and Media of Our Most Explosive Decade*. New York: Washington Square Press, 1982.
    Readings selected to give the reader a total sense of the 1960s. Readings are divided into four groups: the politicization of culture; some new sensibilities; the exploding arts; and messages from the media. Writers selected include Paul Goodman, Herbert Marcuse, Eldridge Cleaver, Norman Mailer, Tom Wolfe, R.D. Laing, Susan Sontag, Pauline Kael, Albert Goldman, Marshall McLuhan, and many others.

42. Jaffe, Harold, and John Tytell. *The American Experience: A Radical Reader*. New York: Harper & Row, Publishers, 1970.
    A selection of readings from sixties writers covering black consciousness, student activists, the counterculture, the arts, and literature.

43. Jones, Landon Y. *Great Expectations: America and the Baby Boom Generation.* New York: Coward-McCann, 1980.
    The baby boom generation are those people born between 1946 and 1964. The youth of the 1960s were a part of this generation. In every stage of their lives they have had a significant impact because of their great numbers. Jones analyzes this group and the results of its dominance, both in the past and as they enter middle-age and older. An interesting look at the generation, but some of the predictions have already proven wrong.

44. Joseph, Peter. *Good Times: An Oral History of America in the Sixties.* New York: Charterhouse, 1973.
    Like *Working* by Studs Turkel, this is a history of the sixties told in vignettes by the people who lived through the times. Some of the people are famous; some are not.

45. Katzman, Allen, ed. *Our Time: An Anthology of Interviews from the East Village Other.* New York: Dial Press, 1972.
    Interviews with such sixties people as Timothy Leary, Alan Watts, Kate Millett, Andy Stapp, Abbie and Anita Hoffman, Jerry Rubin, and many others to try to show what was happening in 1960s life.

46. Kennedy, Robert F. *To Seek a Newer World.* Garden City, NY: Doubleday, 1967.
    Speeches and writings from Kennedy while in the Senate from 1965 on. Subjects include youth, urban crisis, Alliance for Progress, nuclear control, and Vietnam.

47. Kopkind, Andrew. *America: The Mixed Curse.* New York: Penguin Books, 1969.
    Magazine articles written during the 1960s covering many of the crises, acts of resistance, and key players i.e., racial riots, the New Left, Wallace, Reagan, McCarthy, Kennedy, Nixon, the Pueblo, the Gulf of Tonkin, the Democratic national convention of 1968, and others.

48. Kopkind, Andrew, and James Ridgeway, eds. *Decade of Crisis: America in the '60s.* New York: World Publishing, 1972.
    All articles from the weekly newspaper *Hard Times* during the last two years of the 1960s. The articles touch on the crises in politics, the crises of resources, the crisis of the military, the crises of imperialism, and different crises of consciousness.

49. Kostelanetz, Richard, ed. *Beyond Left and Right: Radical Thought for Our Times.* New York: William Morrow, 1968.
    A collection of essays dealing with the future. It was Kostelanetz's belief that because of technology, life would be so different that there would have to be new radical thought, neither left nor right, to make the most of society.

50. Leonard, George. *Walking on the Edge of the World*. Boston: Houghton Mifflin, 1988.
    Leonard, a writer for *Look* magazine in the 1960s, covered many stories on what was happening at the time. He wrote about youth's revolt, civil rights, and education. He got very involved with the human potential movement, especially Esalen. This book is his memoirs, which not only contain his recollections about outside events, but also his own inner journey, as one who is still active in the human development movement.

51. Leuchtenburg, William. *A Troubled Feast: America Since 1945*. Boston: Little, Brown, 1973.
    A short history up to 1973. The "troubled" in the title refers to the troubles of assassinations, Asian war, violence, and social ills. The "feast" refers to the abundance of the times. Photos included.

52. Levitas, Michael. *America in Crisis*. New York: Holt, Rinehart & Winston, 1969.
    A photojournalistic overview of America in the 1960s. The crisis is the clash between the American dream of success and equality and the realities of American life.

53. McGovern, George. *A Time of War/A Time of Peace*. New York: Random House, 1968.
    Mostly speeches and articles from 1963 to 1967 on issues of the times--American security, the arms race, an end to the draft, foreign relations in Cuba, China, and Vietnam--from McGovern's first years in the Senate.

54. McReynolds, David. *We Have Been Invaded by the 21st Century*. New York: Praeger Publishers, 1970.
    Essays on issues of the 1960s--racism, student rebellion, mores, and the invasion of technology.

55. Manchester, William. *The Glory and the Dream: A Narrative History of America, 1932-1972*. Boston: Little, Brown, 1974.
    This is a fascinating history which, in the sections on the sixties, covers JFK/LBJ, Spock, Nader, and Nixon, as well as the events of the period. Very comprehensive.

56. Marías, Julián. *America in the Fifties and Sixties: Julián Marías on the United States*. Translated by Blanche De Puy and Harold C. Raby. University Park, PA: Pennsylvania State UP, 1972.
    Commentary from a Spanish intellectual on how he saw the U.S. In the sixties section, he touches on the blacks, the North and the South, Vietnam, literature, the hippies, the suburbs, American women, and the university.

57. Matusow, Allen J. *The Unraveling of America: A History of Liberalism in the 1960s.* New York: Harper & Row, Publishers, 1984.
    A lengthy assessment of the liberal years, the Kennedy-Johnson years in the U.S. Matusow looks at domestic programs, like The War on Poverty, and finds that on the whole these years failed to significantly enrich the lives of the people of the U.S.

58. Mead, Margaret. *Culture and Commitment.* New York: Doubleday, 1970.
    Although this book does not directly address the 1960s culture, Mead offers an interesting explanation of the changes in culture and commitment that may have resulted in the 1960s culture.

59. Meltzer, Richard. *Gulcher: Post-Rock Cultural Pluralism in America (1649-1993).* New York: Citadel Press, 1990.
    Meltzer was an observer of contemporary culture with a talent for writing. In this book he covers a diverse array of pop topics--boxing, monster movies, wallets, prophylactics, bowling, cigarette packs--leaving the reader with a unique view of some of the icons of the 1960s.

60. Morrison, Joan, and Robert K. Morrison. *From Camelot to Kent State: The Sixties Experience in the Words of Those Who Lived It.* New York: Random House-Times Books, 1987.
    Interviews with over 55 people who lived or were growing up in the 1960s and in some way participated in the activities. Included are interviews with William Sloan Coffin, Philip Berrigan, Elizabeth McAlister, Jack Weinberg, Jerry Rubin, Abbie Hoffman, Carl Oglesby, Eldridge Cleaver, Jeff Jones, and Bill Ayres.

61. Mungo, Raymond. *Total Loss Farm: A Year in the Life.* New York: E.P. Dutton, 1970.
    During this year Mungo, the founder of Liberation News Service (a counter-UPI), travelled with friends all over the country and in Europe. During his travels, he reflects on his experiences in the 1960s.

62. Newfield, Jack. *Bread and Roses Too.* New York: E.P. Dutton, 1971.
    A collection of newspaper pieces, mostly for *The Village Voice*, on such 1960s issues as the southern civil rights movement, the New Left, the counterculture, Vietnam, the media, prisons, and some of the famous names of the times.

63. O'Brien, Geoffrey. *Dream Time: Chapters from the Sixties.* New York: Viking Press, 1988.
    An interior view of the 1960s, told as more of a dreamscape from one person's inner view of the era than as an analytical history of the period.

64. Obst, Lynda R., ed. *The Sixties: The Decade Remembered Now, By the People Who Lived It Then.* New York: Rolling Stone Press, 1976.

> A year-by-year grouping of essays and photographs of individual aspects --people, movements, events--of the sixties. Each year begins with a calendar of events for that particular year.

65. O'Neil, Doric C., ed. *Life in the '60s.* Boston: Little, Brown, 1989.
    A photohistory of the 1960s taken from *Life* magazine's photo collection, including civil rights, the Kennedy years, music, protest, fads and fashions, space exploration, 1968, and Vietnam.

66. O'Neill, William L., ed. *American Society Since 1945.* Chicago: Quadrangle Books, 1969.
    A collection of essays by such writers as Joan Didion, Hunter Thompson, Vance Packard, and Thomas Pynchon on various aspects of American culture--civil rights, the right and the left, students, religion, and cults--which span the 1950s and 1960s.

67. ---. *Coming Apart: An Informal History of America in the 1960's.* New York: Quadrangle Books, 1969.
    Maybe informal, but certainly comprehensive. Covers all aspects of the 1960s, including Ralph Nader, space exploration, sports, Hell's Angels, religion, and organized medicine. One of the first histories written. Unfortunately, it ended before the events of 1970 and Watergate.

68. Quinn, Edward and Paul J. Dolan, eds. *The Sense of the Sixties.* New York: Free Press, 1968.
    Readings on a broad range of topics important in the 1960s. Writers include Paul Goodman, Staughton Lynd, John F. Kennedy, Tom Wicker, Tom Wolfe, Sargent Shriver, Jimmy Breslin, John Updike, Robert Lowell, John Barth, Marshall McLuhan, and many others.

69. Editors of Ramparts. *Conversations with the New Reality: Readings in the Cultural Revolution.* San Francisco: Canfield Press, 1971.
    A selection of essays which discuss various aspects of the cultural revolution of the 1960s, e.g., communes, deserters, hippies, drugs, rock music and festivals, the underground press, television. Writers include Paul Goodman, Jerry Rubin, Ralph Gleason, and Andrew Kopkind.

70. Sayre, Nora. *Sixties Going on Seventies.* New York: Arbor House, 1973.
    A compilation of journalism pieces from this writer spanning the years between 1965 and 1972. She tries to capture the spirit of those transitional years with such topics as the Chicago Democratic Convention, Watts, Black Panthers, Frank Rizzo and Philadelphia, the John Birch Society, John Lindsay, the New York blackout of 1965, Ayn Rand, George Wallace, Harlem, theater, and movies.

71. Sayres, Sohnya, et al. *The 60's Without Apology.* Minneapolis: U of Minnesota P, 1984.
    A collection of essays, some very philosophical, on movements of the 1960s, both in the U.S. and internationally.

72. Shachtman, Tom. *Decade of Shocks: Dallas to Watergate, 1963 - 1974.* New York: Poseidon Press, 1983.
    An account of some of the crucial periods during the 1960s and an analysis of how that decade changed the American consciousness. Photos included.

73. Slater, Philip E. *The Pursuit of Loneliness: American Culture at the Breaking Point.* Boston: Beacon Press, 1976.
    The first edition was published in 1970, and it contained more of the stresses of the 1960s--university revolt, the counterculture, political confrontations. In both editions, Slater was examining the forces that he said were "unraveling" American society. The Vietnam war was one force he left in the 1976 edition.

74. Steinem, Gloria. *Outrageous Acts and Everyday Rebellions.* New York: Holt, Rinehart & Winston, 1983.
    A collection of Steinem's writings, starting with her first 1962 article on being a Playboy bunny and including many of her feminist articles.

75. Stent, Gunther S. *The Coming of the Golden Age: A View of the End of Progress.* Garden City, NY: Natural History Press, 1969.
    By analyzing genetics, art, philosophy, science, and Polynesia, Stent concludes that man in the 1960s was entering a golden age, rather than an end to the Iron Age and further degeneration.

76. Stern, Jane and Michael. *Sixties People.* New York: Alfred A. Knopf, 1990.
    The Sterns categorize the different cultures of sixties people and describe, at times humorously, each type. They include perky girls, playboys, young vulgarians, surfers and party animals, folkniks, British imitators, hippies, rebels, and Mr. & Mrs. Average. Photos included.

77. Stone, I.F. *In a Time of Torment.* New York: Random House-Vintage Books, 1967.
    Essays from Stone's *Weekly*, 1962-1967. Subjects include John Kennedy, the Missile Crisis, Johnson, race relations, Vietnam, Fulbright, young activists, the press, China, and Latin America.

78. ---. *Polemics and Prophecies, 1967-1970.* Boston: Little, Brown, 1970.
    Selections from Stone's *Weekly* from 1967-1970. The main topics are Nixon, the war, the Middle East, and the campus rebels.

79. Thompson, Hunter S. *Fear and Loathing in Las Vegas: A Savage Journey to the Heart of the American Dream.* New York: Random House, 1971.
    Thompson did New Journalism one step further, creating what he called Gonzo journalism. This is his most famous book of Gonzo journalism, chronicling his own experiences in the 1960s world of sex and drugs and rock 'n' roll.

80. ---. *The Great Shark Hunt: Strange Tales from a Strange Time.* New York: Fawcett Popular Library, 1979.
    A gathering of Thompson's writings, many from the 1960s. These writings represent Gonzo at its best.

81. Thompson, William Irwin. *At the Edge of History.* New York: Harper & Row, Publishers, 1971.
    A description of how the imagination of history affects society, especially the revolutionary behavior of 1960s America.

82. Toffler, Alvin. *Future Shock.* New York: Random House, 1970.
    Explores the effects of the rapid rate of change in our society. Unless people are prepared to deal with these changes, there will be "massive adaptational breakdown." "Future shock" refers to this breakdown caused by too much change. Toffler posits a broad theory to help cope with these changes.

83. Trilling, Diana. *We Must March My Darlings: A Critical Decade.* New York: Harcourt Brace Jovanovich, 1977.
    A collection of essays written 1965-1975 on such subjects as John F. Kennedy's death, Dr. Leary, campus rebellion, homosexuality, *Easy Rider*, women's liberation, modern culture, and marriage.

84. Viorst, Milton. *Fire in the Streets: America in the 1960's.* New York: Simon & Schuster, 1979.
    A good history of the 1960s, beginning with the civil rights struggle and ending with Kent State and the spring of 1970. Focuses on many people important to the decade so that the reader gets to know people as well as events. More political than social.

85. Von Hoffman, Nicholas. *Left at the Post.* Chicago: Quadrangle Books, 1970.
    A collection of von Hoffman's columns from the *Washington Post* touching on all aspects of the culture of the 1960s and offering a left of center opinion of the country's condition.

86. Wallechinsky, David. *Midterm Report: The Class of '65 Chronicles an American Generation.* New York: Viking Press, 1986.
    Wallechinsky gathered stories of people all over the country who graduated from high school in 1965. He chose to publish stories from a diverse array of people, both those radically affected by the events of the '60s, and those whose lives were apparently untouched by those events.

87. Warhol, Andy and Pat Hackett. *Popism: The Warhol '60s.* New York: Harcourt Brace Jovanovich, 1980.
    Warhol tells his story of the 1960s culture as he saw it. He looks at painting, movies, fashion, music, and the people who made it all happen. Photos included.

88. Wolfe, Tom. *The Electric Kool-Aid Acid Test; The Kandy-Kolored Tangerine-Flake Streamline Baby; and Radical Chic & Mau-Mauing the Flak Catchers.* New York: Quality Press, 1990.
These are Wolfe's most famous 1960s books, chronicling the decade in his unique New Journalism style. The first book is an account of Ken Kesey's Merry Pranksters. The last two include many essays on all aspects of American culture.

89. ---. *The Purple Decades: A Reader.* New York: Berkley Publishing, 1982.
A collection of Wolfe's writings from the 1960s and 1970s. Using his humorous New Journalism style and his instinct for selecting the most appropriate cultural symbols, Wolfe has been one of the best writers to capture the flavor of the period.

90. Wright, Lawrence. *In the New World: Growing Up With America From the Sixties to the Eighties.* New York: Random House, 1987.
An autobiography of Wright taking the reader from the assassination of Kennedy, through the Vietnam war, the sexual revolution, civil rights, and Watergate to the emergence of Reagan. Wright is a journalist who grew up in Texas and his story is undoubtedly representative of his generation

91. Zahler, Kathy A. and Diane Zahler. *Test Your Countercultural Literacy.* New York: Simon & Schuster-Arco, 1989.
A quiz book on the culture of the sixties covering the roots of the counterculture, protest, civil rights, geography, art and the media, music, lifestyles, symbols, and literature. Photos and graphics included.

The Political, Social
and Economic Milieu

92. Agee, Philip. *Inside the Company: CIA Diary*. Baltimore: Penguin Books, 1975.
    Agee served in the CIA for ten years, during most of the 1960s. He was stationed in Ecuador, Uruguay, and France. During his 10-year stint, he became disillusioned with the CIA and the United States. In this diary, he reveals everything about the CIA and its activities that he was familiar with.

93. Arendt, Hannah. *Crises of the Republic: Lying in Politics, Civil Disobedience, On Violence, Thoughts on Politics and Revolution*. New York: Harcourt Brace Jovanovich, 1972.
    Short works on the Pentagon Papers, on student protesters, on revolution, and on what Arendt sees as an increasing turn to violence in solving social problems. She speaks specifically of the New Left, black power, and the Third World.

94. Aronowitz, Stanley. *False Promises: The Shaping of American Working Class Consciousness*. New York: McGraw-Hill, 1973.
    An analysis of the working class in that period and its relation to society and radical movements.

95. Attewell, Paul A. *Radical Political Economy Since the Sixties: A Sociology of Knowledge Analysis*. New Brunswick, NJ: Rutgers UP, 1984.
    An examination of the effects of the 1960s on what became a new political economy of the 1970s.

96. Baker, Bobby, with Larry L. King. *Wheeling and Dealing: Confessions of a Capitol Hill Operator*. New York: W.W. Norton, 1978.
    This story of capitol hill scandal only serves to show that Watergate really was not the beginning--that corruption had flourished in the federal government at least in the 1950s and 1960s.

97. Barnet, Richard J. *Intervention and Revolution: The United States in the Third World*. New York: World Publishing, 1968.
    Barnet says he is not giving theories as to why the U.S. chooses to become involved in Third World countries' insurgencies. Instead, he has written about U.S. practices in these areas.

98. Berrigan, Philip. *A Punishment for Peace*. New York: Macmillan Publishing, 1969.
    A discussion of American imperialism as it relates to industrialism. Berrigan argues that this industrialism leads to aggression and poverty for its victims, both blacks and Vietnamese, and that government, industry, and even the Church work together to survive and prosper under this system.

99. Blackstock, Nelson. *Cointelpro: The FBI's Secret War on Political Freedom*. New York: Anchor Foundation-Pathfinder Press, 1988.
    A short, in-depth look at Cointelpro, the FBI's counterintelligence program to undermine and disrupt New Left activities. Documents are included.

100. Bohlen, Charles E. *Witness to History, 1929-1969*. New York: W.W. Norton, 1973.
    An ambassador to the U.S.S.R. recounts his experiences of American-Soviet relations during the U-2 incident, the Cuban missile crisis, and all through the 1960s.

101. Bookchin, Murray. *Limits of the City*. New York: Harper & Row, Publishers, 1974.
    A Marxist history of the development of the city. The author argues that today's metropolises are a function of and also influence the society; the metropolis is the negation of city life.

102. ---. *Post-Scarcity Anarchism*. Berkeley: Ramparts Press, 1971.
    Bookchin foresaw the subcultures that emerged in the 1960s as harbingers of the utopian society that would be a result of the social revolution which would eliminate need, hierarchy, and capitalism.

103. Brenton, Myron. *The Privacy Invaders*. Greenwich, CT: Fawcett-Crest, 1964.
    An examination of the ways private life was being invaded by others in the marketplace, in the workplace, and around the community.

104. Brooks, John. *The Go-Go Years*. New York: Weybright & Talley, 1973.
    A look at the happenings on Wall Street during the 1960s.

105. Colfax, J. David, and Jack L. Roach, eds. *Radical Sociology*. New York: Basic Books, 1971.
    Papers on radical sociology, a non-clinical, participatory sociology. It demands that sociologists go out and organize, interpret, and build alternative societies.

106. Cowan, Paul. *The Making of an Un-American: A Dialogue with Experience*. New York: Viking Press, 1967.
    A personal account of the writer's disillusionment with the U.S., his time in the Peace Corps in the early 1960s, and the problems with American attitudes toward other countries and people.

107. ---, et al. *State Secrets: Police Surveillance in America.* New York: Holt, Rinehart & Winston, 1974.
      Surveillance and political repression in the 1960s. Includes documents on the operations of the FBI.

108. Cray, Ed. *The Big Blue Line: Police Power vs. Human Rights.* New York: Coward-McCann, 1967.
      A study of police malpractice in cities in the United States from 1960 to 1966.

109. Deutsch, Stephen E., and John Howard, eds. *Where It's At: Radical Perspectives in Sociology.* New York: Harper & Row, Publishers, 1970.
      A collection of readings selected to help define radical sociology. Such areas as the distribution of power, the distribution of wealth, educational opportunities, work opportunities, the welfare system, bureaucracy, and the third world are examined.

110. Domhoff, G. William. *Who Rules America?* Englewood Cliffs, NJ: Prentice Hall, 1967.
      A sociological study analyzing the upper class in America and the way its members rule the country.

111. Drucker, Peter F. *Men, Ideas and Politics.* New York: Harper & Row, Publishers, 1971.
      Essays on such diverse topics as the new markets of the 1960s, Kierkegaard, Henry Ford, the Japanese economics, and the '60s "Romantic Generation." The author says they all share the common theme of "political (or social) ecology" in which "society, polity, and economy are a genuine environment . . . in which everything relates to everything else and in which men, ideas, and institutions must always be seen together . . . to be understood."

112. Easterlin, Richard A. *Population, Labor Force, and Long Swings in Economic Growth: The American Experience.* New York: Columbia UP (for National Bureau of Economic Research), 1968.
      Many of these statistics are from before the 1960s, but the book may be of interest because of its analysis of the fertility decline in the '60s and its projections for labor force growth.

113. Esfandiary, F.M. *Optimism One: The Emerging Radicalism.* New York: W.W. Norton, 1970.
      Arguments against the ideas that modern man is alienated and cut off from nature. Esfendiary felt that urban, technological man is much more free to be individualistic and humanistic.

114. Feldman, Saul D., and Gerald W. Theilbar, eds. *Life Styles: Diversity in American Society.* Boston: Little, Brown, 1972.

Essays that touch on various aspects of American life, e.g., consumerism, civil religion, violence, Canadian relations, class systems, sex roles, the family, and race and ethnicity.

115. Flaherty, Joe. *Managing Mailer.* New York: Coward-McCann, 1969.
Flaherty managed Norman Mailer's campaign for mayor of New York City on a ticket with Jimmy Breslin in 1969. This book chronicles that somewhat crazy campaign.

116. *Fortune* editors. *America in the Sixties: The Economy and the Society.* New York: Harper & Row, Publishers, 1960.
Predictions for what the 1960s would be like economically. Amazingly, many of the predictions were right on target, even without the foresight of the social and political upheavals to come.

117. Gavin, James M. in collaboration with Arthur T. Hadley. *Crisis Now.* New York: Random House, 1968.
Gavin saw two crises--the Vietnam war and the disintegration of United States cities--as related to what he calls "the scientific revolution." This book explains these crises and offer suggestions for solving them.

118. Gettleman, Marvin E., and David Mermelstein, eds. *The Failure of American Liberalism After the Great Society.* New York: Random House, 1967.
A collection of readings on the crises facing American society in the 1960s and liberalism's failure to deal with them. Writers included Lyndon Johnson, Sargent Shriver, Bayard Rustin, Tom Hayden, and Eldridge Cleaver.

119. Goodman, Walter. *The Committee: The Extraordinary Career of the House Committee on Un-American Activities.* New York: Farrar, Straus & Giroux, 1968.
A history of HUAC up to 1966.

120. Halperin, Morton H., et al. *The Lawless State: The Crimes of the U.S. Intelligence Agencies.* New York: Penguin Books, 1976.
Descriptions of the ways in which the CIA and FBI were secretly involved in matters such as Allende's overthrow in Chile, the secret war in Laos, the attempted overthrow of Castro, the use of drugs and behavior modification, the SCLC and Martin Luther King, Jr., and the Vietnam war protesters.

121. Houghton, Neal D., ed. *Struggle Against History: U.S. Foreign Policy in an Age of Revolution.* New York: Washington Square Press, 1968.
A collection of essays on American foreign policy in the 1960s, including colonialism, the Cold War, mass media, the Cuban revolution, Latin America, Asia, and the Vietnam war.

122. Kaufman, Arnold S. *The Radical Liberal: The New Politics: Theory and Practice.* New York: Simon & Schuster-Clarion, 1968.
An exploration of the new politics. Kaufman argues that for liberalism to remain effective, it must turn toward radicalism.

123. Kennedy, Senator Edward M. *Decisions for a Decade: Policies and Programs for the 1970s.* Garden City, NY: Doubleday, 1968.
Kennedy makes suggestions for improvements in the U.S., based on problems of the times--dissenting students, crime, civil rights, Asia, Latin America, and worldwide poverty.

124. Klare, Michael. *War Without End: Planning for the Next Vietnams.* New York: Alfred A. Knopf, 1972.
A study of America's intervention in the revolutionary struggle in Vietnam and of plans for involvement in other struggles in developing countries. Klare's theory is that for economic reasons the U.S. will continue to involve itself in a long series of "limited" conflicts.

125. Konvitz, Milton R. *Expanding Liberties: Freedom's Gains in Postwar America.* New York: Viking Press, 1966.
A study of new freedoms gained in America after WWII, including academic freedom, the Communist Party, censorship, racial equality, and free speech.

126. Krause, Patricia A., ed. *Anatomy of an Undeclared War: Congressional Conference on the Pentagon Papers.* New York: International Universities Press, 1972.
An examination of the power of Congress to control the foreign policy decisions of the President, especially with regard to information on the Vietnam war.

127. Ladd, Bruce. *Crisis in Credibility.* New York: NAL, 1968.
A look at various "crises in credibility" in U.S. government in the 1960s. Ladd sees the greatest part of the problem as the extension of executive power. He also sees three aspects of the credibility gap in the executive branch of government: secrecy, lying, and news management.

128. Lamott, Kenneth. *Anti-California: Report from Our First Parafascist State.* Boston: Little, Brown, 1971.
Reflections on life in California in the 1960s. Lamott was not a hippie or a college revolutionary, though he sympathized with many of their issues. However, he felt that life in California was a bad experience and shows his reader why he felt that way.

129. Lazo, Mario. *Dagger in the Heart: American Policy Failures in Cuba.* New York: Funk & Wagnalls, 1968.
An account and analysis of the Bay of Pigs invasion and the Cuban missile crisis from an anti-Castro Cuban lawyer.

130. Lubell, Samuel. *The Hidden Crisis in American Politics.* New York: W.W. Norton, 1970.
Studies of the effects of rapid social change on the political and social American spheres.

131. McCarthy, Senator Eugene J. *The Limits of Power: America's Role in the World.* New York: Holt, Rinehart & Winston, 1967.
McCarthy argues that the U.S. should be more restrained in its foreign relations: that international agencies should be used more often; that the use of agencies like the CIA should be more restricted; and that distribution and sale of arms to foreign nations should be limited.

132. McPherson, William. *Ideology and Change: Radicalism and Fundamentalism in America.* Palo Alto, CA: National Press, 1973.
McPherson explores parallels in social movements. Through a selection of readings he compares old radicals and fundamentalists with new. Many readings come from books cited in this bibliography; the interest in them lies in their treatment in the context of McPherson's goals.

133. McQuaid, Kim. *The Anxious Years: America in the Vietnam-Watergate Era.* New York: Basic Books, 1989.
McQuaid takes a close look at the 1968 presidential campaign, the Vietnam war, and Watergate as representative of the failures of the American power establishment.

134. Magdoff, Harry. *The Age of Imperialism: The Economics of U.S. Foreign Policy.* New York: Monthly Review Press, 1969.
Magdoff relates U.S. foreign policy aggressiveness to the international expansion of U.S. business. But he also suggests that economics is not everything--that the U.S. intervened in Vietnam because all of Asia is important to the U.S.

135. Melman, Seymour. *Our Depleted Society.* New York: Holt, Rinehart & Winston, 1965.
A critical analysis of the American policy that spent more resources on the Cold War than on American domestic problems.

136. Mileur, Jerome M., ed. *Liberal Tradition in Crisis: American Politics in the Sixties.* Lexington, MA: Heath, 1974.
Mileur sees liberalism, which had been dominant in American politics, in a crisis because it is not only being challenged by the right, but also by the left, those most likely to champion it. In this collection, he has brought together readings from such liberals as Arthur Schlesinger, Jr., Jack Newfield, Daniel Moynihan, John Kenneth Galbraith, C. Wright Mills, and Michael Harrington.

137. Oglesby, Carl. *The Yankee and Cowboy War: Conspiracies from Dallas to Watergate.* Kansas City: Sheed & Ward, 1976.

Oglesby argues that Dallas and Watergate were links in a chain of conspiracies of coup and countercoup among the American elites.

138. O'Neill, Robert M. *Free Speech: Responsible Communication under Law.* Indianapolis, IN: Bobbs-Merrill, 1966.
      A gathering of legal materials and principles of free speech. Includes free speech on college campuses, obscenity, libel, and radio, television, and politics.

139. Pachter, Henry M. *Collision Course: The Cuban Missile Crisis and Coexistence.* New York: Praeger Publishers, 1963.
      An account of the crisis and the people involved in it and an analysis with suggestions for dealing with conflicts in the nuclear age. Pachter was a U.N. correspondent during the crisis.

140. Parenti, Michael. *The Anti-Communist Impulse.* New York: Random House, 1969.
      An examination of anti-Communism. The author finds it just as alarming as far left or right ideologies.

141. Pearson, Drew, and Jack Anderson. *The Case Against Congress: A Compelling Indictment of Corruption on Capitol Hill.* New York: Simon & Schuster, 1968.
      The authors write about corruption in Congress, naming names such as Thomas Dodd, Everett Dirksen, Adam Clayton Powell, Bob Kerr, and many others.

142. Powers, Gary, with Curt Gentry. *Operation Overflight: The U-2 Spy Pilot Tells His Story for the First Time.* New York: Holt, Rinehart & Winston, 1970.
      Powers flew a U-2 plane during the Eisenhower administration. Here he tells about his plane being shot down over the U.S.S.R. and his captivity there as a U.S. spy. He was returned to the U.S. in 1962.

143. Reischauer, Edwin O. *Beyond Vietnam: The United States and Asia.* New York: Random House-Vintage Books, 1967.
      Suggestions for U.S. foreign relations with Japan, China, and the rest of Asia which should follow as a result of the Vietnam war.

144. *Assassination and Political Violence; Report to the National Commission on the Causes and Prevention of Violence.* By James F. Kirkham, Sheldon G. Levy, and William Crotty. Washington, DC: U.S. Government Printing Office, 1969.
      A study of political assassination including definitions, factors conducive to assassinations, a description of each assassination attempt on a U.S. officeholder, an analysis of presidential assassinations, cross-cultural comparisons, and analysis of the factors that underlie such a high incidence of assassination in the U.S.

145. Schiller, Herbert I., and Joseph D. Phillips, eds. *Super-State: Readings in the Military-Industrial Complex*. Urbana: U of Illinois P, 1970.
    Essays examining the relationship of defense and industry, the U.S. reliance on a defense economy, and the alternatives to the Military-Industrial Complex.

146. Sigel, Roberta S., ed. *Learning about Politics: A Reader in Political Socialization*. New York: Random House, 1970.
    Although this is a textbook on socialization, it does offer essays on reactions to John F. Kennedy's assassination, student protest, and the Radical Right. Writers include Richard Flacks and Seymour M. Lipset.

147. Stark, Rodney. *Police Riots: Collective Violence and Law Enforcement*. Belmont, CA: Focus Publishing, 1972.
    A very detailed analysis of police and police riots using examples from Berkeley, the Chicago Democratic Convention, and the Detroit riots. Stark also gives some suggestions for improving police forces to lessen the chances for police brutality.

148. Thompson, Hunter S. *Hell's Angels: A Strange and Terrible Saga*. New York: Ballantine Books, 1967.
    Thompson spent almost a year with the Angels in 1966. He got to know many of them and gave wonderful descriptions of the men and their activities. In the end, the reader is left unsure of whether Thompson admired them, pitied them, feared them, or hated them--maybe a little of each. New Journalism style.

149. Turner, William W. *Hoover's F.B.I. The Men and the Myth*. Los Angeles: Sherbourne Press, 1970.
    An exploration of Hoover and his FBI by an ex-agent.

150. Winslow, Robert W. *Crime in a Free Society: Report by the President's Commission on Law Enforcement and Administration of Justice*. Belmont, CA: Dickenson Press, 1968.
    A report on crime in the U.S. in the 1960s.

151. Wolff, Robert P. *The Poverty of Liberalism*. Boston: Beacon Press, 1969.
    Political concerns of liberalism in 1960s society.

Presidencies

GENERAL WORKS

152. Bruno, Jerry, and Jeff Greenfield. *The Advance Man*. New York: William Morrow, 1971.
    Bruno was an advance man in the democratic campaigns of Kennedy, Johnson, Humphrey, and Robert Kennedy. In this book he and Greenfield describe what kinds of politicking helped to make successful campaigns during the 1960s.

153. Burke, John P., and Fred I. Greenstein. *How Presidents Test Reality: Decision in Vietnam, 1954 and 1965*. New York: Russell Sage Foundation, 1989.
    An analysis of the differing ways that Eisenhower and Johnson made decisions on U.S. involvement in Vietnam.

154. Gulley, Bill, with Mary Ellen Reese. *Breaking Cover*. New York: Simon & Schuster, 1970.
    Gulley was head of the Military Office in the White House through the Johnson, Nixon, and Ford years. As such, he was privy to information most people never knew about. In this book, he talks about his years in the White House, the secrets he knows, and adds his information to the political biographies of Johnson and Nixon.

155. O'Brien, Lawrence F. *No Final Victories: A Life in Politics from John F. Kennedy to Watergate*. Garden City, NY: Doubleday, 1974.
    O'Brien was Director of Congressional Relations for Kennedy and Johnson, Postmaster General under Johnson, and twice Democratic National Chairman. It was his office that the Watergate burglars broke into. However, he says he wrote this book, a memoir of those years, to show that politics does not have to be bad.

156. Reedy, George. *The Twilight of the Presidency*. New York: World Publishing, 1970.
    A picture of the presidency, not of one particular man, but in general from one who served as a presidential assistant in the White House in the 1960s.

157. Schlesinger, Arthur M., Jr. *The Imperial Presidency*. New York: Popular
     Library, 1974.
     Schlesinger looks at the rise of presidential power in relation to the
     Vietnam war and to Watergate. He believes that the U.S. needs a strong
     president, but a president within Constitutional limitations.

158. Wicker, Tom. *JFK and LBJ: The Influence of Personality Upon Politics*. New
     York: William Morrow, 1968.
     A comparison and analysis of the presidencies of both men. It is
     Wicker's theory that the escalation of the Vietnam war was an
     inevitable result of Johnson's succession.

THE CHARISMA OF KENNEDY

159. Abel, Elie. *The Missile Crisis*. Philadelphia: J.B. Lippincott, 1966.
     An account of the Cuban Missile Crisis of 1962, day-by-day. Based on
     interviews with the people involved, especially Robert Kennedy.

160. Agronsky, Martin, et al. *Let Us Begin: The First 100 Days of the Kennedy
     Administration*. New York: Simon & Schuster, 1961.
     A photodocumentary of the first 100 days of JFK's presidency.

161. Allison, Graham T. *Essence of Decision: Explaining the Cuban Missile
     Crisis*. Boston: Little, Brown, 1971.
     A theoretical analysis and investigation of the Cuban Missile Crisis as a
     case study on United States foreign policy. The author was from
     Harvard University and the book represents his work with primary and
     secondary sources and interview.

162. Baker, Leonard. *The Johnson Eclipse: A President's Vice Presidency*. New
     York: Macmillan Publishing, 1966.
     A detailed description and analysis of Johnson as vice-president during
     the Kennedy years.

163. Bernstein, Irving. *Promises Kept: John F. Kennedy's New Frontier*. New
     York: Oxford UP, 1991.
     Bernstein argues that Kennedy, had he lived, would have been a very
     successful president, at least with regard to domestic issues.

164. Brauer, Carl M. *John F. Kennedy and the Second Reconstruction*. New York:
     Columbia UP, 1977.
     The author compares the early 1960s to the Reconstruction period after
     the Civil War. In many ways the two eras differed, but they were alike
     in that in both periods there was movement to give black Americans
     their rights as citizens and as people. This book examines John F.
     Kennedy's role in this second reconstruction.

165. Burner, David, and Thomas R. West. *The Torch Is Passed: The Kennedy Brothers and American Liberalism.* New York: Atheneum Publishers, 1984.
     A study of liberalism--with John and then Robert Kennedy. The book concludes with a look at Ted Kennedy's liberalism.

166. Collier, Peter, and David Horowitz. *The Kennedy's: An American Drama.* New York: Summit Books, 1984.
     A chronicle of the entire Kennedy family, beginning with Joe and Rose and ending with the death of David Kennedy (son of Robert) in 1984.

167. Exner, Judith, as told to Ovid Demaris. *My Story.* New York: Grove Press, 1977.
     Judy Exner tells the story of her affairs with Sam Giancana and with Jack Kennedy in the early 1960s.

168. Fairlie, Henry. *The Kennedy Promise: The Politics of Expectation.* Garden City, NY: Doubleday, 1973.
     Fairlie argues that the energy of the Kennedy men was bad for the nation and that they created expectations for the Presidency that could not be met.

169. Fuller, Helen. *Year of Trial: Kennedy's Crucial Decisions.* New York: Harcourt Brace Jovanovich, 1962.
     The crucial decisions that Kennedy made during his first year as President.

170. Hilsman, Roger. *To Move a Nation: The Politics of Foreign Policy in the Administration of John F. Kennedy.* Garden City, NY: Doubleday, 1967.
     A study, based on case studies, of foreign policy decisions regarding the Bay of Pigs, Cuba, the Congo, China, Indonesia, Malaysia, and Vietnam. Hilsman was Assistant Secretary of State for Far Eastern Affairs, so this book could be considered a memoir of his experiences.

171. Johnson, Haynes, et al. *Bay of Pigs: The Leaders' Story of Brigade 2506.* New York: W.W. Norton, 1964.
     The history of the Bay of Pigs invasion as told by the men who took part in it.

172. Kennedy, Robert F. *Thirteen Days: A Memoir of the Cuban Missile Crisis.* New York: NAL, 1969.
     Robert Kennedy's account of the Cuban Missile Crisis. Photos included.

173. Lasky, Victor. *John F.K.: The Man and the Myth.* New York: Macmillan Publishing, 1963.
     An early political biography of Kennedy written before his assassination. Lasky is very unfavorable towards Kennedy, presenting him as ineffectual and duplicitous.

174. MacNeil, Robert, ed. *The Way We Were: 1963, the Year Kennedy Died.*
New York: Carroll & Graf, 1988.
Photographs and interviews that cover just about every aspect of 1963
from one of the nation's leading journalists. Arranged month by
month.

175. Parmet, Herbert S. *JFK: The Presidency of John F. Kennedy.* New York: Dial
Press, 1983.
Kennedy's political life beginning with his presidential nomination in
1960 and moving through his campaign and presidency.

176. Reeves, Thomas C. *A Question of Character: A Life of John F. Kennedy.*
New York: Free Press, 1991.
Reeves claims to have researched Kennedy's life to try to find the truth
about whether or not Kennedy was the hero or the immoral cheat. His
conclusion is that Kennedy's life was more gray than simply black and
white, and that Americans should be ready to accept the truth.

177. Salinger, Pierre. *With Kennedy.* Garden City, NY: Doubleday, 1966.
Salinger was Kennedy's press secretary while he was president. This
book is Salinger's memoirs of his history with JFK. Photos included.

178. Sidey, Hugh. *John F. Kennedy, President.* New York: Atheneum Publishers,
1964.
A narrative account of Kennedy's time as president. Sidey was a
journalist who had covered Kennedy as a senator and then as president.
He says his story was reviewed and approved by Kennedy.

179. Sorenson, Theodore C. *Kennedy.* New York: Harper & Row, Publishers,
1965.
Sorenson was a friend of Kennedy's, as well as his Special Counsel. This
is his story of Kennedy's presidency. The sources were primarily
Sorenson's own files and recollections.

180. ---. *The Kennedy Legacy.* New York: Macmillan Publishing, 1969.
A description of John and Robert Kennedy's public lives and an
argument for their importance in American history.

181. Wofford, Harris. *Of Kennedy and Kings.* New York: Farrar, Straus &
Giroux, 1980.
Wofford worked closely with Sargent Shriver in the inception of the
Peace Corps. He also worked with John Kennedy and Martin Luther
King in the civil rights movement. Finally, he was dedicated to Robert
Kennedy, concluding that he would have made a better president than
his brother Jack. This book is a professional and personal memoir of
Wofford's work with Shriver, King, and the Kennedys.

John F. Kennedy's Assassination

182. Anson, Robert Sam. *They've Killed the President: The Search for the Murderers of John F. Kennedy.* New York: Bantam Books, 1975. Anson argues for a conspiracy of organized crime and the CIA in the assassination of JFK.

183. Ayers, Bradley Earl. *The War That Never Was: An Inside Account of CIA Covert Operations Against Cuba.* Indianapolis: Bobbs-Merrill, 1976. Ayers was a member of the CIA and a secret "advisor" to the people involved in paramilitary operations against Castro's Cuba. Ayers believed that there was a relationship between the CIA's actions against Castro and the assassinations of John and Robert Kennedy.

184. Belin, David W. *November 22, 1963: You are the Jury.* New York: Quadrangle Books, 1973 Belin was one of the lawyers involved in the Warren Commission investigation. He uses transcripts from the investigation to answer the conspiracy "sensationalists" and to prove that Oswald alone killed Kennedy and Tippett.

185. Belli, Melvin M., with Maurice C. Carroll. *Dallas Justice: The Real Story of Jack Ruby and His Trial.* New York: David McKay, 1964. Belli was Jack Ruby's defense lawyer. He felt that Ruby was convicted because of the politics of Dallas. His case rested on medical testimony that Ruby suffered from a form of epileptic seizures. His book is an indictment of the Dallas legal structure.

186. Blakey, G. Robert, and Richard N. Billings. *The Plot to Kill the President.* New York: New York Times, 1981. Blakey was Chief Counsel and Staff Director of the House Select Committee on Assassinations and this book represents his view that organized crime plotted to kill John Kennedy.

187. Buchanon, Thomas G. *Who Killed Kennedy?* New York: G.P. Putnam's, 1964. Using comparisons with other presidential assassinations, Buchanon argues that Kennedy's assassination was also a conspiracy--of Americans who were against him and saw him as an obstacle to the Vietnam war.

188. Canfield, Michael, with Alan J. Weberman. *Coup D'Etat in America: The CIA and the Assassination of John F. Kennedy.* New York: Third Press, 1975. In this book the theory is that the Kennedy assassination was linked to the Watergate scandal by the people involved in both, e.g., E. Howard Hunt, Frank Sturgis, and others. Photos and documents included.

189. *Dallas Morning News. November 22: The Day Remembered.* Dallas, TX: Taylor Publishing, 1990

A concise summary of the issues surrounding the assassination and a very detailed schedule for the day itself, as well as the next three days. Compiled from interviews with those who were there. Many photos.

190. Davison, Jean. *Oswald's Game.* New York: W.W. Norton, 1983.
A look at Oswald's life to determine why he might have assassinated J.F.K. Davison challenges conspiracy theories. Photos included.

191. Epstein, Edward Jay. *Counterplot.* New York: Viking Press, 1969.
A study of the Jim Garrison investigation of the John Kennedy assassination.

192. ---. *Inquest: The Warren Commission and the Establishment of Truth.* New York: Viking Press, 1966.
Epstein challenges the thoroughness and effectiveness of the investigation into John Kennedy's assassination. His concern is with the process of fact-finding the Commission used.

193. ---. *Legend: The Secret World of Lee Harvey Oswald.* New York: McGraw-Hill, 1978.
Epstein examines Oswald's connections to the Soviet KGB, though in his reconstruction of the assassination he follows the line that the Warren Commission endorsed. He specifically dwells on the story of Juri Nosenko, a Soviet defector who said he had been in charge of the Oswald files when he was in Russia.

194. Fensterwald, Bernard, Jr., with Michael Ewing. *Coincidence or Conspiracy?* New York: Zebra, 1977.
Fensterwald looks at the assassination theories in a unique way, taking a particular group or theory said to be related to the assassination, e.g., the Warren Commission, the Mafia, Links to Watergate, and sketching each person who might have played a part, including photographs when possible.

195. Flammonde, Paris. *The Kennedy Conspiracy: An Uncommissioned Report on the John Garrison Investigation.* New York: Meredith Press, 1969.
Garrison was able to open the Kennedy assassination case in New Orleans and actually had some people arrested and tried as part of the conspiracy. However, the person Garrison accused was found innocent. Flammonde wrote his conspiracy book about the Garrison investigation.

196. Ford, Gerald R., and John R. Stiles. *Portrait of the Assassin.* New York: Simon & Schuster, 1965.
Ford was a part of the Warren Commission, In this book, he reconstructs Oswald's later life to show that Oswald certainly had the personality to kill Kennedy. Ford spends some time defending the Warren Commission report.

197. Garrison, Jim. *A Heritage of Stone*. New York: G.P. Putnam's, 1970.
Garrison argues that John Kennedy's assassination was not the work of one lone man, but was in fact a *coup d'etat*, an assassination carried out by America's military powers for its own survival and progress.

198. ---. *On the Trail of the Assassins*. New York: Sheridan Square Press, 1988.
The movie *JFK* was based on this book and is Garrison's story of his investigation of the Kennedy assassination and prosecution of Clay Shaw. Photos included.

199. Greenberg, Bradley, and Edwin B. Parker, eds. *The Kennedy Assassination and the American Public: Social Communication in Crisis*. Stanford, CA: Stanford UP, 1965.
Readings and studies from social scientists and journalists on reporting during the assassination, on the ways in which people got their news during that four-day weekend, and surveys of responses to and effects of the assassination.

200. Joesten, Joachim. *Oswald: Assassin or Fall Guy?* New York: Marzani and Munsell, 1965.
Joesten's theories match Garrison's but Joesten's book was written before the Warren Commission had concluded its investigation.

201. Jones, Penn, Jr. *Forgive My Grief*. Midlothian, TX: Midlothian *Mirror*, vol. 1, 1966; vol. 2, 1967; vol. 3, 1968; vol. 4, 1974.
"A Critical Review of the Warren Commission Report on the Assassination of President John F. Kennedy." From 1963 to 1974, Jones, owner of the Midlothian (Texas) *Mirror*, wrote about the conspiracy to kill John Kennedy. He was convinced that Johnson and even Nixon were involved in the conspiracy and kept a running count of the strange deaths of people associated with the assassination in any way.

202. Kantor, Seth. *Who Was Jack Ruby?* New York: Everest House, 1978.
This book focuses on Jack Ruby and his place in the Kennedy assassination. Kantor believes Ruby was paid by the Mafia to kill Oswald.

203. Kirkwood, James. *American Grotesque: An Account of the Clay Shaw-Jim Garrison Affair in New Orleans*. New York: Simon & Schuster, 1970.
This was the only trial on the Kennedy assassination. Clay Shaw was charged by Garrison, but was acquitted of conspiring to kill Kennedy. Photos included.

204. Lane, Mark. *A Citizen's Dissent: Mark Lane Replies*. New York: Holt, Rinehart & Winston, 1968.
Lane replies to those people who continued to maintain that Oswald was the lone Kennedy assassin after Lane's *Rush to Judgment*. Lane argues that this indicates the U.S. is moving toward a closed society, with media and the government the sources of fact and public opinion.

205. ---. *Rush to Judgment.* New York: Holt, Rinehart & Winston, 1966.
    Lane was asked by Oswald's mother to serve as her son's lawyer before
    the Warren Commission. Although he was not officially accepted in
    such a role, in this book he critiques the Warren Commission Report to
    shed doubt that Oswald was the assassin.

206. Lawrence, Lincoln. *Were We Controlled?* New Hyde Park, NY: University
    Books, 1967.
    Lawrence argues that Oswald and Ruby were both victims of mind
    control techniques in their assassination activities.

207. Leek, Sybil, and Bert R. Sugar. *The Assassination Chain.* New York: Corwin
    Books, 1976.
    A survey of the assassination theories surrounding JFK, Martin Luther
    King, RFK, and the attempted assassination of George Wallace. The
    authors speculate that there could have been one mastermind--possibly
    Howard Hughes.

208. Lewis, Richard Warren. *The Scavengers and Critics of the Warren Report.*
    Based on an investigation by Lawrence Schiller. New York: Delacorte,
    1967.
    A refutation of most of the people who argued that Oswald did not
    murder Kennedy on his own.

209. Lifton, David S. *Best Evidence: Disguise and Deception in the Assassination
    of John F. Kennedy.* New York: Macmillan Publishing, 1980.
    A chronological account of Lifton's investigation into the John F.
    Kennedy assassination, The basis of his argument is that one of the
    bullets that hit Kennedy was surgically removed before the autopsy.
    Photos included.

210. McDonald, Hugh C., as told to Geoffrey Bocca. *Appointment in Dallas: The
    Final Solution to the Assassination of JFK.* New York: Zebra, 1975.
    McDonald claimed to have spoken to a hired gunman who told him the
    story that he (the gunman) assassinated JFK from a building next to the
    Texas Book Depository, that Oswald was set up to be a patsy, and that
    Oswald was supposed to have been killed by the gunman right after he
    shot Kennedy.

211. Manchester, William. *The Death of a President: November 20 - November
    25.* New York: Harper & Row, Publishers, 1967.
    Jackie Kennedy commissioned Manchester to write this book. In it he
    recounts in minute detail the events of those six days in Dallas, the
    White House, and the government in Washington.

212. Marrs, Jim. *Crossfire: The Plot That Killed Kennedy.* New York: Carroll &
    Graf, 1989.
    A thorough compilation of all the information surrounding the
    Kennedy assassination from books and periodicals published up to 1989.

Marrs believes, based on his research, that there was a conspiracy. Photos included.

213. Melanson, Philip H. *Spy Saga: Lee Harvey Oswald and U.S. Intelligence.* New York: Praeger Publishers, 1990.
An extensive examination of Oswald to prove that he had been a CIA operative. Photos included.

214. Newman, Albert H. *The Assassination of John F. Kennedy: The Reasons Why.* New York: C.N. Potter, 1970.
Newman argues that Oswald was alone in assassinating Kennedy, that he did kill Officer Tippet and tried to kill Major General Edwin Walker, an extreme rightist living in Dallas, and that Oswald and Ruby were not linked. He also offers a motive for the assassination.

215. Popkin, Richard H. *The Second Oswald.* New York: Avon Books, 1966.
An argument for the fact that there were two Oswalds--the real one and one who looked very much like him--at the assassination and that each played a part in the murder.

216. Roffman, Howard. *Presumed Guilty: Lee Harvey Oswald in the Assassination of President Kennedy.* Cranbury, NJ: Associated UP, 1975.
Roffman argues that the Warren Commission operated under the assumption that Oswald was guilty and ignored or distorted any evidence contrary to this basic premise. He does not offer any theories as to who actually did assassinate JFK.

217. Sauvage, Leo. *The Oswald Affair: An Examination of the Contradictions and Omissions of the Warren Report.* New York: World Publishing, 1966.
Sauvage disputes that Oswald was given the same considerations in the Warren investigation as he would have been given in a regular trial.

218. Scheim, David E. *Contract on America--The Mafia Murders of John and Robert Kennedy.* Silver Spring, MD: Argyle Press, 1983.
Mostly focused on Jack Ruby's associations with the underworld, Scheim presents evidence that the mob--and Jack Ruby--conspired in John Kennedy's death. The final chapter brings in some evidence that the mob was also responsible for the deaths of Malcolm X, Martin Luther King, Jr., and Robert Kennedy.

219. Scott, Peter Dale. *Crime and Cover-up: The CIA, the Mafia, and the Dallas-Watergate Connection.* Berkeley: Westworks, 1977.
An examination of the connection between the CIA and the Mafia and between Kennedy's assassination and the Watergate scandal.

220. Summers, Anthony. *Conspiracy*. New York: McGraw-Hill, 1980.
     Written after the investigation by the assassination committee of
     Congress in 1978, this book argues for conspiracy and focuses on the
     assassination's link with the Cuban situation.

221. Thornley, Kerry. *Oswald*. Chicago: New Classics House, 1965.
     Thornley was in the Marines with Oswald after he returned from Japan.
     He had also started a novel whose main character was based on Oswald.
     In this book, he reflects on Oswald's character and personality, uses parts
     of his book to further explain Oswald, and includes his testimony to the
     Warren Commission.

222. United Press International and *American Heritage Magazine*. *Four Days*.
     New York: American Heritage, 1964.
     A photo-documentary covering November 22 - November 25, 1963--the
     Kennedy assassination and funeral.

223. United States. Warren Commission. *Hearings before the President's
     Commission on the Assassination of President Kennedy*. 26 volumes.
     Washington, DC: U.S. Government Printing Office, 1964.
     The complete testimony before the Warren Commission on the
     assassination of John F. Kennedy.

224. ---. *Report of the Warren Commission on the Assassination of President
     Kennedy*. New York: McGraw-Hill, 1964.
     The final report of the Warren Commission.

225. Weisberg, Harold. *Whitewash: A Report on the Warren Report*.
     Hyattstown, MD: Weisberg, 1966.
     A refutation of the Warren Report based on what it did and did not
     investigate. Weisburg's theory is that Oswald could not have killed
     Kennedy alone.

JOHNSON'S GREAT SOCIETY

226. Alsop, Stewart. *The Center: People and Power in Political Washington*.
     New York: Harper & Row, Publishers, 1968.
     A book about the center of power in this country--Washington, DC.
     Alsop goes back into history, but also gives interesting insights into
     1960s Washington power--the social circles, the President, the State
     Department, McNamara as head of Defense, the press corps, the CIA, the
     Cabinet, Congress, and the Supreme Court.

227. Austin, Anthony. *The President's War*. New York: J.B. Lippincott, 1971.
     "The Story of the Tonkin Gulf Resolution." This encounter of North
     Vietnamese boats and American ships on August 4, 1964, created the
     circumstances for which the United States, in effect, went to war with
     North Vietnam.

228. Belfrage, Sally. *Freedom Summer*. New York; Viking Press, 1965.
     A narrative account of Freedom Summer, from basic training to jail, to
     the end of the summer, from a participant's point of view.

229. Berman, Larry. *Lyndon Johnson's War: The Road to Stalemate in Vietnam*.
     New York: W.W. Norton, 1989.
     Berman went back to 1967-68 to explore Johnson's war and the
     incompatibility between Johnson's foreign and domestic policies.

230. Bishop, Jim. *A Day in the Life of President Johnson*. New York: Random
     House, 1967.
     An hour-by-hour account of a typical day in the life of Johnson in his
     presidency. Also includes background information and an account of a
     weekend at the LBJ ranch.

231. Conkin, Paul. *Big Daddy from the Pedernales: Lyndon Johnson*. Boston:
     Twayne Publishers, 1986.
     A scholarly biography. Conkin sees Johnson as a complex person,
     neither good not bad. He also sees him as somewhat out of his time--a
     throwback to frontier America.

232. Davie, Michael. *LBJ: A Foreign Observer's Viewpoint*. New York: Duell,
     Sloan and Pearce, 1966.
     Reflections on Johnson the man and president. On the whole, Davie
     views him positively.

233. Divine, Robert. *The Johnson Years*. Lawrence: UP of Kansas, 1987.
     An extensive collection of readings on all aspects of the Johnson
     administration, e.g., foreign policy, "The Great Society," Vietnam, the
     environment, and science. There is also a short catalog of materials in
     the LBJ library.

234. Evans, Rowland, and Robert Novak. *Lyndon B. Johnson: The Exercise of
     Power*. New York: NAL, 1966.
     A political biography of Johnson covering the years from 1953 to 1965.

235. Geyelin, Philip. *Lyndon B. Johnson and the World*. New York: Praeger
     Publishers, 1966.
     An examination of how Johnson approached foreign affairs and foreign
     policy.

236. Goldman, Eric F. *The Tragedy of Lyndon Johnson*. New York: Alfred A.
     Knopf, 1969.
     An account of Johnson's years in the White House. According to
     Goldman, Johnson was the classic tragic figure, "the strong man
     overwhelmed by forces, from within and without."

237. Goldwater, Senator Barry. *Where I Stand*. New York: McGraw-Hill, 1964.
Goldwater describes his views and positions on public policy as he
begins his 1964 campaign for the presidency. Included is his acceptance
speech at the 1964 Republic National Convention.

238. Goulden, Joseph C. *Truth Is the First Casualty: The Gulf of Tonkin Affair--
Illusion and Reality*. Chicago: Rand McNally, 1969.
Goulden makes a case for his belief that the United States acted hastily,
with incomplete information, in the Gulf of Tonkin incident.

239. Graff, Henry. *The Tuesday Cabinet: Deliberation and Decision on Peace and
War under Lyndon B. Johnson*. Englewood Cliffs, NJ: Prentice Hall,
1970.
On Tuesdays, Johnson's chief advisors gathered together for lunch and
discussion, mostly about the Vietnam war. These meetings proved to be
very important in policy-making about the war. Included at the
meetings were Dean Rusk, Robert McNamara, McGeorge Bundy, Bill
Moyers, and Richard Helms.

240. Haley, J. Evetts. *A Texan Looks at Lyndon: A Study in Illegitimate Power*.
Canyon, TX: Palo Duro Press, 1964.
Haley argues, early in Johnson's presidency, that Texans who were not
the rich and powerful, distrusted Johnson and felt he was dishonest and
designing.

241. Henggeler, Paul R. *In His Steps: Lyndon Johnson and the Kennedy
Mystique*. Chicago: Ivan R. Dee, 1991.
Henggeler claims Johnson had a feeling of ambivalence about the
Kennedy mystique. On the one hand, he saw John as the "good"
Kennedy who had helped Johnson's career; yet, he saw Robert as the
"bad" Kennedy who could usurp Johnson's power. This book explores
that theory of ambivalence.

242. Hoopes, Townsend. *The Limits to Intervention*. New York: David McKay,
1969.
An account of Johnson's decisions not to escalate the number of troops
in Vietnam in 1968, to initiate a bombing halt, and not to run for a
second term as president.

243. Johnson, Lyndon B. *The Vantage Point*. New York: Holt, Rinehart &
Winston, 1971.
Johnson's own story of his presidency. Photographs included.

244. Kearns , Doris. *Lyndon Johnson and the American Dream*. New York:
Harper & Row, Publishers, 1976.
A biography and examination of the ways Johnson's private and public
selves interacted.

245. Krosney, Herbert. *Beyond Welfare: Poverty in the Supercity.* New York: Holt, Rinehart & Winston, 1966.
     A description and analysis of Johnson's War on Poverty program and the needs of the U.S. to deal with poverty.

246. Levitan, Sar A., and Garth L. Mangum. *Federal Training and Work Programs in the Sixties.* Ann Arbor: Institute of Labor & Industrial Relations, University of Michigan, 1969.
     The manpower programs were an effort to improve the employability of the disadvantaged. The authors trace the development of manpower programs, review the seven major programs individually, and make recommendations for their continued effectiveness.

247. Levitan, Sar A., and Robert Taggart. *The Promise of Greatness.* Cambridge: Harvard UP, 1976.
     An analysis of the components of the Great Society programs. The authors argue that those 1960s programs and policies were good and that the U.S. should continue such policies.

248. Lokos, Lionel. *Hysteria 1964: The Fear Campaign against Barry Goldwater.* New Rochelle, NY: Arlington House, 1967.
     Lokos argues that the Goldwater opponents used fear tactics rather than facts to build opposition to Goldwater. He takes several issues, e.g., nuclear weapons, civil rights, social security, extremism, and claims to explore what Goldwater actually said about these issues.

249. Marris, Peter, and Martin Rein. *Dilemmas of Social Reform, Poverty and Community Action in the United States.* New York: Atherton Press, 1967.
     The two authors examine community action programs funded by the Ford Foundation and the President's Committee on Juvenile Delinquency. They concentrate their analysis on the process of reform, rather than on results.

250. Moynihan, Daniel P. *Maximum Feasible Misunderstanding: Community Action in the War on Poverty.* New York: Free Press, 1969.
     The title is based on a definition of "Community Action" as that "which is developed and conducted with the maximum feasible participation of the residents of the areas" involved. Moynihan writes about the Community Action Programs that were a part of Johnson's War on Poverty.

251. Roberts, Charles. *LBJ's Inner Circle.* New York: Delacorte, 1965.
     A study of Johnson's early White House staff and advisors.

252. Sherrill, Robert. *The Accidental President.* New York: Grossman Publishers, 1967.
     Sherrill explores the ambivalence that most people felt toward Johnson. He calls Johnson unappealing and dangerous and yet explores why he

and others like him will probably work and vote for Johnson in the 1968 election.

253. Valenti, Jack. *A Very Human President.* New York: W.W. Norton, 1975.
Valenti was a friend of Johnson's for many years and was a member of his White House staff. These are his memoirs of Johnson, beginning with Johnson's first day as president. Photos included.

254. VanDeMark, Brian. *Into the Quagmire: Lyndon Johnson and the Escalation of the Vietnam War.* New York: Oxford UP, 1991.
An analysis of LBJ's decisions to escalate the war in Vietnam, November 1964-July 1965.

255. White, Theodore H. *The Making of the President, 1964.* New York: NAL-Signet Books, 1964.
White reports on the presidential campaigns of 1964--from the death of Kennedy and Johnson's succession, through the primaries, the conventions, and the election. Throughout this election year were heard the sounds of the civil rights revolution and rioting in the streets.

256. White, William S. *The Professional: Lyndon B. Johnson.* Boston: Houghton Mifflin, 1964.
An account of Johnson's transition into the presidency after Kennedy's death.

THE NIXON YEARS

257. Agnew, Spiro T. *Frankly Speaking.* New York: Public Affairs Press, 1970.
Speeches Agnew made as Vice President.

258. Ambrose, Stephen E. *Nixon. Volume Two: The Triumph of a Politician, 1962-1972.* New York: Simon & Schuster, 1989.
A political biography based on Nixon's memoirs, tape-recorded conversations, and reports from associates. Ambrose admits that Nixon is a study in contradictions and that his purpose is only to point out these contradictions.

259. Blaustein, Arthur I., and Geoffrey Faux. *The Star Spangled Hustle: The Story of a Nixon Promise.* Garden City, NY: Doubleday-Anchor Books, 1973.
American issues in the beginning of the Nixon administration. Primarily concerned with poverty.

260. Cohen, Richard M., and Jules Witcover. *A Heartbeat Away: The Investigation and Resignation of Vice President Spiro T. Agnew.* New York: Viking Press, 1974.
Agnew left office before Nixon as a result of kickbacks he had been paid by Maryland businessmen. Cohen and Witcover tell the story of that

whole process, which went back as far as Agnew's beginnings in public office.

261. Coyne, John R., Jr. *The Impudent Snobs: Agnew vs. the Intellectual Establishment.* New Rochelle, NY: Arlington House, 1972.
Coyne uses the speeches of Agnew and the reactions to his attacks to suggest that there is a "new mood stirring in the country," that liberalism is dying and the assaults Agnew made on the liberals reflected the feelings of the people.

262. Dean, John W., III. *Blind Ambition: The White House Years.* New York: Simon & Schuster, 1976.
John Dean, counsel to Nixon, tells his story of Nixon's administration and of his part and others' in the Watergate scandal. Photos included.

263. Drury, Allen, and Fred Maroon. *Courage and Hesitation: Notes and Photographs of the Nixon Administration.* Garden City, NY: Doubleday, 1971.
An informal account of the first three years of Nixon's presidency. Generally a positive point of view. Extensive photographs by Fred Maroon.

264. Ehrlichman, John. *Witness to Power: The Nixon Years.* New York: Simon & Schuster, 1982
Ehrlichman's account of his years with Nixon. Although he was one of Nixon's most loyal assistants, his account shows that in the end he had totally lost respect for his president.

265. Ellsberg, Daniel. *Papers On the War.* New York: Simon & Schuster, 1972.
An attempt to help the public understand the foreign policy and bureaucratic issues that kept the United States involved in the Vietnam war in the face of all the resistance to it.

266. Evans, Rowland, Jr., and Robert D. Novak . *Nixon In the White House.* New York: Random House, 1971.
An account of Nixon's first three years as President.

267. Gordon, Kermit, ed. *Agenda for the Nation.* Garden City, NY: Doubleday, 1968.
Essays which examine the domestic and foreign policy issues confronting the new 1968 (Nixon) administration. Writers include Charles Schultze, Kenneth Clark, Clark Kerr, and Henry Kissinger.

268. Henderson, Charles P., Jr. *The Nixon Theology.* New York: Harper & Row, Publishers, 1972.
Henderson explores Nixon's religious beliefs and the conflict between his actions as President and his wish always to be righteous.

269. Hersh, Seymour M. *The Price of Power: Kissinger in the Nixon White House*. New York: Summit Books, 1983.
A very detailed account of U.S. foreign policy during the Nixon years.

270. Hoffman, Abbie, Jerry Rubin, and Ed Sanders. *Vote!* New York: Warner Books, 1972.
An account of the 1972 Democratic and Republican conventions as seen through the eyes of these three yippies. It is also a call to all the hippies, yippies, etc., to get out and vote for McGovern.

271. Kalb, Marvin, and Bernard Kalb. *Kissinger*. Boston: Little, Brown, 1974.
The Kalbs give a detailed account of the five years that Kissinger served Nixon--as Senior Advisor and as Secretary of State. There is a great deal of information on Kissinger's foreign relations in Vietnam, in China, and in the Middle East. The book ends before Nixon's resignation.

272. Kissinger, Henry. *White House Years*. Boston: Little, Brown, 1979.
Kissinger's story of his years as security advisor to Nixon and head of the Department of State. He focuses on foreign policy, particularly Vietnam, Russia, China, Europe, and the Middle East. Photographs are included.

273. McGinniss, Joe. *The Selling of the President, 1968*. New York: Pocket Books,1969.
An interesting look at the public relations effort that went into Nixon's 1968 presidential campaign. Documents included.

274. Mailer, Norman. *St. George and the Godfather*. New York: Arbor House, 1972.
This is Mailer's account of the 1972 Democratic and Republican conventions.

275. Mankiewicz, Frank. *U.S. vs. Richard M. Nixon: The Final Crisis*. New York: Quadrangle Books, 1975.
The story of Nixon's political career from the point of view that Nixon was the most corrupt President and ran the most corrupt administration in U.S. history.

276. Moffett, Toby. *The Participation Put-on: Reflections of a Disenchanted Washington Youth Expert*. New York: Dell Publishing, 1971.
Moffett, at 25, was appointed head of the Office of Students and Youth in HEW, to serve as an advocate for youth. In 1970, right after Nixon announced the U.S. invasion into Cambodia, he resigned. In this book he chronicles his disillusionment at working for change within the Nixon government.

277. Schell, Johathan. *Observing the Nixon Years*. New York: Random House-Vintage Books, 1989.

Schell focuses on the Vietnam war in this analysis of the Nixon years. He looks at protest against the war, the Nixon administration, and the war's links to the Watergate crisis. He covers the time period 1969-1975, including the period after Nixon's resignation and the end of the war.

278. ---. *The Time of Illusion.* New York: Alfred A. Knopf, 1975.
Schell looks at the Nixon years by trying to make into a whole the fragments that were told to the American public and those that were kept secret by the Nixon administration.

279. Staff of the *New York Times. The End of a Presidency.* New York: Bantam Books, 1974.
Articles by *New York Times* staffers on the end of Nixon's and the beginning of Ford's presidencies. Includes Nixon's resignation speech, Ford's inaugural statement, the Articles of Impeachment, and some of the White House transcripts.

280. Nixon, Richard M. *RN: The Memoirs of Richard Nixon.* 2 vols. New York: Grosset & Dunlap , 1978.
Nixon's autobiography up to 1974, the end of his presidency. Based on written diaries, tapes, and recollections. Photos included.

281. Osborne, John. *The Last Nixon Watch.* Washington, DC: New Republic Books, 1975.
From columns in *The New Republic* in 1974, the transition from Nixon to Ford. Osborne was convinced that Nixon was becoming mentally unbalanced.

282. Rather, Dan, and Gary Paul Gates. *The Palace Guard.* New York: Harper & Row, Publishers, 1974.
A political analysis of Nixon's presidency which stresses the network of aides surrounding Nixon and his isolation from the Congress and other politicians.

283. Schrag, Peter. *Test of Loyalty: Daniel Ellsberg and the Rituals of Secret Government.* New York: Simon & Schuster, 1974.
The story of Daniel Ellsberg's publishing of the Pentagon Papers and of what happened to him afterwards.

284. Smith, Gerard. *Doubletalk: The Story of the First Strategic Arms Limitation Talks.* Garden City, NY: Doubleday, 1980.
Nixon considered these talks, lasting from 1969 to 1972, to be one of his most momentous accomplishments. Smith was the head of the U.S. delegation to the talks.

285. Thompson, Hunter S. *Fear and Loathing on the Campaign Trail '72.* New York: Popular Library, 1973.

Not an analysis but a first-hand record of the 1972 presidential campaign. Thompson uses his own style of "gonzo" journalism to create an account both passionate and hilarious.

286. Staff of the *Washington Post*. *The Fall of a President*. New York: Delacorte, 1974.
The story of Nixon's years in power as seen by members of the press.

287. Whalen, Richard J. *Catch the Falling Flag: A Republican's Challenge to His Party*. Boston: Houghton Mifflin, 1972.
Whalen worked for Nixon's election in 1967. Nevertheless, in a year when Nixon was again running for office, Whalen published this book as an argument against Nixon's reelection on the grounds that his administration was providing no original ideas or "guiding ideals."

288. White, Theodore H.. *The Making of the President, 1972*. New York: Atheneum Publishers, 1973.
White covers the campaigns of Nixon and McGovern. He concentrates more on Nixon, possibly because Nixon was such an interesting character, he won by such a landslide, and he got himself involved in Watergate.

289. Wicker, Tom. *One of Us: Richard Nixon and the American Dream*. New York: Random House, 1991.
A consideration of Nixon from after his defeat in California in 1962 until the end of his presidency. Wicker does not concentrate on Watergate, but instead on Nixon the man and what made him an important political figure.

290. Wills, Garry. *Nixon Agonistes: The Crisis of the Self-Made Man*. New York: NAL, 1979.
First published in 1969, this book is an analysis of Nixon's political life to that time. Wills seems to have felt a degree of sympathy for Nixon, the man, while being appalled by Nixon, the politician.

291. Zumwalt, Elmo. *On Watch*. Chicago: Quadrangle Books, 1976.
After four years as Chief of Naval Operations, Zumwalt wrote to make public what he found to be deception of the administration (Nixon, Kissinger, and others) about the SALT talks, the Vietnam war, and U.S. military strength and readiness.

Watergate

292. Breslin, Jimmy. *How the Good Guys Finally Won: Notes from an Impeachment Summer*. New York: Viking Press, 1975.
An account of Nixon's last days in office, but with emphasis on the good guys who won, the people bringing about the impeachment charges, especially Tip O'Neill.

293. Chester, Lewis, et al. *Watergate: The Full Inside Story*. London: Andre
     Deutsch, 1973.
     Written before Nixon resigned, an interesting account of the Watergate
     happenings from a British journalist. Chester believes Watergate was a
     result of the administration's obsession with surviving at the expense of
     ethics and principles.

294. Colson, Charles. *Born Again*. Old Tappan, NJ: Chosen Books, 1976.
     Colson served as Special Counsel to the President during Nixon's first
     term in office and was reportedly involved in Watergate. This is his
     memoir of this period, half about his political life and half about his
     experience of conversion as a born-again Christian soon after he left the
     White House.

295. ---. *Life Sentence*. Lincoln, VA: Chosen Books, 1972.
     The story of Colson's connections with the Nixon White House, his
     time in prison for Watergate, and his commitment to Christianity.

296. Gold, Gerald, ed. *The White House Transcripts*. New York: Bantam Books,
     1973.
     The full text of all the White House tapes made by Nixon and submitted
     to the Committee on the Judiciary of the House during the Watergate
     Hearings.

297. Haldeman, H.R., with Joseph DiMona. *The Ends of Power*. New York: Dell
     Publishing, 1978.
     Haldeman claims this is the true story of Watergate from Nixon's
     closest aide.

298. Jaworski, Leon. *The Right and the Power: The Prosecution of Watergate*.
     New York: Reader's Digest Press, 1976.
     An account of the behind-the-scenes battles in the prosecution of
     Watergate, by the Special Watergate Prosecutor.

299. Kutler, Stanley I. *The Wars of Watergate: The Last Crisis of Richard Nixon*.
     New York: Alfred A. Knopf, 1990.
     An account of Watergate and an analysis of the reasons for Nixon's
     downfall. Very detailed and comprehensive.

300. Lasky, Victor. *It Didn't Start with Watergate*. New York: Dial Press, 1977.
     An argument that whatever Nixon was guilty of in the Watergate affair
     was not something new in presidencies, but that all presidents,
     especially Democratic ones, had been just as guilty of other sins.

301. Liddy, G. Gordon. *Will*. New York: St. Martin's Press, 1980.
     Liddy was probably the strangest of the Watergate criminals. This book
     is his autobiography, presenting his version of Watergate. He was one
     of the few involved who never informed on his co-conspirators.

302. Lukas, J. Anthony. *Night-Mare: The Underside of the Nixon Years.* New York: Viking Press, 1976.
A comprehensive account of the Watergate affair. Lukas' information comes from published sources, the Nixon tapes, and interviews.

303. McCarthy, Mary. *The Mask of State: Watergate Portraits.* New York: Harcourt Brace Jovanovich, 1974.
Reports on the Watergate investigation and portraits of the major characters involved. McCarthy's final conclusion was that Nixon had to have been behind both the break-in and the cover-up.

304. McCord, James W. *A Piece of Tape, the Watergate Story, Fact and Fiction.* Rockville, MD: Washington Media Services, 1974.
McCord had had a life in the FBI and the CIA before he became head of security for Nixon's Committee to Re-elect the President. This is his story of Watergate, including his testimony in the investigation.

305. Sussman, Barry. *The Great Cover-Up: Nixon and the Scandal of Watergate.* New York: NAL-Signet Books, 1974.
Sussman was editor in charge of city news at the *Washington Post* when the Watergate fiasco began. He concentrates in this book on the time immediately following the break-in to prove that it was then that Nixon took charge of the cover-up. Photos included.

306. Szulc, Tad. *Compulsive Spy: The Strange Career of E. Howard Hunt.* New York: Viking Press, 1974.
A biography of Hunt, who was for years a CIA agent and was then one of the prime Watergate criminals.

307. Weissman, Steve, ed. *Big Brother and the Holding Company: The World Behind Watergate.* Palo Alto, CA: Ramparts Press, 1974.
Readings which support the argument that by forgetting Watergate when Nixon resigned, Americans were ignoring the bigger problems of big business and the military, which were undermining U.S. democratic processes.

308. White, Theodore H. *Breach of Faith: The Fall of Richard Nixon.* New York: Atheneum Publishers, 1975.
The story of the Nixon presidency and the forces that led him to the cover-up of Watergate.

309. Woodward, Bob, and Carl Bernstein. *All the President's Men.* New York: Simon & Schuster, 1974.
The famous story of the uncovering of the Watergate scandal by the two Washington Post reporters who helped keep the story going.

Youth

GENERAL WORKS

310. Aiken, Jonathan, and Michael Beloff. *Short Walk on the Campus.* New York: Atheneum Publishers, 1966.
    In 1964 the two authors were awarded Oxford University scholarships for a debating tour of the U.S. This book records their tour and their interesting reactions to the American students of the early 1960s all over the country.

311. Aldridge, John W. *In the Country of the Young.* New York: Harper's Magazine, 1970.
    An essay in which Aldridge argues that though their ideals may have seemed virtuous, youth had lost the ability to question life issues qualitatively because they had very little relationship with their physical and cultural surroundings.

312. Bayer, Alan E., Alexander W. Astin, and Robert F. Boruch. *Social Issues and Protest Activity: Recent Student Trends.* Washington, DC: ACE, 1970.
    Surveys of freshman student attitudes and characteristics, 1967-1969. Students were asked questions about the campus, the role of science, the family and population control, the military, crime, urban problems, and racial crises.

313. Berger, Bennett. *Looking for America: Essays on Youth, Suburbia, and Other American Obsessions.* Englewood Cliffs, NJ: Prentice Hall, 1971.
    A sociological analysis of youth, suburbia, leisure, and black culture. Berger's topics are based on what he calls "cultural resonance," or the ability to "evoke deep emotional response. . . from large numbers of people because they touch something vital or important. . . in the common life."

314. Berger, Peter L., and Richard John Neuhaus. *Movement and Revolution.* Garden City, NY: Doubleday, 1970.
    Actually two separate analyses of movement and revolution done by first a conservative (Berger) and then a liberal (Neuhaus). They do speak specifically of the 1960s movements.

315. Bernstein, Saul. *Youth on the Streets: Work with Alienated Youth Groups.*
New York: Association Press, 1964.
A study of lower-class youth in Chicago, Cleveland, Los Angeles, San
Francisco, Detroit, New York, Philadelphia, Washington, DC, and
Boston. Even in the early 1960s, Bernstein saw a huge gap between
lower-class youth and middle-class adults. Bernstein looked at ways to
cope with the increasing problems of the youth he studied.

316. Birmingham, James, ed. *Our Time Is Now: Notes from the Highschool
Underground.* New York: Praeger Publishers, 1970.
Articles from high school underground papers on such subjects as
student power, black power, educational reform, and youth culture.

317. Bryant, Barbara E. *High School Students Look at Their World: Issues,
Government, School, Family, Future.* Columbus, OH: R.H. Goettler,
1970.
A study of Ohio high school students' attitudes on 1960s social and
political issues.

318. Butz, Otto, ed. *To Make a Difference: A Student Look at America, Its Values,
Its Society, and Its Systems of Education.* New York: Harper & Row,
Publishers, 1967.
A series of talks given by students at San Francisco State during winter
1965-66 on their concerns about themselves, society, and higher
education.

319. Cooper, John Charles. *The New Mentality.* Philadelphia: Westminster
Press, 1969.
Cooper argues that the 1960s was not just another instance of the
restlessness of youth, but it was the beginning of a new evolutionary
phase of mentality and morality.

320. Cottle, Thomas J. *Time's Children: Impressions of Youth.* Boston: Little,
Brown, 1971.
Essays giving impressions of youth in the 1960s from an American
educator.

321. Dector, Midge. *Liberal Parents, Radical Children.* New York: Coward-
McCann, 1975.
The author calls this "an essay in fictionalized sociology." An
interesting book in which the author speculates, through fictionalized
family portraits, on the causes of the unhappiness of the 20-30 year olds
and their parents with the younger generation's inability to take their
positions as leaders of society. The accounts are too one-sided to be
believable.

322. Dietze, Gottfried. *Youth, University, and Democracy.* Baltimore: Johns
Hopkins UP, 1970.

A philosophical overview of the crises of youth, the place of the university, and the feasibility of democracy.

323. *Federal Executive Branch Review of the Recommendations of the 1971 White House Conference on Youth.* Washington, DC: U.S. Government Printing Office, 1972.
A review of the recommendations put forth by the White House Conference on Youth and a response from the agencies that would be responsible for implementing each recommendation.

324. Foley, James A., and Robert K. Foley. *The College Scene: Students Tell It Like It Is.* New York: Cowles Books, 1969.
A compilation of all the findings of the College Poll, a survey of student views on such issues as Vietnam and the draft, sex, riots, drugs, faculty, religion, voting, hippies, and fraternities and sororities.

325. Fox, Jack, ed. *Youthquake.* New York: Look-UPI-Cowles Books, 1967.
From the editors, reporters, and photographers of UPI and Cowles, a look at what the 1960s younger generation was up to. Topics included drugs, young marriage, God, the Beatles, sex and others. Photos included.

326. Friedenberg, Edgar Z. *Coming of Age in America: Growth and Acquiescence.* New York: Random House, 1965.
A classic study of adolescents in the mid-1960s. Friedenberg was especially interested in adolescents' responses to authority.

327. ---, ed. *The Anti-American Generation.* New Brunswick, NJ: Trans-action Books, 1972.
The anti-American generation was the middle-class youth of the U.S. The essays explore this generation from the pages of *Trans-action* magazine.

328. Greene, Bob. *Be True to Your School: A Diary of 1964.* New York: Atheneum Publishers, 1987.
A reconstruction of the diary Greene kept while he was in high school in Ohio in 1964. It is representative of what it was like being a high school kid, part of the baby boomers, back in the early 1960s.

329. Greene, Thayer A. *Modern Man in Search of Manhood.* New York: Association Press, 1967.
Greene explores the idea of masculinity in 1960s society. Part of youth's rebellion is the striving for identity and masculinity in a society which extends adolescence and offers no guideposts along the way to attainment of manhood.

330. Handel, Gerald. *College Confidential.* New York: Trident Press, 1969.
An alternative guide to colleges, with information on new trends, getting in, taking achievement tests, choosing college courses, studying,

fraternities and sororities. School listings give information such as admission standards, strong programs, social milieu, and political leanings of the students and faculty.

331. Hansel, Robert R. *Like Father, Like Son--Like Hell!* New York: Seabury Press, 1969.
Hansel argues that instead of a generation gap, conflict was caused by the "Assumption Gap." There were the "Searching People" and the "Settled People, " rather than the young and the old.

332. Hendin, Herbert. *The Age of Sensation.* New York: W.W. Norton, 1975.
A study of college youth in America. Hendin studied regular students, revolutionaries, homosexuals, drug users, and student suicides. This is a psychological study using samples of students in clinical interviews.

333. Hofmann, Hans F. *Discovering Freedom.* Boston: Beacon Press, 1969.
An argument for placing more emphasis on human values rather than the depersonalization of external values that has become part of society. Believing that is one reason why youth rebel, Hofmann argues for inner freedom and external liberation.

334. Holmes, Douglas, Monica Holmes, and Lisa Appignanesi. *The Language of Trust: Dialogue of the Generations.* New York: Science House, 1971.
A book for middle-class parents and adolescents to help them deal with the generation gap in the 1960s. Devotes a great deal of attention to drug use.

335. Horowitz, David. *Student.* New York: Ballantine Books, 1962.
An interesting look at what was causing the disillusionment that characterized the students of the 1950s and early 1960s. Horowitz refers to the "irrelevance of knowledge" in America, to universities as factories, and to the academic world as status-seeking and conforming.

336. Hyman, Sidney. *Youth in Politics: Expectations and Realities.* New York: Basic Books, 1972.
Hyman studied the role of youth in the 1970 congressional elections. He expected that what was learned from this election would provide information on the course of the 1972 presidential election, and other elections in the 1970s.

337. Jacobs, Paul, and Saul Landau. *The New Radicals: A Report with Documents.* New York: Random House-Vintage Books, 1966.
Descriptions of the various groups that radical youth were involved in or sympathetic to: SNCC, SDS, FSM, war protesters, and others. The documents further explain the aims and ideologies of these groups and include documents from SNCC, "The Port Huron Statement," interviews, and proclamations. A chronology of movement events covers 1954-1965.

338. Kavanaugh, Robert. *The Grim Generation*. New York: Trident Press, 1970.
     Kavanaugh has presented--sympathetically--several types of portraits of
     American students in the 1960s: "The kept generation" who would not
     be changed by their college experiences; campus hippies, the anti-
     materialists, the "walking dead"; and others. Very interesting, but not
     very practical.

339. Keniston, Kenneth. *The Uncommitted: Alienated Youth in American
     Society*. New York: Harcourt Brace Jovanovich, 1965.
     Keniston analyzes the alienation he found so prevalent in youth of the
     period. He feels that youth chose to be alienated by rejecting the values
     of their elders. This book is cited in many other sources on this era.

340. Klein, Alexander, ed. *Natural Enemies? Youth and the Clash of
     Generations*. Philadelphia: J.B. Lippincott, 1969.
     Readings from both sides of the generation gap on the generation gap.
     Contributors include N. Hentoff, D. Moynihan, M. Mead, A.
     Schlesinger, Jr., T. Hayden, M. Bundy, A. Buchwald, E. Fromm, B. Spock,
     M. McLuhan, R.B. Fuller, N. Mailer, H. Miller, K.A. Porter, H. Hefner,
     R.F. Kennedy, D.D. Eisenhower, J.D. Rockefeller 3rd, J. Lennon and P.
     McCartney, E. McCarthy, and many others.

341. Lorber, Richard, and Ernest Fladell. *The Gap*. New York: McGraw-Hill, 1968.
     Reflections of an older man (Fladell) and his nephew (Lorber) living
     together for the summer, and their experiences of the generation gap.

342. Madsen, Brigham O. *The Now Generation: Student Essays on Social Change
     in the Sixties*. Salt Lake City: University of Utah, 1971.
     Essays by college students in an honors class. Topics include
     consumerism, the space age, existentialism, the arts, media, the New
     Left, the student movement, poverty, minorities, drugs, and the law.

343. Medved, Michael, and David Wallechinsky. *What Really Happened to the
     Class of '65*. New York: Ballantine Books, 1976.
     In 1965, *Time Magazine* chose the senior class of Palisades High School
     as the focus of its cover story on "Today's Teenagers." Ten years later,
     two of those seniors, who also happened to be writers, interviewed 30 of
     those class members. If the members of this high school class were
     typical of the American student in 1965, they were also typical of the
     kinds of paths they followed after high school.

344. Mehnert, Klaus. *Twilight of the Young: The Radical Movements of the
     1960s and Their Legacy*. New York: Holt, Rinehart & Winston, 1967.
     Written by a non-American about international movements. Several
     sections on the U.S. from the Beats to the occult and self-awareness
     movements.

345. Nobile, Philip, ed. *The Con III Controversy: The Critics Look at The
     Greening of America*. New York: Pocket Books, 1971.

Con III refers to Consciousness III, the '60s generation Reich described in *The Greening of America*. Gathered here are criticisms of that book from people such as Nicholas Von Hoffman, Garry Wills, Herbert Marcuse, Tom Hayden, and many others.

346. Rapson, Richard L., ed. *The Cult of Youth in Middle-Class America.* Lexington, ME: Heath, 1971.
   A collection of essays examining American childhood with a view to its relation to American society. Writers include Alexis de Tocqueville, Jane Addams, John Dewey, Richard Hofstadter, Bruno Bettelheim, Theodore Roszak, and Benjamin DeMott.

347. Robertson, James Louis. *What Generation Gap? A Dialogue on America.* Washington, DC: Acropolis Books, 1970.
   A debate between the younger and older generations on the problems between the two generations. Robertson gave a speech on the older generation's failure to properly educate youth and this book includes the text of the speech, letters he received about his speech, and his responses to the letters. Although Robertson writes from a fairly conservative point of view, he does seem interested in keeping an open dialog between the generations.

348. Seidenbaum, Art. *Confrontation on Campus: Student Challenge in California.* Los Angeles, CA: Ward Ritchie, 1969.
   In 1968 Seidenbaum toured the large California universities for a series of magazine articles. He looked at each school in terms of student upheavals, and he ended up with a humane accounting of the students he interacted with.

349. Stanford, Gene, ed. *Generation Rap: An Anthology abnout Youth and the Establishment.* New York: Dell Publishing, 1971.
   Selection of writings from youth to the establishment and vice versa. Writers include Paul Goodman, Eldridge Cleaver, Jerry Rubin, Kurt Vonnegut, Jr., Leo Rosten, I.F. Stone, Irving Howe, Spiro Agnew, Norman Cousins, and Rollo May.

350. Stinchcombe, Arthur L. *Rebellion in a High School.* Chicago: Quadrangle Books, 1964.
   A study of the causes and dimensions of high school rebellion. It is interesting because it deals with the group of high school students who were also rebellious in the 1960s in colleges and universities.

351. Strouse, Jean. *Up Against the Law: The Legal Rights of People Under Twenty-one.* New York: NAL-Signet Books, 1970.
   A manual of the rights of youth including areas such as student rights, parents, marriage, drugs, sex, driving, employment, contracts, and the draft.

352. Taylor, Robert N. *This Damned Campus: As Seen by a College Chaplain.*
     Philadelphia: Pilgrim Press, 1969.
     A school chaplain discusses his experiences with students and their
     actions. His view is that universities are taking the place of churches as
     places to learn morality and ethics.

353. *Thoughts of Young Radicals.* New York: Pitman Publishing, 1966.
     In 1966, *The New Republic* published a series of articles from America's
     young radicals--Charlie Cobb, Todd Gitlin, Stokely Carmichael, Tom
     Hayden, Casey Hayden, Richard Flacks, and Jean Smith. They were
     asked to respond to four questions about their analysis and projections
     for America. These essays have been collected in this book, with
     comments by some of the "older generation," such as Michael
     Harrington.

354. Walton, George H. *Wasted Generation.* Philadelphia: Chilton Books, 1965.
     The wasted generation were the young men of military age in the U.S.
     in the 1960s. Walton discusses the rise in failures for induction
     physicals (both for physical and mental reasons) illiteracy, early
     marriage, teen-age drinking, school dropouts, and juvenile delinquents.
     He cites these as examples of the failure of American families and
     schools to properly ground youth in the necessities for becoming
     productive members of society.

355. Wein, Bibi *The Runaway Generation.* New York: David McKay, 1970.
     A look at several of the kids who left the mainstream during the 1960s
     and got involved with drugs, dropped out of high school, and/or ran
     away from their homes.

356. Wilkerson, David. *Hey, Preach . . . You're Comin' Through.* New York:
     Pyramid Books, 1968.
     For teen-agers, a message about the generation--the problems and the
     possibilities. Wilkerson was looking to the future to a spiritual
     revolution among youth.

357. Williams, Paul. *Pushing Upwards.* New York: Links, 1973.
     Reflections on life in the 1960s by the originator of *Crawdaddy.*
     Williams' concerns about human relationships, war, media, arts, music,
     self-identity, and self-growth are representative of the concerns of many
     young people of the times.

358. Yankelovich, Daniel. *Generations Apart.* New York: Columbia
     Broadcasting System, 1969.
     A study done by Yankelovich for a CBS news series. He found that there
     were a significant number of youth critical of U.S. economic and
     political systems and of authorities. The more radical the political
     values of a youth, the more critical of tradition and social values he
     tended to be. Very short, but full of statistical data.

359. *The Young Americans: Understanding the "Upbeat" Generation.* New York:
Time, 1966.
Time-like articles on youth in the 1960s. Photographs included.

EDUCATION

360. Abeles, Elvin. *The Student and the University: A Background Book on the
Campus Revolt.* New York: Parents' Magazine, 1969.
A history of higher education and an analysis of the relationship of the
background of higher education to the 1960s student protest.

361. Ackerman, Nathan W., et al. *Summerhill: For and Against.* New York:
Hart Publishing, 1970.
In 1960, A.S. Neill wrote about an experimental school in which
children were encouraged in their curiosity and could learn or not learn
as they chose. Youth of the 1960s picked up on this as a way for children
to be raised. In this book we hear from leading thinkers, such as Max
Rafferty, Ashley Montagu, Bruno Bettelheim, Paul Goodman, and Erich
Fromm, their opinions about a Summerhill type of learning experience.

362. American Civil Liberties Union. *Academic Freedom, Academic
Responsibility, Academic Due Process in Institutions of Higher
Learning.* New York: ACLU, 1966.
Policy statements by the ACLU for use as guides for discussions and
decisions.

363. Axelrod, Joseph, et al. *Search for Relevance: The Campus in Crisis.* San
Francisco: Jossey-Bass, 1969.
A look at the issues in higher education in the late 1960s--student
development, curriculum problems, relationships between students and
faculty, and activist students.

364. Barzun, Jacques. *The American University: How It Runs, Where It is Going.*
New York: Harper & Row, Publishers, 1968.
An overview of the structures and responsibilities of higher education
institutions in the 1960s.

365. Ben-David, J. *Trends in American Higher Education: Directions Old and
New.* New York: McGraw-Hill, 1972.
This is primarily a survey of American higher education. However,
Ben-David does address the problems of the "bohemian" community
which often surrounds the university and the politicization of the
university.

366. Birenbaum, William M. *Overlive: Power, Poverty and the University.* New
York: Delacorte, 1969.
A look at "bigger is better" and other such phenomena in American
society and how they related to 1960s educational institutions.

367. Bolton, Charles D., and Kenneth C.W. Kammeyer. *The University Student: A Study of Student Behavior and Values.* New Haven, CT: College and University Press, 1967.
     A study of what students did with their informal time, to see if any of their classroom content spread into their personal lives.

368. Buchanan, James M., and Nicos E. Devletoglou. *Academia in Anarchy: An Economic Diagnoses.* New York: Basic Books, 1970.
     An economic analysis of the turmoil on campuses in the 1960s.

369. Cantelon, John E. *College Education and the Campus Revolution.* Philadelphia: Westminster Press, 1969.
     An examination of the value of the liberal arts college, especially within a large university, in the education of the young.

370. Capaldi, Nicholas, ed. *Clear and Present Danger: The Free Speech Controversy.* New York: Pegasus, 1970.
     Readings in defense of free speech. Included are readings on censorship. It was Capaldi's theory that universities may have been losing their academic freedom by taking political sides on such issues as the Vietnam war, and this theory is also explored.

371. Committee on the Student in Higher Education. *The Student in Higher Education.* New Haven, CT: Hazen Foundation, 1968.
     A report criticizing the university for not being more concerned with the human development of students. It makes recommendations for how schools could take on the responsibility of "Developmental Education."

372. Dennis, Lawrence E., and Joseph F. Kaufman, eds. *The College and the Student.* Washington, DC: American Council on Education, 1966.
     A collection of readings which focus on the student's position in the academic community. Several papers are on the student and academic freedom.

373. Estrada, Jacquelyn, ed. *The University Under Siege.* Los Angeles: Nash Publishing, 1971.
     An analysis of the New Left's activities on American campuses based on the principles of Ayn Rand's Objectivism. The writers were against campus unrest and tried to posit solutions to the problems they saw.

374. Farber, Jerry. *The Student As Nigger: Essays and Stories.* New York: Pocket Books, 1969.
     Jerry Farber's essay, "The Student As Nigger," became famous for its explanation of the powerlessness of students against the socializing influence of the schools. All of these essays follow this same theme of students and the influence of schools, not in what they teach, but in how they teach.

375. Footlick, Jerrold K. *The College Scene Now.* Silver Spring, MD: Dow Jones, 1967.
    A book describing what was happening in colleges and universities in 1967. Profiles of eight colleges: Bryn Mawr, Colorado State, Dartmouth, El Camino, Fordham, Indiana, Vanderbilt, and Wooster.

376. Frankel, Charles. *Education and the Barricades.* New York: W.W. Norton, 1968.
    An examination of where American higher education should go after all the turmoils of the 1960s.

377. Full, Harold, ed. *Controversy in American Education: An Anthology of Crucial Issues.* New York: Macmillan Publishing, 1967.
    Readings on issues in education at every level during the 1960s.

378. Goheen, Robert. *The Human Nature of a University.* Princeton, NJ: Princeton UP, 1969.
    Reflections from the man who was president of Princeton during the 1960s. He offers a justification for a liberal education for the youth of the times.

379. Graubard, Stephen R., and Geno A. Ballotti, eds. *The Embattled University.* New York: George Braziller, 1970.
    Readings on student issues, university governance, faculty involvement, university purpose, and university support, all raised in the 1960s. Writers include Edgar Friedenberg, Clerk Kerr, Morris Abram, Erik Erikson, and Daniel Bell.

380. Hefferlin, J.B. Lon. *Dynamics of Academic Reform.* San Francisco: Jossey-Bass, 1969.
    Study of educational reform in colleges and universities. How does reform occur? What are its causes?

381. Hodgkinson, Harold L. *Institutions in Transition: A Profile of Change in Higher Education.* New York: McGraw-Hill, 1971.
    Sponsored by the Carnegie Commission on Higher Education, a study of changes in higher education. Included is one chapter on student protests.

382. Hook, Sidney. *In Defense of Academic Freedom.* New York: Pegasus, 1970.
    A gathering of readings on the dangers to academic freedom that were the result of violence on university campuses. Writers include Bruno Bettelheim, Henry Steele Commager, Jacques Barzun, and Kenneth Clark.

383. Institute on College Self Study, University of California, Berkeley. *Order and Freedom on the Campus: The Rights and Responsibilities of Faculty and Students.* Edited by Owen A. Knorr, and W. John Mintner.

Boulder, CO: Western Interstate Commission for Higher Education, 1965.
Papers that explore rights and responsibilities of faculty and students, academic freedom, student discontent, institutional accountability, and the Berkeley uprisings in 1964.

384. Jencks, Christopher, and David Riesman. *The Academic Revolution.* Garden City, NY: Doubleday, 1968.
A study of the evolution of higher education and of its relation to American society.

385. Jervey, Edward D. *Three Way Street.* New York: Vantage Press, 1969.
An argument for the cooperation of students, faculty, and administration in the policy-making of the colleges and universities of America.

386. Katz, Joseph, et al. *No Time for Youth: Growth and Constraints in College Students.* San Francisco: Jossey-Bass, 1968.
A four-year study of undergraduates, both in and out of the classroom. Includes a chapter on the student activists of 1964.

387. Kerr, Clark. *The Uses of the University.* Cambridge, MA: Harvard UP, 1972.
A study of the changes in universities that was first published in 1963. In 1972, the book was republished with an extra chapter in which Kerr gave his reactions to the uprisings in the universities and listed several things he wished he would have said in 1963.

388. Krueger, Marlis, and Frieda Silvert. *Dissent Denied: The Technocratic Response to Protest.* New York: Elsevier, 1975.
A study of black and white student protest and an assessment of the socio-political significance of that protest.

389. Lee, Calvin B.T. *The Campus Scene: 1900-1970.* New York: David McKay, 1970.
History of the different ethos on American college campuses during the 20th century. The last four sections deal with the 1960s.

390. McGrath, Earl J. *Should Students Share the Power? A Study of Their Role in College and University Governance.* Philadelphia: Temple UP, 1970.
A study of existing practices of student participation in university governance, a look at the effects of these practices, and recommendations for policies on student governance.

391. Mallery, David. *Ferment on the Campus: An Encounter with the New College Generation.* New York: Harper & Row, Publishers, 1966.
A study of students and faculty on seven U.S. campuses to get a feeling for what students were thinking and doing, politically and socially, in the mid-1960s.

392. Menashe, Louis, and Ronald Radosh, eds. *Teach-Ins: USA: Reports, Opinions, Documents.* New York: Praeger Publishers, 1967.
An exploration of the teach-in movement, which began in the early sixties as a way for faculty and students to learn more about important issues and to communicate with each other less formally.

393. Metzger, Walter P., et al. *The Dimensions of Academic Freedom.* Urbana, IL: U of Illinois P, 1969.
A discussion of academic freedom which touches on the role of faculty in student uprisings and the new student in the 1960s.

394. Postman, Neil and Charles Weingartner. *The Soft Revolution: A Student Handbook for Turning Schools Around.* New York: Dell Publishing, 1971.
A handbook on changing the structures of education without the use of violence. It was written for students who were unhappy with their educations and wanted constructive ideas for change.

395. Ridgeway, James. *Closed Corporation: American Universities in Crisis.* New York: Random House, 1969.
An exploration of the relationship of universities and faculty to society. Are the universities "central to industrial society?"

396. Roszak, Theodore, ed. *The Dissenting Academy.* New York: Random House-Pantheon Books, 1968.
A group of writers address the question of the academic community's social responsibility, especially with regard to war. Writers include Staughton Lynd, Gordon Zahn, and Noam Chomsky.

397. Sanford, Nevitt. *Where Colleges Fail: A Study of the Student as Person.* San Francisco: Jossey-Bass, 1967.
Sanford argues that individual development should be the aim of education. He also discusses the processes of developmental change in students and looked at outside pressures on colleges and universities.

398. Schwab, Joseph J. *College Curriculum and Student Protest.* Chicago: U of Chicago P, 1969.
A look at student protest as it relates to the curriculum and specific recommendations for curricular change to help ameliorate some of the problems.

399. Scimecca, Joseph, and Roland Damiano. *Crisis at St. John's: Strike and Revolution on the Catholic Campus.* New York: Random House, 1967.
The crisis was not student protest, but a faculty strike that lasted about a year. The authors were part of the striking faculty and wrote this book with the aim of making St. John's crisis an example of the problems facing Catholic universities in the 1960s.

400. Taylor, Harold. *Students Without Teachers: The Crisis in the University.*
New York: McGraw-Hill, 1969.
Taylor makes the argument that universities were neglecting their
students. He felt that universities needed to provide more leadership to
help their students make decisions and deal with change.

401. Tussman, Joseph. *Experiment at Berkeley.* New York: Oxford UP, 1969.
A description of the Experimental Program instituted by Berkeley in
1965. It gave faculty full determination of the curriculum to try to solve
some of the educational problems associated with the first two college
years and with student dissatisfaction with their curriculum.

402. Von Hoffman, Nicholas. *The Multiversity: A Personal Report on What
Happens to Today's Students at American Universities.* New York:
Holt, Rinehart & Winston, 1966.
An attempt to describe the impact of the large university on students,
faculty, and administration. Von Hoffman believed that universities
could easily add new services and programs, but found it very difficult
to change existing ones. The school he used as an example was the
University of Illinois.

403. Wallerstein, Immanuel, and Paul Starr, eds. *The University Crisis Reader.* 2
vols. New York: Random House, 1971.
Documents from debates at Columbia University in the late 1960s on the
crisis in the university. Coverage includes the business aspects of the
university, its relationship with government, racisim in the university,
university governance, changes in education, SDS and the left, faculty
roles, and student movements.

404. Weaver, Gary R., and James H. Weaver, eds. *The University and
Revolution.* Englewood Cliffs, NJ: Prentice Hall, 1969.
A collection of readings on the impact of the university on
revolutionary movements and vice versa. Writers include Seymour
Lipset, Jack Newfield, Mark Rudd, Eldridge Cleaver, and others.

405. Williams, Sylvia Berry. *Hassling.* Boston: Little, Brown, 1970.
An account of high school issues of conflict in a Palo Alto, California,
high school, 1967-1969.

406. Wilson, Bryan. *The Youth Culture and the Universities.* London: Faber,
1970.
Although primarily about Britain, there seem to have been enough
similarities between youth and universities in both countries that this
book would be valuable in its analysis for the U.S.

407. Wolff, Robert Paul. *The Ideal of the University.* Boston: Beacon Press, 1969.
An exploration of what a university should be and do and some
observations about the universities and university education in the
1960s.

408. Yamamoto, Kaoru, ed. *The College Student and His Culture: An Analysis.*
     Boston: Houghton Mifflin, 1968.
     A collection of readings about higher education and students. Writers
     include Clark Kerr, Kenneth Keniston, Nevitt Sanford, and David
     Riesman.

Protest

GENERAL WORKS

409. Abrahamsen, David. *Our Violent Society*. New York: Funk & Wagnalls, 1970.
     A study of violence in American society in the 1960s. Abrahamsen looks at violence in relation to sex, race, assassins, the American dream, and Lee Harvey Oswald.

410. Aiken, M., N.J. Demerath III, and G. Marwell. *Dynamics of Idealism: White Activists in a Black Movement*. San Francisco: Jossey-Bass, 1971.
     Although this study is primarily concerned with civil rights activities, the research speaks more generally about activists and how their activities shape them. It is of interest because many of the civil rights activists went on later to non-civil rights activism.

411. Anderson, Walt, ed. *The Age of Protest*. Pacific Palisades, CA: Goodyear Publishing, 1969.
     In the preface, Kenneth Boulding posits several propositions for a possible theory of protest. A number of readings are collected about protest from writers such as Paul Goodman, Theodore Roszak, Herbert Marcuse, Martin Luther King, Jr., I.F. Stone, Stokely Carmichael, Eldridge Cleaver, Nat Hentoff, and Abraham Maslow.

412. Armstrong, Gregory, ed. *Protest: Man Against Society*. New York: Bantam Books, 1969.
     A broad array of readings, from the *Bible* to Jerry Rubin, on man's right and responsibility to protest. Included are essays, poems, fiction, and song lyrics.

413. Bedau, Hugo Adam, ed. *Civil Disobedience: Theory and Practice*. New York: Pegasus, 1969.
     A collections of essays on civil disobedience. Part I explores Thoreau's essay on civil disobedience; Parts II and III explore civil disobedience in the U.S. in the civil rights and peace movements. The last part is a justification of civil disobedience.

414. Berke, Joseph, ed. *Counter Culture*. London: Peter Owen, 1969.
A handbook for those who want to live revolutionary lives. Essays by
Tuli Kupferberg, Julian Beck, Allen Ginsberg, Stokely Carmichael, and
others.

415. Bienen, Henry. *Violence and Social Change*. Chicago: U of Chicago P, 1968.
A review of what had been written about violence related to
fundamental societal change.

416. Boorstin, Daniel J. *The Decline of Radicalism: Reflections on America
Today*. New York: Random House, 1969.
Boorstin argues that the protesters of the 1960s were not radicals but
were "barbarians" seeking not meaning, but power.

417. Boskin, Joseph, and Robert A. Rosenstone, eds. *Protest in the Sixties*.
Philadelphia: American Academy of Political and Social Science, 1969.
A special issue of *The Annals of the American Academy of Political and
Social Science* with articles on racial, social, political, and educational
movements of the 1960s.

418. Bowers, John Waite, and Donovan J. Ochs. *The Rhetoric of Agitation and
Control*. Reading, MA: Addison-Wesley Publishing, 1971.
The authors studied how agitators and establishments work to gain or
keep control. Specific examples used were the Democratic National
Convention of 1968, the San Francisco State strike, and the Birmingham
bus boycott.

419. Brustein, Robert. *Revolution as Theatre: Notes on the New Radical Style*.
New York: Liveright, 1971.
A look at student demonstrations as dramatic presentations. Brustein
was a drama critic and teacher and so saw the demonstrations as a form
of drama rather than strictly political acts. He was also a leftist, though
he disagreed with many 1960s activities.

420. Buckhout, Robert, and 81 concerned Berkeley students, eds. *Toward Social
Change: A Handbook for Those Who Will*. New York: Harper & Row,
Publishers, 1971.
A manual for change in areas such as violence, alienation, alternative
life styles, drugs, mental health, population control, and education.
Includes a glossary of hip slang.

421. Buckman, Peter. *The Limits of Protest*. Indianapolis, IN: Bobbs-Merrill,
1970.
An analysis of American leftist protest.

422. Butler, Ed. *Revolution Is My Profession*. Los Angeles: Twin Circle, 1968.
A handbook for revolution.

423. Campbell, James S., Joseph R. Sahid, and David P. Stang. *Law and Order Reconsidered*. Washington, DC: U.S. Government Printing Office, 1970. Report of the Task Force on Law and Law Enforcement to the National Commission on the Causes and Prevention of Violence. A study of the weaknesses in U.S. institutions and laws leading to violence, and recommendations for strengthening those weaknesses.

424. Canning, Jeremiah W., ed. *Values in an Age of Confrontation*. Columbus, OH: Merrill Publishing, 1970.
     An exploration of the value conflicts that the editors feel were responsible for national and international confrontations in the 1960s.

425. Cantor, Norman F. *The Age of Protest: Dissent and Rebellion in the 20th Century*. New York: Hawthorn Books, 1969.
     A survey of protest in the twentieth century. The last section focuses on protest movements of the 1960s.

426. Conant, Ralph W. *The Prospects for Revolution: A Study of Riots, Civil Disobedience, and Insurrection in Contemporary America*. New York: Harper's Magazine, 1971.
     A study of protest as a way of securing redress against a power structure that restricts opportunity. Focused on blacks and student protests.

427. Cooney, Robert, and Helen Michalowski. *The Power of the People: Active Nonviolence in the United States*. Philadelphia: New Society, 1967.
     A visual history on the practice of nonviolence in the United States. Includes biographical sketches of nonviolent leaders.

428. Cooper, David, ed. *To Free a Generation: The Dialectics of Liberation*. New York: Macmillan Publishing, 1968.
     Essays that analyze destruction--self-destruction and destruction of others--focusing on racism, greed, war, and repression. Essayists include R.D. Laing, Paul Goodman, Stokely Carmichael, Herbert Marcuse, and others.

429. Dellinger, David. *Revolutionary Nonviolence*. Indianapolis, IN: Bobbs-Merrill, 1970.
     A collection of essays by one of the most well-known of the anti-war activists. The essays cover the period from 1943 to 1970 and such topics as WWII, Vietnam, Cuba and China, nonviolence and the Movement, and the Chicago convention. Dellinger has always been one of the leading proponents of nonviolence.

430. Denisoff, R. Serge, ed. *The Sociology of Dissent*. New York: Harcourt Brace Jovanovich, 1974.
     A collection of essays which examine dissent from both the left and the right. Although many of the writers look generally at the subject, a few look specifically at students, the New Left and the Old, the black revolution, and women's liberation.

431. Douglas, William O. *Points of Rebellion.* New York: Random House, 1970.
Essays on dissent. Douglas discusses how Americans look at dissent,
who was leading the dissent, and he gives suggestions for restructuring
society as an answer to the dissent.

432. Flacks, Richard. *Conformity, Resistance, and Self-Determination: The
Individual and Authority.* 2d ed. Boston: Little, Brown, 1973.
Readings of seminal thinkers on the general subject of authority,
including several essays from the 1960s by such writers as Kenneth
Keniston, Flacks, Todd Gitlin, Carl Oglesby, and Ivan Illich.

433. Fortas, Abe. *Concerning Dissent and Civil Disobedience.* New York: NAL-
Signet Books, 1968.
A very thorough explanation of the "principles governing dissent"--
when dissent is or is not constitutional and how it can most effectively
be carried out.

434. Franklin, Bruce. *From the Movement / Toward Revolution.* New York:
Van Nostrand-Reinhold, 1971.
Documents from various "revolutionary" movements of the 1960s--
civil rights, antiwar, women's liberation, the Black Panthers,
Venceremos, Weather Underground. Includes pictures, posters, comics,
and other graphics.

435. Freeman, Howard E., and Norman R. Kurtz, eds. *America's Troubles: A
Casebook on Social Conflict.* Englewood Cliffs, NJ: Prentice Hall, 1969.
Essays describing social conflicts of the 1960s, e.g., the poor, blacks,
miseducation, homosexuals, abortion, youth in trouble, hippies, and
others.

436. Gerassi, John, ed. *The Coming of the New International: A Revolutionary
Anthology.* New York: World, 1971.
Selections from revolutionaries both before and during the 1960s,
including Lenin, Mao Tse-Tung, Chou En-Lai, Giap, Frantz Fanon,
Nelson Mandela, Ché Guevara, Fidel Castro, Huey Newton, Eldridge
Cleaver, and many others.

437. Gold, Robert S. ed. *The Rebel Culture.* New York: Dell Publishing, 1971.
Prose, poetry, and cartoon selections that represent the 1960s rebel
culture. Contributors include Leonard Cohen, Jules Feiffer, William
Zinsser, Russell Baker, Allen Ginsberg, Abbie Hoffman, and many
others.

438. Goodman, Mitchell, ed. *The Movement Toward a New America: The
Beginnings of a Long Revolution.* New York: Alfred A. Knopf, 1970.
A handbook for activists including a history of movements,
biographical information about people involved in them, and models of
what to do and how to do it.

439. Hare, A. Paul, and Herbert H. Blumberg. *Nonviolent Direct Action: American Cases: Social-Psychological Analyses.* Washington, DC: Corpus Books, 1968.
A case study approach to the study of nonviolence. First is an introduction to nonviolence, then cases for civil rights and for peace. The last part gives various analyses of nonviolence.

440. Hayden, Tom. *Rebellion and Repression.* Cleveland: World, 1969.
Transcripts of Hayden's testimony at two government hearings: the House Un-American Activities Committee and the National Commission on the Causes and Prevention of Violence. Both testimonies took place after the Chicago Democratic Convention and before Hayden's indictment as a conspirator.

441. Hendel, Samuel, ed. *The Politics of Confrontation.* New York: Appleton-Century-Crofts, 1971.
A systematic study of confrontation politics as exemplified by 1960s issues such as the role of the university, women's liberation, the draft, ROTC on campus, and student power.

442. *The History of Violence in America: Report of the National Commission on the Causes and Prevention of Violence.* Edited by Hugh Davis Graham and Ted Robert Gurr. New York: Praeger Publishers, 1969.
A study of violence in America which addresses violence used to protest the Vietnam war and other 1960s issues, as well as violence used against the protesters.

443. Hoffman, Abbie. *Revolution For the Hell of It.* New York: Dial Press, 1968.
Writings from Hoffman on revolution, the March on the Pentagon (1967), Yippies, the Chicago Democratic convention, and other subjects.

444. Hormachea, C.R., and Marion Hormachea, eds. *Confrontation: Violence and the Police.* Boston: Holbrook Press, 1971.
A group of readings that explore and analyze the factors involved in violent confrontation, particularly civil rights, anti-Vietnam war, and other campus demonstrations. The editors confess that they favor the police establishment.

445. Johnson, Chalmers. *Revolutionary Change.* Boston: Little, Brown, 1966.
A systems study of revolutions. Johnson believed that revolution could be avoided by responsiveness from the political and social systems to the need for change.

446. Kane, Frank. *Voices of Dissent: Positive Good or Disruptive Evil?* Englewood Cliffs, NJ: Prentice Hall, 1970.
A look at dissent, its history, examples of it, its causes, theories about it, reactions to it, and possible ways of dealing with it.

447. Kaplan, Judy, and Linn Shapiro, eds. *Red Diaper Babies: Children of the Left.* Somerville, MA: Red Diaper Productions, 1985.
      Although this is not specifically about the '60s, it is interesting because many of the '60s activists were Red Diaper Babies. The participants in this conference show how their parents' and grandparents' politics shaped their own lives and influenced their own activism.

448. Kaplan, Morton. *Dissent and the State in Peace and War.* New York: Dunellen, 1970.
      An exploration of dissent which is based not only on sentiment, but also on reason. Kaplan also explores how education relates to dissent.

449. Katope, Christopher G. and Paul G. Zolbrod, eds. *Beyond Berkeley: A Sourcebook on Student Values.* New York: Harper & Row, Publishers, 1966.
      Essays on the Berkeley student rebellion in 1964. Authors include Nathan Glazer, Paul Goodman, Mario Savio, Clark Kerr, and Irving Howe.

450. Lynd, Staughton, ed. *Nonviolence In America: A Documentary History.* Indianapolis, IN: Bobbs-Merrill, 1966.
      A selection of writings demonstrating the American tradition of nonviolence. Writers include William Lloyd Garrison, Thoreau, Emma Goldman, William James, Clarence Darrow, A.J. Muste, Martin Luther King, Jr., Bayard Rustin, Reinhold Niebuhr, and David Dellinger.

451. Methuin, Eugene H. *The Riot Makers: The Technology of Social Demolition.* New Rochelle, NY: Arlington House, 1970.
      A detailed explanation of the planned staging of riots. Covered many periods in American history, but primarily the university and civil rights riots of the 1960s.

452. Miller, Albert J. *Confrontation, Conflict and Dissent: A Bibliography of a Decade of Controversy, 1960-1970.* Metuchen, NJ: Scarecrow Press, 1972.
      The emphasis is on confrontation and includes the categories "Confrontation, General," "Firearms, Control and Regulation," "The Gap in Generations and the Drug Dilemma," "Police-Community Relations," "The Pregnant Question--Sex Education," "Student Dissent," "Anti-Ballistic Missile Systems," "Civil Disobedience, Violence, and Nonviolence," "Military Service--Compulsory and Voluntary," and "List of Alternative Tabloids." Older materials are included. A few short annotations.

453. Nieburg, H.L. *Political Violence: The Behavioral Process.* New York: St. Martin's Press, 1969.
      A study of violence to discover what it says about society and how it relates to the whole continuum of political behavior.

454. Oppenheimer, Martin, and George Lakey. *A Manual for Direct Action*. Chicago: Quadrangle Books, 1964.
    A training manual for nonviolent action. Specifically for civil rights action, but the author says it would be valuable for other movements, i.e., peace, student. Appendices include "The Bill of Rights and Civil rights," "Amendments 13, 14, and 15 to the Constitution," and "The Civil Rights Act of 1964."

455. Roberts, Myron. *The Roots of Rebellion: A Study of Existential America*. Dubuque, IA: Wm. C. Brown, 1969.
    A clear description of existentialism and its relation to rebellion in the U.S. Concludes with recommendations for goals for the next decade.

456. Rossman, Michael. *The Wedding within the War*. Garden City, NY: Doubleday, 1971.
    A volume of journalistic pieces done during the 1960s. They define the movement and its changes and reflections on the demonstrations.

457. Rubenstein, Richard F. *Rebels in Eden: Mass Political Violence in the United States*. Boston: Little, Brown, 1970.
    A history of violent movements in America, including the movements in the sixties.

458. Rush, Gary B., and R. Serge Denisoff. *Social and Political Movements*. New York: Appleton-Century-Crofts, 1971.
    A text on the development and lifespan of political movements.

459. Schultz, Bud, and Ruth . *It Did Happen Here: Recollections of Political Repression in America*. Berkeley: U of California P, 1989.
    Interviews with people who have faced political repression in the U.S., including several about repression in the 1960s.

460. *Trials of the Resistance*. Essays by Noam Chomsky, et al. New York: Random House-New York Review of Books, 1970
    Essays about the types of crimes that were generating major publicity in the 1960s--the editor calls them the times that "impel defendants to stand forth as judges of the courts which try them." Topics include: Captain Levy, an Army captain who refused to train Special Forces aidmen and who worked for civil rights and talked down the Vietnam war among Army personnel; Michael Ferber and the Boston Conspiracy Trial; the trial of the Oakland Seven; the Ultra-Resistance; and the trial of Bobby Seale.

461. Waskow, Arthur I. *Running Riot: Official Disaster and Creative Disorder in American Society*. New York: Herder & Herder, 1970.
    A "journey" through the sixties. The book is divided into two parts, one dealing with the civil rights movement and the other with the student/peace/radical movement.

462. Wright, Nathan. *Ready to Riot.* New York: Holt, Rinehart & Winston, 1968.
A study of riots in American cities--both black and white riots.

463. Zimmer, Timothy W.L. *Letters of a C.O. from Prison.* Valley Forge, PA: Judson Press, 1969.
Zimmer, a student at Earlham College, went to prison in 1967 for refusing conscription. His letters show him to be a serious, sincere, intelligent young man struggling with the choice he made at such an early age.

YOUTH

464. Altbach, Philip G., and David H. Kelley. *American Students: A Selected Bibliography on Student Activism and Related Topics.* Lexington, MA: Heath, 1973.
A bibliography focusing on student activism in the 1960s. It includes a section on the student left.

465. Altbach, Philip G., and Robert S. Laufer, eds. *The New Pilgrims: Youth Protest in Transition.* New York: David McKay, 1972.
A group of essays examining the youth movement, primarily in the U.S., and placing it within an historical context. Not limited to university students, it examines the broader context of generational conflict.

466. Aptheker, Bettina. *The Academic Rebellion in the United States.* Secaucus, NJ: Citadel Press, 1972.
An exploration of campus revolts. Aptheker was a communist and took part in the Free Speech Movement at Berkeley. She sees the revolts as being indicative of a change in the class position of intellectuals. She places the Black Liberation Movement at the core of student radicalism, rather than seeing it as a separate issue.

467. Avorn, Jerry L., and members of the staff of the *Columbia Daily Spectator.* *Up against the Ivy Wall, a History of the Columbia Crisis.* New York: Atheneum Publishers, 1968.
An account of the student revolt at Columbia in April and May of 1968. This was one of the most famous student revolts of the decade and the coverage is based on interviews with the people involved. The fact that this was written so soon after the events described gives the account a special perspective.

468. Baker, Michael A., et al. *Police on Campus: The Mass Police Action at Columbia University, Spring, 1968.* New York: New York Civil Liberties Union, 1969.
An account of the violent actions of the police to break up the Columbia University student protesters in April, 1968. Based on eyewitness testimony.

469. Bander, Edward J., ed. *Turmoil on the Campus.* New York: H.W. Wilson, 1970.
     Essays from a wide range of writers on student unrest, including early essays on Kent State.

470. Barlow, William, and Peter Shapiro. *An End to Silence: The San Francisco State College Student Movement in the '60s.* Indianapolis, IN: Bobbs-Merrill, 1971.
     In 1968 students went on strike at San Francisco State to defend the needs of the non-white communities of the Bay Area. This book is a history and analysis of the conditions leading up to the strike, as representative of conditions at other American colleges and universities. The writers were students at San Francisco State and were deeply involved with the strikes.

471. Bayer, Alan E., and Alexander W. Astin. *Campus Disruption during 1968-69.* Washington, DC: American Council on Education, 1969.
     A survey and study of campus unrest from representative American colleges and universities.

472. Becker, Howard S., ed. *Campus Power Struggle.* [n.p.]: Trans-Action Books, 1970.
     Articles from *transaction* magazine. For the most part the articles are about campus uprisings at Berkeley, Columbia, San Francisco State, and Cornell Universities. There are also articles on racism on campus, drugs, young conservatives, psychiatric help for students, and student power.

473. Bell, Daniel, and Irving Kristol, eds. *Confrontation: The Student Rebellion and the Universities.* New York: Basic Books, 1969.
     Essays by Talcott Parsons, Seymour Lipset, Nathan Glazer, Bell, Kristol, and others on the student movement of the 1960s. Separate chapters on Berkeley, San Francisco State, Columbia, and Cornell.

474. Bloomberg, Edward. *Student Violence.* Washington, DC: Public Affairs Press, 1970.
     Bloomberg places the blame for the turmoil on college campuses on faculty and administration who were too permissive with students.

475. Boruch, Robert F. *Faculty Role in Campus Unrest.* Washington, DC: American Council on Education, 1969.
     A study of faculty participation in student protest.

476. Brickman, William W., and Stanley Lehrer, eds. *Conflict and Change on the Campus: The Response to Student Hyperactivism.* New York: School and Society Books, 1970.
     Readings which examine the scope and nature of student unrest in the 1960s. Part I focuses on American students; Part II on the international scene. Various documents are also included.

477. Brown, Michael. *The Politics and Anti-Politics of the Young.* Beverly Hills, CA: Glencoe Press, 1969.
A collection of readings tracing the origins of youth activists and drop-outs. Writers include Theodore Roszak, Mario Savio, Tom Hayden, Amitai Etzioni, and Kenneth Keniston.

478. Cain, Arthur H. *Young People and Revolution.* New York: John Day, 1970.
Writing for young people, Cain says he wants to cheer the revolutionaries on, but he also wants to make young readers aware of their alternatives and to give them knowledge of the thoughts and actions of influential men of the past.

479. Califano, Joseph A., Jr. *The Student Revolution: A Global Confrontation.* New York: W.W. Norton, 1970.
A short examination of student unrest in several countries in Europe, Africa, the Middle East, and Asia. Califano lists the common elements he detected among student in all of these countries. He concludes by outlining the differences and similarities of the causes of unrest in the U.S. His arguments are persuasive and logical, but they are, nevertheless, based on generalizations of the observations of one man.

480. Carling, Francis. *Move Over: Students, Politics, Religion.* New York: Sheed & Ward, 1969.
The author says he is "concerned with the intersection of politics and religion." He believes that religion and politics are very much related in the youth movement. His book examines what factors led to both political and religious activism among students and the implications of that activism.

481. Carnegie Commission on Higher Education. *Dissent and Disruption: Proposals for Consideration by the Campus.* New York: McGraw-Hill, 1971.
"Concentrates on how dissent on campus may be protected and disruption may be prevented." There are specific recommendations that would protect the rights of students and faculty to dissent, but would also keep the campuses from being disrupted in the course of this dissent.

482. Clark, Ted, and Dennis T. Jaffe. *Toward a Radical Therapy: Alternate Services for Personal and Social Change.* New York: Gordon & Breach, 1973.
The authors set up a youth crisis center in 1969. They wrote this book to propose alternative strategies for helping young people respond to the changes inherent in trying to live the countercultural lifestyle.

483. Cooper, John Charles. *A New Kind of Man.* Philadelphia: Westminster Press, 1972.

An exploration of what the author calls "the new mentality" of American youth in the 1960s. Cooper believes that the moral concerns of this generation indicate an awakening of religious consciousness.

484. Cox Commission. *Crisis at Columbia. Report of the Fact-Finding Commission Appointed to Investigate the Disturbances at Columbia University in April and May 1968.* New York: Random House-Vintage Books, 1968.
A very detailed report of the uprising with the Commission's observations and recommendations. The conclusion was not anti-student, but focused on the need for students and faculty to feel they have a say in the University's administration.

485. Coyne, John R., Jr. *The Kumquat Statement.* New York: Cowles Books, 1970.
An allusion to James Kunen's *The Strawberry Statement* (see entry 523). Coyne wrote about Berkeley in the 1960s from the point of view of a student not involved in the revolutionary activism and appalled by what the activists were doing to American education.

486. Crick, Bernard, and William A. Robson, eds. *Protest and Discontent.* Baltimore: Penguin Books, 1970.
Interesting as a general approach to youth's protest, but focuses on Britain. There is one chapter on American protest by David C. Rapoport titled "Generations in America."

487. Cutler, Richard L. *The Liberal Middle Class: Maker of Radicals.* New Rochelle, NY: Arlington House, 1973.
Examination of radical youth, both political and social, and an exploration of the danger of them to the American political system.

488. Davidson, Carl. *The New Radicals in the Multiversity: An Analysis and Strategy for the Student Movement.* Chicago: Students for a Democratic Society, 1968.
A short essay on strategies for building student movements in large universities.

489. DeConde, Alexander, ed. *Student Activism: Town and Gown in Historical Perspective.* New York: Charles Scribner's Sons, 1971.
Although this group of readings was gathered to give a history of student activism worldwide, the last two chapters focus on Berkeley and Cornell in the 1960s.

490. Divale, William Tulio, with James Joseph. *I Lived Inside the Campus Revolution.* New York: Cowles Books, 1970.
The story of campus insurrection from a man who rose to power in the "revolution," and who ended up believing in a lot of what he was doing, while at the same time being an FBI informer.

491. Douglas, Bruce, ed. *Reflections on Protest: Student Presence in Political Conflict.* Richmond, VA: John Knox Press, 1967.
     A guide for strategic thinking for students who wished to become involved in student movements. Includes theory and case studies. Particularly focused on Christian movements.

492. Draper, Hal. *Berkeley: The New Student Revolt.* New York: Grove Press, 1965.
     The history of the Free Speech Movement and demonstrations at Berkeley. Introduction by Mario Savio. Also included are various selections from other people about the revolt of the students at Berkeley. Written by a member of the library staff.

493. Ehrenreich, Barbara and John. *Long March, Short Spring: The Student Uprising at Home and Abroad.* New York: Monthly Review Press, 1969.
     This book covers the U.S., England, France, Germany, and Italy. It includes information from interviews on student uprisings and radicalism. In the U.S., it focuses on Columbia University.

494. Eichel, Lawrence E., et al. *The Harvard Strike.* New York: Houghton Mifflin, 1970.
     An account of the events which led to the confrontation of students at Harvard in 1969 and of the confrontation itself. Photos included.

495. Epstein, Cy. *How to Kill a College.* Los Angeles: Sherbourne Press, 1971.
     Epstein taught at California State College, Fullerton, and reports on the uprisings that took place there in 1970.

496. Erlich, John and Susan, eds. *Student Power, Participation and Revolution.* New York: Association Press, 1970.
     Student writings about their concerns--racism, poverty, militarism, environmental pollution. Includes high school students.

497. Esler, Anthony. *Bombs, Beards, and Barricades: 150 Years of Youth in Revolt.* New York: Stein and Day, 1971.
     Esler begins with the first student revolt in Germany in 1815. His thesis is that what happened in the 1960s was but part of a continuum of youth revolt and shared the same characteristics with what had gone before.

498. Executive Systems, Inc. *The Establishment Meets Students.* Lawrenceville, IL: Ad-Ventures, 1970.
     Speeches from two conferences that brought together students, businessmen, academic administrators, and government officials to talk about student revolt. Speakers include Tom Hayden, Julian Bond, and others.

499. Feuer, Lewis S. *The Conflict of Generations: The Character and Significance of Student Movements.* New York: Basic Books, 1969.

A history of student movements. As a sociologist Feuer describes the common traits of the student activists and he outlines the stages of such movements. Although he claims all student movements have been similar, he does focus on a few, e.g., the New Student Left and the Berkeley uprising in 1964-1966.

500. Fish, Kenneth L. *Conflict and Dissent in the High School*. New York: Bruce Publishing, 1970.
A study of student unrest in high schools in the 1960s. Includes specific accounts of various schools.

501. Flacks, Richard. *Youth and Social Change*. Chicago: Markham Publishing, 1972.
An account of the transformation of college campuses of the 1950s to the political centers of activity of the 1960s. Although the writer is sympathetic to the radical student movement, he claims the book is based on thorough research. Flacks was a graduate student at the University of Michigan at the beginning of the 1960s and was a member of SDS from its first days.

502. *Fortune* editors. *Youth in Turmoil*. New York: Time-Life Books, 1969.
A collection of essays analyzing youth protesters from the perspective of the business world. The collection reflects the more conservative view and shows the concern that efforts be made to bring the protesters back into the mainstream of established society.

503. Foster, Julian, and Durward Long, eds. *Protest! Student Activism in America*. New York: William Morrow, 1970.
A study and description of student activism. Part of the book is made up of case studies of protests at Indiana University, the University of Wisconsin, San Francisco State, the University of Colorado, Princeton, Howard, and Ohio State Universities.

504. Gerzon, Mark. *The Whole World Is Watching: A Young Man Looks at Youth's Dissent*. New York: Viking Press, 1969.
Gerzun tries to describe the attitudes of the 1960s generation to history, mass society, politics, questions of identity, drugs, marriage, the draft, and the whole range of cultural issues affecting youth.

505. Glazer, Nathan. *Remembering the Answers: Essays on the American Student Revolt*. New York: Basic Books, 1970.
An exploration of the role of colleges and universities in the radical political movements of the 1960s.

506. Gold, Alice Ross, Richard Christie, and Lucy Norman Friedman. *Fists and Flowers: A Social Psychological Interpretation of Student Protest*. New York: Academic Press, 1976.
A research study of the political attitudes of student protesters and the process of radicalization.

507. Grant, Joanne. *Confrontation on Campus: The Columbia Pattern for the New Protest*. New York: NAL, 1969.
    A story of the Columbia take-over in a narrative-day-to-day account. Several documents relating to the strike are also included.

508. Hanff, Helene. *The Movers and Shakers: The Young Activists of the Sixties*. New York: S.G. Phillips, 1970.
    This book is about the movements of the 1960s seeking to reform a corrupt establishment--specifically the military, the political, and the academic establishments.

509. Hart, Richard L., and J. Galen Saylor, eds. *Student Unrest: Threat or Promise?* Washington, DC: Association for Supervision and Curriculum Development, NEA, 1970.
    Essays on the subject of student unrest in the secondary schools.

510. Heath, Louis G., ed. *Vandals In the Bomb Factory: The History and Literature of the Students for a Democratic Society*. Metuchen, NJ: Scarecrow Press, 1966.
    A history of SDS and forty documents which serve to show the group's thoughts and activities during the 1960s.

511. Heirich, Max. *The Beginning: Berkeley, 1964*. New York: Columbia UP, 1968.
    Using the Berkeley Free Speech Movement uprisings in 1964 as a model, Heirich analyzes collective action in a conflict setting. Photos included.

512. ---. *The Spiral of Conflict: Berkeley, 1964*. New York: Columbia UP, 1971.
    A study of the Berkeley conflict and of the movement from a small dispute to a major confrontation. Photographs included.

513. Hersey, John. *Letter to the Alumni*. New York: Alfred A. Knopf, 1970.
    Hersey wrote to Yale alumni about his reflections on the uprisings at Yale, and universities all over the country, in the aftermath of Kent State, spring, 1970.

514. Hook, Sidney. *Academic Freedom and Academic Anarchy*. New York: Cowles Books, 1970.
    Hook argues that student unrest of the 1960s had nothing to do with bettering education, but that it, in fact, threatened academic freedom and the democratic process.

515. Horowitz, Irving Louis, and William H. Friedland. *The Knowledge Factory: Student Power and Academic Politics in America*. Chicago: Aldine Publishing, 1970.
    The authors examine student activism for decision-making power on campuses as a result of their models and experiences in the black power and anti-war movements.

516. Howe, Irving, ed. *Student Activism.* Indianapolis, IN: Bobbs-Merrill, 1967.
A group of writings providing information and opinion about 1960s student rebellion. Writers include Clark Kerr, Nathan Glazer, Carl Oglesby, and Howe. Each essay ends with questions for discussion and writing.

517. Jacqueney, Mona G. *Radicalism on Campus: 1969-1971: Backlash in Law Enforcement and in the Universities.* New York: Philosophical Library, 1972.
A careful analysis of student unrest in the three years, 1969-1971, the dynamics of the relationships between universities and law enforcement, and a review of what federal and state government did to deal with campus unrest.

518. Kelman, Steven. *Push Comes To Shove: The Escalation of Student Protest.* Boston: Houghton Mifflin, 1970.
Kelman was a student at Harvard beginning in 1966. Although he felt he was a socialist, he did not agree with SDS ideology and methodology. This book is his memoir of his Harvard life up to the strike of 1969 and his analysis of why SDS and the strike hurt rather than helped Harvard and ultimately the future of America.

519. Keniston, Kenneth. *Young Radicals: Notes on Committed Youth.* New York: Harcourt Brace Jovanovich, 1968.
Observations of the work of Vietnam Summer, a group organizing other groups to oppose the Vietnam war during the summer of 1967. Specifically, Keniston studies the politicization and commitment of a small group of leaders of the Summer.

520. ---. *Youth and Dissent: Rise of a New Opposition.* New York: Harcourt Brace Jovanovich 1971.
A study of youth opposition within a psycho-historical framework.

521. Kennan, George F. *Democracy and the Student Left.* Boston: Little, Brown, 1968.
In 1968 the *New York Times* published a speech Kennan made in which he was critical of the student radicals of the times. This speech begins this book with responses from students and adults, largely disagreeing with Kennan. The book ends with Kennan's response to the responses.

522. Kerpelman, Larry C. *Activists and Nonactivists: A Psychological Study of American College Students.* New York: Behavioral Publications, 1972.
A study of the psychological factors that might lead a student to become activist.

523. Kunen, James Simon. *The Strawberry Statement: Notes of a College Revolutionary.* New York: Avon Books, 1968.
A diary of Columbia in the summer of 1967 by one of its activist students.

524. Lauter, Paul, and Florence Howe. *The Conspiracy of the Young.* New York: World, 1970.
     An exploration of student turmoil in America and the repressive institutions that led them to revolt. Generally sympathetic to youth.

525. Levine, Maryl, and John Naisbitt. *Right On! A Documentary on Student Protest.* New York: Bantam Books, 1970.
     A photodocumentary. Throughout the book there are statistics from the Urban Research Corporation on college protests. Much of the book is focused on black student protest.

526. Levitt, Morton, and Ben Rubinstein, eds. *Youth and Social Change.* Detroit: Wayne State UP,1972.
     Sociological and psychological studies on youth's protest in the 1960s. Writers include Zbigniew Brzezinski, Nathan Glazer, Edgar Friedenberg, and many others.

527. Libarle, Marc, and Tom Seligson. *The Highschool Revolutionaries.* New York: Random House, 1970.
     A collection of writings and interviews from high school students all over the country on their own feelings about American society. Most of the participants were active, protesting students. Not just universities suffered from student protests.

528. Liebert, Robert. *Radical and Militant Youth: A Psychoanalytic Inquiry.* New York: Praeger Publishers, 1971.
     Liebert studied the students involved in the Columbia strike in 1968. He was trying to determine the profiles of the student activists--what caused some to protest and what determined the form that protest would take.

529. Light, Donald, Jr., and John Spiegel, et al. *The Dynamics of University Protest.* Chicago: Nelson-Hall, 1977.
     Review and analysis of student protests in the 1960s.

530. Lipset, Seymour Martin. *Rebellion in the University.* Boston: Little, Brown, 1971.
     An analysis of student protest including "Sources of Student Activism," "Who Are the Activists," "Historical Background," "Faculty and Students," and consequences of student activism.

531. ---, ed. *Student Politics.* New York: Basic Books, 1967.
     Although the essays in this book focus on student politics in developing countries, there are several essays of interest to researchers in U.S. student politics.

532. Lipset, Seymour Martin, and Philip G. Altbach, eds. *Students In Revolt.* Boston: Houghton Mifflin, 1969.

Readings on international student rebellion in the 1960s. Richard E. Peterson contributes a long, informative essay on American student protest in higher education.

533. Lipset, Seymour Martin and Gerald M. Schaflander. *Passion and Politics: Student Activism in America*. Boston: Little, Brown, 1971.
Discussion of student activism and recommendations for solutions. Lipset gives a short history of activism since the Revolutionary War. Since the writers do not completely agree in their analyses, each writer was responsible for his own half of the book.

534. Lipset, Seymour Martin and Sheldon S. Wolin, eds. *The Berkeley Student Revolt: Facts and Interpretations*. Garden City, NY: Doubleday-Anchor Books, 1965.
Essays about the 1964 uprising at Berkeley and the Free Speech Movement. Writers include Lipset, Clark Kerr, Mario Savio, Jack Weinberg, Nathan Glazer, Paul Goodman, Wolin, and many others.

535. Lombardi, John. *Student Activism in Junior Colleges: An Administrator's Views*. Washington, DC: American Association of Junior Colleges, 1969.
Lombardi gave a "description and interpretation" of what was happening and could potentially happen at junior colleges. He felt the junior college students were imitating their counterparts in the larger institutions.

536. Louis, Debbie. *And We Are Not Saved*. Garden City, NY: Doubleday, 1970.
Although much of this book focuses on civil rights, the author claims to be trying to analyze the reasons why the student movement was so strong in the early 1960s, but disintegrated in the later part of the decade.

537. Lunsford, Terry. *The "Free Speech" Crisis at Berkeley, 1964-65: Some Issues for Social and Legal Research*. Berkeley: University of California, Center for Research and Development in Higher Education, 1965.
An examination of the issues involved in the Berkeley student protest in the mid-1960s. The purpose is to study the issues surrounding this particular event and to stimulate research on these issues.

538. McGill, William J. *The Year of the Monkey: Revolt on Campus 1968-69*. New York: McGraw-Hill, 1982.
A view of campus unrest at the University of California-San Diego in 1969, told from the perspective of the man who was chancellor of the University. We get a view of Angela Davis, Eldridge Cleaver, and Herbert Marcuse, as well as the impact of the People's Park riots in Berkeley on the UCSD campus administration.

539. Miles, Michael W. *The Radical Probe: The Logic of Student Rebellion*. New York: Atheneum Publishers, 1971.

A study of student rebellion, both black and white. Miles challenges the theory that student radicals were only a small minority of the students.

540. Momboisse, Raymond M. *Control of Student Disorders*. Sacramento, CA: MSM Enterprises, 1968.
A manual to aid in the struggle for colleges to take action against the militants (both student and faculty) who threaten to destroy the schools.

541. Nagel, Julian, ed. *Student Power*. London: Merlin, 1969.
Although the focus here is on international student unrest, there are two chapters, one on the American student movement and one on American hippies.

542. Nichols, David C., ed. *Perspectives on Campus Unrest*. Washington, DC: American Council on Education, 1970.
A collection of readings about how to ease campus tensions. Writers include Kenneth Boulding, Kenneth Keniston, Seymour Martin Lipset, Clark Kerr, Harris Wofford, and many others.

543. Orrick, William. *Colleges in Crisis*. California. State College, San Francisco. Study Team Concerning the San Francisco State College Strike, 1970.
A history of the 1968-69 strike at San Francisco State College.

544. Rader, Dotson. *I Ain't Marchin' Anymore*. New York: David McKay, 1969.
A personal memoir of 1967-1968 at Columbia and the rest of New York. Rader was a political activist and tells of his experiences in the 1967 march on Washington, the Columbia uprising, and life in New York City.

545. Rand, Ayn. *The Cashing-in: The Student Rebellion*. New York: Nathaniel Branden Institute, 1965.
A book about what Rand believed were the roots of student rebellion. She was against the rebelliousness, and blamed it on the philosophy and ideology taught them by the existentialist philosophers.

546. Rogan, Donald L. *Campus Apocalypse: The Student Search Today*. New York: Seabury Press, 1969.
An examination of students of the sixties using the theory that students were seeking salvation, but not in the traditional sense. They were seeking to be saved from the lives their parents were leading, a dreary, depersonalized existence.

547. Rorabaugh, W. J. *Berkeley at War: The 1960s*. New York: Oxford UP, 1989.
A history of the sixties in Berkeley, one of the centers of the upheaval, beginning with the Free Speech Movement in 1964. Includes photos and a glossary of organizations.

548. Rosencranz, Richard. *Across the Barricades*. Philadelphia: J.B. Lippincott, 1971.

Portraits of several of the people involved in the Columbia uprisings and a look at each one's reasons for joining the movement.

549. Rossner, Robert. *The Year without an Autumn: Portrait of a School in Crisis.* New York: R.W. Baron, 1969.
In 1968-69, the Bronx High School of Science was one of several high schools across the country which experienced teacher and student strikes over a number of issues. This account is written by one of the teachers at Science--one more committed to student issues than to conservative teachers.

550. Sampson, Edward E., and Harold K. Korn, eds. *Student Activism and Protest.* San Francisco: Jossey-Bass, 1970.
Essays which analyze and describe student protest and protesters, which look for sources of dissent, and which survey contemporary research on dissent.

551. Scott, Marvin B., and Stanford M. Lyman. *Revolt of Students.* Columbus, OH: Merrill Publishing, 1970.
A scholarly description of student revolt using the game-theory model of analysis.

552. Searle, John. *The Campus War: A Sympathetic Look at the University in Agony.* New York: World, 1971.
An analysis of student protest in the 1960s. Searle starts from the assumptions that: 1) each revolt is not an isolated event, but they they all manifest certain "formal mechanisms"; and 2) the unrest is a search for the "sacred."

553. Shinto, William Mamotu *The Drama of Student Revolt.* Valley Forge, PA: Judson Press, 1970.
A look at youth's unrest as a drama. The hippies displayed the comedic style; the activists the tragic. Blacks exemplified the epic style. The farcical style belonged to the silent majority.

554. Spender, Stephen. *The Year of the Young Rebels.* New York: Random House, 1969.
Reflections on student revolts all over the world, including Columbia. Spender discusses many philosophical and practical issues, including the role of the Third World in the student revolution, the significance of the "generation gap," and the ideals of youth.

555. Urban Research Corporation. *Legislative Response to Student Protest.* Chicago: Urban Research Corp., 1970.
A summary of legislation proposed and passed at the federal and state levels as a result of campus protests in 1969.

556. ---. *Student Protests, 1969. Summary.* Chicago: Urban Research Corp., 1970.
Profiles of all the student protest activity from January through June,
1969. Findings based on analyses of the protests are given. Surprising
are the findings that the cause raised most often was black rights and in
only two percent of the protests was the Vietnam war an issue. The 232
campuses in the study are listed.

557. Wallerstein, Immanuel . *University in Turmoil: The Politics of Change.*
New York: Atheneum Publishers, 1969.
A discussion of the issues--university and government, university and
national social change, governance of the university--that were at the
root of many campus protests.

558. Warshaw, Steven, *The Trouble in Berkeley.* Berkeley: Diablo Press, 1965.
"The complete history, in text and pictures, of the great student rebellion
against the 'new university.'" A photodocumentary of the Free Speech
Movement.

559. Westby, David L. *The Clouded Vision: The Student Movement in the
United States in the 1960s.* Lewisburg, PA: Bucknell UP, 1976.
An analysis of student activism of the 1960s based on research studies
with a search for underlying causes and hypotheses to describe the
theories of the movement.

560. Wood, James L. *The Sources of American Student Activism.* Lexington,
MA: Heath, 1974.
Examines many theories of student activism in the 1960s through
empirical studies. The author develops his own theory of activism
combining a radical socialization theory and family conflict theory.

561. Zorza, R. *The Right to Say "We": The Adventures of a Young Englishman
at Harvard and in the Youth Movement.* New York: Praeger
Publishers, 1970.
The years between 1966 and 1972 at Harvard and across America from
the perspective of a young, privileged Englishman.

Kent State

562. Bills, Scott L. *Kent State/May 4: Echoes through a Decade.* Kent, OH: Kent
State UP, 1982.
Essays and interviews that reflect the wide range of responses to the May
4 tragedy at Kent State--emotional and political. Some of the interviews
use oral history format. A very good bibliography of primary materials
is included.

563. Bills, Scott L., Tim Smith, and S.R. Thulin, eds. *Kent State: Ten Years After.*
Kent, OH: Kent Popular Press, 1980.

A collection of essays on various aspects of the Kent State occurrence written in 1980, 10 years after the shootings. The writers were, for the most part, students or faculty at Kent State in 1970. The essays are short and most of them are not research articles. Three essays describe various collections of Kent State documents and one essay is a description of the course being taught on the May 4 activities. Included is a reprint of the "Statement of 23 Concerned Faculty" and a chronology of events.

564. Casale, Ottavio M., and Louis Paskoff, eds. *The Kent Affair: Documents and Interpretations.* Boston: Houghton Mifflin, 1971.
A selection from the huge mass of material reported about the shootings at Kent State. Includes local and national newspaper reports, radio and television broadcasts, state and federal documents from the investigations, editorials, articles, letters, maps, and photographs.

565. Davies, Peter. *The Truth about Kent State: A Challenge to the American Conscience.* New York: Farrar, Straus & Giroux, 1973.
The challenge is to the reader to demand more action from the U.S. government to at least find the reasons for the Kent State shootings. Almost 80 pages of photographs of the campus incident.

566. Eszterhas, Joe, and Michael D. Roberts. *Thirteen Seconds: Confrontation at Kent State.* New York: Dodd, Mead, 1970.
Written right after the Kent State killings, this book is an account of the events surrounding the incident and a look at the four students killed.

567. Gordon, William A. *The Fourth of May: Killings and Coverups at Kent State.* Buffalo, NY: Prometheus Books, 1990.
After a quick summary of the Kent State uprising, Gordon devotes the book to explaining points that were raised about the events to condemn or exonerate the students and the guardsmen. Photos included.

568. Grant, Edward J., and Mike Hill. *I Was There: What Really Went on at Kent State.* Lima, OH: CSS Publishing Co., 1974.
Grant and Hill were in the National Guard at Kent State on May 4. This book presents their side of the story.

569. Hare, A. Paul, ed. *Kent State: The Non-Violent Response.* Haverford, PA: Center for Nonviolent Conflict Resolution, 1973.
This is an account of the training in nonviolent response that was given to students at Kent State after the May 4 shootings. Also included are documents of the institutional responses to the violence of May, 1970.

570. Hensley, Thomas R., et al. *The Kent State Incident: Impact of the Judicial Process on Public Attitudes.* Westport, CT: Greenwood Press, 1981.
Actual research studies of the impact of judicial decisions about Kent State on Kent State students. Much of this book was already published

in Hensley and Lewis, *Kent State and May 4: A Social Science Perspective.*

571. Hensley, Thomas R., and Jerry M. Lewis, eds. *Kent State and May 4th: A Social Science Perspective.* Dubuque, IA: Kendall-Hunt, 1978.
A look at the Kent State shootings, including an overview, an essay on the legal aftermath, and sociological studies based on the incident.

572. Kelner, Joseph, and James Munves. *The Kent State Coverup.* New York: Harper & Row, Publishers, 1980.
Kelner was chief counsel for the Kent State victims in the 1975 trial. He argues in this book that many governmental agencies acted to suppress information that would have shown the shootings to be unjustified. Photos included.

573. Michener, James A. *Kent State: What Happened and Why.* New York: Fawcett-Crest, 1971.
An early look at what happened at Kent State and recommendations for how to avoid a repeat. Photos included.

574. Payne, J. Gregory. *Mayday: Kent State.* Dubuque, IA: Kendall-Hunt, 1981.
Divided into three parts, the event, the people, and the movie, this book provides a detailed look at Kent State from the perspective of the person who was involved as an historical consultant in the production of the television movie on Kent State.

575. Stone, I.F. *The Killings at Kent State: How Murder Went Unpublished.* New York: New York Review, 1971.
An attempt to expose a conspiracy by Ohio officials and others to obstruct justice in the shootings at Kent State University in 1970. Interesting because it comes so soon after the shootings. Includes the full text of the Justice Department's secret summary of the F.B.I. findings, and other excerpts from primary source material.

576. Taylor, Stuart, et al. *Violence at Kent State, May 1 to 4, 1970.* New York: College Notes and Texts, 1971.
A survey study of the attitudes and feelings of Kent State students after the shootings.

ECONOMICS

577. Dunne, John Gregory. *Delano: The Story of the California Grape Strike.* New York: Farrar, Straus & Giroux, 1967.
The story of the strike of the migrant grape pickers led by Cesar Chavez in California in 1965.

578. Fusco, Paul, and George D. Horwitz. *La Causa: The California Grape Strike.* New York: Macmillan Publishing, 1970.
    A photodocumentary of the strikers and the strike in 1969.

579. Matthiessen, Peter. *Sal Si Puedes: Cesar Chavez and the New American Revolution.* New York: Random House, 1969.
    The story of Cesar Chavez's fight to develop the United Farm Workers Association in the 1960s.

580. Nabokov, Peter. *Tijerina and the Courthouse Raid.* Albuquerque: U of New Mexico P, 1969.
    The story of a Spanish-American uprising in New Mexico in 1967 over old land rights, prejudice, and poverty.

EXTREMISTS

581. American Jewish Committee. *Extremism in America Today.* New York: AJC, 1968.
    An analysis of the dangers of extremism by Clifford Case, Robert Kennedy, and Morris Abram. Done in an interview format.

582. Archer, Jules. *The Extremists: Gadflies of American Society.* New York: Hawthorn Books, 1969.
    A definition and history of extremism in the U.S. The last chapter outlines the types of extremism operating in the 1960s.

583. Castellucci, John. *The Big Dance: The Untold Stody of Kathy Boudin and the Terrorist Family That Committed the Brink's Robbery Murders.* New York: Dodd, Mead, 1986.
    Although this book focuses on a 1981 incident, the characters involved in the robbery were a part of the Weather Underground and so it is of interest in tracing the changes in these revolutionaries of the 1960s.

584. Jacobs, Harold, ed. *Weatherman.* Berkeley: Ramparts Press, 1970.
    A history and analysis of the Weatherman movement. Articles, photographs, cartoons, and communiques from the group.

585. Raskin, Jonah, ed. *The Weather Eye: Communiques from the Weather Underground May 1970 - May 1974.* New York: Union Square, 1974.
    A history of the Weatherpeople as well as statements from them.

586. Sinclair, John. *The Guitar Army: Street Writings/Prison Writings.* New York: Douglas Books, 1972.
    Sinclair started the White Panther movement, the Rainbow People's Party, and managed MC5, a revolutionary rock and roll band from Michigan. In 1969, he was sentenced to ten years imprisonment for possession of marijuana. These writings were published in several

underground papers--some before and some after he was sent to prison. They attempt to explain his revolutionary theories.

587. Stern, Susan. *With the Weathermen: The Personal Journey of a Revolutionary Woman*. Garden City, NY: Doubleday, 1975.
Susan Stern was involved with the Weathermen from their beginnings in 1969 until 1972. This is the story of her experiences.

588. Weather Underground. *Prairie Fire: The Politics of Revolutionary Anti-Imperialism*. [n.p.]: Weather Underground,1974.
The political statement of this revolutionary group. It includes such issues as why revolution is necessary, how to achieve it, the issues of Vietnam, the Third World, the environment, racism, women, and youth.

The Counterculture

GENERAL WORKS

589. Belasco, Warren J. *Appetite for Change: How the Counterculture Took on the Food Industry, 1966-1988.* New York: Pantheon Books, 1989.
      Belasco traces the contemporary history of health food from the 1960s to its current popularity. He places the beginnings of it in the late 1960s when the counterculture shunned "plastic" foods and took to eating more vegetarian, organic foods.

590. Bugliosi, Vincent with Curt Gentry. *Helter Skelter: The True Story of the Manson Murders.* New York: Bantam Books, 1975.
      Bugliosi was the D.A. who convicted the Manson group for the Tate-LaBianca murders in 1969. His account of the crime and trials reads like a thriller.

591. Copeland, Alan, and Nikki Arai, eds. *People's Park.* New York: Ballantine Books, 1969.
      A photo-documentary of the People's Park incident, including the building of the park, its use, its destruction, and the subsequent riots as a result of its destruction.

592. Cox, Harvey. *The Feast of Fools.* Cambridge, MA: Harvard UP, 1969.
      An examination of the death and re-emergence of festivity and fantasy in the 1960s.

593. Earisman, Delbert L. *Hippies in Our Midst: The Rebellion Beyond Rebellion.* Philadelphia: Fortress Press, 1968.
      A study of the hippies in New York City. The author analyzes the hippies of the 1960s and also tries to put the movement into an historical context.

594. Feigelson, Naomi. *The Underground Revolution: Hippies, Yippies and Others.* New York: Funk & Wagnalls, 1970.
      The story of the U.S. counterculture in the 1960s. Covers most aspects including hippies, yippies, and the Eastern and drug gurus.

595. Felton, David, ed. *Mindfuckers: A Source Book on the Rise of Acid Fascism in America.* San Francisco: Straight Arrow Press, 1972.

A discussion of the communities established by Manson, Victor Baranco (The Institute of Human Abilities) and Mel Lyman (the Fort Hill Community). All three were cultists, instilled fear in their members, and used psychedelics in the groups.

596. Foss, Daniel. *Freak Culture: Life-Style and Politics.* New York: E.P. Dutton: 1972.
An interesting analysis of the freak movements of the 1960s. Freaks are defined as hippies and/or the New Left.

597. Gruen, John. *The New Bohemia: The Combine Generation.* New York: Shorecrest, 1966.
Greenwich Village in the 1960s. The new bohemians were artists and other countercultural types who appreciated the spirit and the cheap rents of the area. Photographs are included.

598. *The Hippies.* By the correspondents of *Time.* Ed. by Joe David Brown. New York: Time Magazine, 1967.
A selection of essays which describe and analyze the hippie movement-- its lifestyles, use of drugs, communal living, music--from Haight-Ashbury to New York City.

599. Hoffman, Abbie. *Square Dancing in the Ice Age.* New York: G.P. Putnam's, 1982.
A selection of the underground writings of this famous American hippie.

600. ---. *Steal This Book.* New York: Pirate, 1971.
A how-to handbook of methods which could be used to cheat the system, such as getting free food, clothing and furniture, and making free long distance phone calls.

601. ---. *Woodstock Nation.* New York: Random House-Vintage Books, 1969.
Hoffman's reflections on the Woodstock Festival as well as on the times and movement people in general.

602. Holmquist, Anders. *The Free People.* New York: Outerbridge & Dienstfrey, 1969.
A collection of photographs, mostly from California, of countercultural people.

603. Horowitz, David, Michael Lerner, and Craig Pyes, eds. *Counterculture and Revolution.* New York: Random House, 1972.
An introduction to the counterculture--not the political activists, but those looking for new life styles. Writers include Horowitz, Lerner, Abbie Hoffman, Timothy Leary, John Sinclair, Robin Morgan, and John Lennon and Yoko Ono.

604. Kesey, Ken. *The Further Inquiry.* New York: Viking Press, 1990.
     Kesey's own story of the Merry Pranksters, written in dialogue as if it
     were a play. Many photos included.

605. Kleps, Art. *Millbrook: The True Story of the Early Years of the Psychedelic
     Revolution.* Oakland, CA: Bench Press, 1977.
     Millbrook was Timothy Leary's commune in upstate New York. Kleps
     was one of the early members who started the Neo-American church,
     based on the use of psychedelic drugs. By the end of his experience with
     Leary, he had a negative opinion of Leary, though not necessarily of the
     idea of Millbrook.

606. Leventman, Seymour, ed. *Counterculture and Social Transformation:
     Essays on Negativistic Themes in Sociological Theory.* Springfield, IL:
     Charles G.Thomas Publisher, 1982.
     A sociological study of counterculture. The phenomena is not viewed
     as a cultural aberration, but as an undercurrent that was sending a
     message to American society of its "disillusionment and discontent."

607. Lukas, J. Anthony. *Don't Shoot--We Are Your Children.* New York:
     Random House, 1968.
     Profiles of ten people who were involved socially or politically in the
     counterculture.

608. Partridge, William L. *The Hippie Ghetto: The Natural History of a
     Subculture.* New York: Holt, Rinehart & Winston, 1973.
     A case study of a hippie community through participation. Partridge did
     not see the hippies as a counterculture but as a definite subculture of
     American society. Photos included.

609. *The People's Park: A Report on a Confrontation at Berkeley.* Office of the
     Governor, Sacramento, CA, 1969.
     An official report on the "People's Park" riots. Probably because of its
     source, it is slanted toward the law enforcers.

610. Perry, Paul. *On the Bus: The Complete Guide to the Legendary Trip of Ken
     Kesey and the Merry Pranksters and the Birth of the Counterculture.*
     New York: Thunder's Mouth Press, 1990
     Using interviews, various written pieces, and photos, Perry has given a
     history of this countercultural phenomenon of 1964, the bus trip that
     many believe was the beginning of the whole 1960s countercultural
     movement.

611. Roszak, Theodore. *Source: An Anthology of Contemporary Materials
     Useful for Preserving Sanity While Braving the Great Technological
     Wilderness.* New York: Harper & Row, Publishers, 1972.
     A selection of readings intended to counter technocratic revolution and
     lead to inward revelation and peace. Writers include Thomas Merton,

Carlos Casteneda, Denise Levertov, Norman O. Brown, Paul Goodman, Pablo Neruda, R.D. Laing, Alan Watts, and others.

612. Rubin, Jerry. *Do It! Scenarios of the Revolution*. New York: Simon & Schuster, 1970.
One of the most famous spokesmen for 1960s youth, Jerry Rubin calls on American youth to create a new world very different from their parents'. Filled with graphics and photos, this was one of <u>the</u> books for youth in the 1960s.

613. Sanders, Ed. *The Family: The Story of Charles Manson's Dune Buggy Attack Battalion*. New York: Avon Books, 1972.
Sanders' account of the Manson family focuses on the relationships Manson forged with California society--the famous and the infamous, and especially the various cult groups from which he seems to have lifted much of his philosophy. While there is a great deal on the development of the family, there is almost nothing on the trials of all the family members.

614. Snyder, Don. *Aquarian Odyssey: A Photographic Trip into the Sixties*. New York: Liveright, 1979.
An artistic photojourney through the countercultural world of the 1960s.

615. Stearn, Jess. *The Seekers*. Garden City, NY: Doubleday, 1969.
A not very flattering look at the counterculture of the 1960s. Stearn focuses on their drug use, constantly pointing out how dangerous even marijuana was.

616. Taylor, Derek. *It Was 20 Years Ago Today*. London: Bantam Books, 1987.
Taylor was press officer and assistant to the Beatles in 1964. As such, he became familiar with the famous of the 1960s. In this book, he tells the story of 1967--its music, its countercultural happenings, the Diggers, the Haight-Ashbury, the Human Be-In, the march on the Pentagon. Includes photographs.

617. Turner, Florence. *At the Chelsea*. London: Hamish Hamilton, 1986.
In the '60s, as in other decades, the Chelsea Hotel in New York City became famous for the people who often stayed there--Janis Joplin, Edie Sedgwick, Bob Dylan, Joan Baez, Patti Smith, and Viva, just to name a few. Turner lived in the Chelsea from 1964 to 1974. In this book she gives a social history of the Hotel (now declared a national landmark) as well as a memoir of her own life during this period.

618. Whitmer, Peter O. *Aquarius Revisited: Seven Who Created the Sixties Counterculture That Changed America*. New York: Macmillan Publishing, 1987.

In this book, Whitmer focuses on the ideas and writing of William Burroughs, Allen Ginsberg, Hunter Thompson, Norman Mailer, Timothy Leary, Ken Kesey, and Tom Robbins. Photos included.

619. Yablonsky, Lewis. *The Hippie Trip*. New York: Pegasus, 1968.
A first-hand account of the "hippie panorama" by a prominent sociologist. Includes interviews and analyses.

THE HAIGHT-ASHBURY

620. Anthony, Gene. *The Summer of Love: Haight Ashbury at Its Highest*. Berkeley: Celestial Arts, 1980.
Photographs and text on life in the Haight-Ashbury district, 1965-1967. Focuses on the Diggers, the San Francisco *Oracle*, the Free Clinic, the Mime Troupe, the Fillmore, the Trips Festival, and the Human Be-In.

621. Becker, Howard, ed. *Culture and Civility in San Francisco*. Chicago: Trans-action Books, 1971.
Analysis of San Francisco in the 1960s. Becker felt that San Francisco was a city more tolerant of odd behavior and that was why so many different lifestyles flourished.

622. Cavan, Sherri. *Hippies of the Haight*. St. Louis: New Critics Press, 1972.
A study of the hippies which focuses on the relationship between their beliefs and their practices. Very theoretical.

623. Ford, Clay. *Berkeley Journal: Jesus and the Street People--A Firsthand Report*. New York: Harper & Row, Publishers, 1972.
Ford worked for the Telegraph Avenue Projects--a program to help street people--in 1970. These are his reflections on was happening in the Haight during that summer. The reference to Jesus is the fact that the project was church-backed and many of Ford's reflections relate to his religious background.

624. Perry, Charles. *The Haight-Ashbury: A History*. NY: Random House, 1984.
A history and interpretation of this hippie haven from 1965-1967.

625. Von Hoffman, Nicholas. *We Are the People Our Parents Warned Us Against*. Chicago: Quadrangle Books, 1968.
A series of vignettes on the people in the Haight-Ashbury during 1967. Von Hoffman uses the New Journalism technique of focusing on personalities rather than events. A lot of attention is given to drug use.

626. Wolf, Leonard. *Voices from the Love Generation*. Boston: Little, Brown, 1968.
Interviews with many people in Haight-Ashbury during the mid-1960s when it was a hippie mecca.

627. Wolfe, Burton H. *The Hippies.* New York: NAL-Signet Books, 1968.
An early account of the hippies in the Haight-Ashbury. The author
used participant observation techniques for his research.

DRUGS

628. Aaronson, Bernard, and Osmond Humphrey, eds. *Psychedelics: The Uses
and Implications of Hallucinogenic Drugs.* Garden City, NY:
Doubleday, 1970.
A selection of readings on psychedelics, dealing with the nature of the
experience, anthropological considerations, psychedelics and religion,
psychedelics and mental functionings, therapeutic applications, and
psychedelics and the current cultural scene.

629. Alpert, Richard, and Sidney Cohen. *LSD.* New York: NAL, 1966.
Answers to questions about LSD from two points of view. Alpert
believed anyone should be able to use the drug; Cohen was in favor of
its use under controlled situations. Photographs included.

630. Andrews, George, and Simon Vinkenoog, eds. *The Book of Grass: An
Anthology on Indian Hemp.* New York: Grove Press, 1967.
A collection of accounts of experiences of people using marijuana, from
the ancient Greeks to Timothy Leary and Richard Alpert. Other users
include Errol Flynn, R.D. Laing, Aldous Huxley, and William
Burroughs.

631. Barber, Bernard. *Drugs and Society.* New York: Russell Sage Foundation,
1967.
A very broad treatment of the subject. Barber does touch on some
functions of drugs, such as political, religious, ideological, and ego-
disrupting, all popular uses for them in the 1960s.

632. Bloomquist, Edward R. *Marijuana.* New Rochelle, NY: Glencoe Press, 1968.
A negative look at marijuana, the physical but mostly the psychological,
social, and cultural effects, from a prosecuting lawyer.

633. Blum, Richard H., et al. *Society and Drugs.* San Francisco: Jossey-Bass, 1969.
An examination of the changing patterns of drug use in society in the
1960s.

634. ---. *Drugs II: Students and Drugs. College and High School Observations.*
San Francisco: Jossey-Bass, 1970.
Studies of drug use on five western U.S. colleges and universities and
four California high schools. Included such issues as motivations,
correlations with other student characteristics, bad outcomes, predicting
who will turn on, and psychiatric problems.

635. ---. *Utopiates: The Use and Users of LSD 25*. New York: Atherton Press, 1964.
    An early look at LSD use. The essayists look at LSD use as a social and cultural phenomena, different from other types of drug use.

636. Braden, William. *The Private Sea: LSD and the Search for God*. Chicago: Quadrangle Books, 1968.
    The author argues that LSD and radical theology are related, that they both challenge orthodox theology, that they have both introduced Eastern religious ideas to the West, that LSD reflects an interest in humanism and a rejection of science and rationalism.

637. Carey, James T. *The College Drug Scene*. Englewood Cliffs, NJ: Prentice Hall, 1968.
    Case studies of college drug users, particularly the drug scenes at Berkeley.

638. Cashman, John. *The LSD Story*. Greenwich, CT: Fawcett-Crest, 1966.
    A short, early treatment of LSD, including its history, its use in clinical settings, Timothy Leary and his associations with it, its relation to religious experiences, and its relation to other drugs.

639. Clark, Walter Houston. *Chemical Ecstasy: Psychedelic Drugs and Religion*. New York: Sheed & Ward, 1969.
    Clark studied the use of psychedelics in the creation of mystical experiences during the Leary studies at Harvard and other places. He felt that such drugs could result in positive experiences and that their use should be continued.

640. Cohen, Sidney. *The Beyond Within: The LSD Story*. New York: Atheneum Publishers, 1970.
    A study of LSD and other hallucinogens, based on reports from people who had taken or were taking the drugs.

641. ---. *The Drug Dilemma*. New York: McGraw-Hill, 1969.
    A history and brief description of drug use. The author gives definitions for different types of dependence. For each drug, the author relates such things as physiological and psychological effects, motivation to use, legal problems, uses, complications, management, and prevention. Treatment is not well documented.

642. ---. *Drugs of Hallucination: The Uses and Misuses of Lysergic Acid Diethylamide*. London: Seeker & Warburg, 1964.
    An examination of LSD and other hallucinogens.

643. Cuskey, Walter R., Arnold William Klein, and William Krasner. *Drug Trip Abroad: American Drug Refugees in Amsterdam and London*. Philadelphia: U of Pennsylvania P, 1972.

Studies and interviews with young Americans who were into the drug scenes in areas where drugs were treated differently than in the U.S.

644. DeBold, Richard C., and Russell C. Leaf, eds. *LSD, Man and Society.* Middletown, CT: Wesleyan UP, 1967.
An examination of LSD and its users. First is a discussion of the individual and LSD, then the society and LSD and finally the biological effects of LSD.

645. Endore, Guy. *Synanon.* Garden City, NY: Doubleday, 1968.
Synanon was started as an organization of ex-drug addicts, ex-felons, who banded together to support one another to lead lives free of drugs and crime. It grew out of Alcoholics Anonymous, but became much more popular in the 1960s because of the spread of drug use. The writer tells its story in a method of participatory observation, using dialog and focusing on various characters involved in Synanon.

646. Fort, Joel. *The Pleasure-Seekers: The Drug Crisis, Youth and Society.* Indianapolis: Bobbs-Merrill, 1969.
Fort argues that drug use should not be a criminal offense. He suggests the society needs to move beyond all drugs, including tobacco and alcohol. He also suggests a program of education about the harmful effects of drugs.

647. Geller, Allen, and Maxwell Boas. *The Drug Beat.* Chicago: Cowles Books, 1969.
The authors focus on marijuana, LSD, and amphetamines. They claim that what separates these drugs was their wide usage by the respectable middle class. The authors look at the properties, characteristics, and influences of these drugs on society. Glossary included.

648. Goldstein, Richard. *One in Seven: Drugs on Campus.* New York: Walker, 1966.
This book claims to give parents the understanding they need about drug use by their children. It speaks mainly to parents of college children.

649. Goode, Erich. *The Marijuana Smokers.* New York: Basic Books, 1970.
A sociological study of the use of marijuana in U.S. society in the 1960s.

650. Grinspoon, Lester, and James B. Bakalar. *Psychedelic Drugs Reconsidered.* New York: Basic Books, 1979.
A look at psychedelic drugs in the late 1970s. The authors felt they needed to be reconsidered, since their popular use in the 1960s had died down. They present a history of psychedelic drug use, including a chapter on the '60s, and discussed their future use in research and treatment.

651. Hentoff, Nat. *A Doctor among the Addicts.* New York: Rand McNally, 1968.
An analysis of the heroin problem in the 1960s and a description of the work of Dr. Marie Hyswander in working with addicts. Contains an early argument for the use of Methadone in treating the addicts.

652. Hollingshead, Michael. *The Man Who Turned on the World.* New York: Abelard-Schuman, 1973.
Michael Hollingshead began taking LSD in 1960, before it was illegal. This book is a narrative of his ten-year odyssey through the 1960s, constantly using LSD and trying to communicate with others who were on their own trips to spiritual enlightenment.

653. Hyde, Margaret O. *Mind Drugs.* New York: McGraw-Hill, 1968.
A handbook on drugs and drug abuse for youth and parents.

654. Inglis, Brian. *The Forbidden Game: A Social History of Drugs.* New York: Charles Scribner's Sons, 1975.
A discussion of shamanism, the priesthood, civilization, alcohol, drug wars, prohibition, and control of all types of drugs.

655. Land, Herman W. *What Can You Do About Drugs and Your Child.* New York: Hart Publishing, 1969.
A guide for parents who are concerned about the possibility of their children using drugs.

656. Laurie, Peter. *Drugs: Medical, Psychological, and Social Facts.* Baltimore: Penguin Books, 1967.
An overview of the knowledge about drugs and the people who used them.

657. Leary, Timothy. *The Politics of Ecstasy.* New York: G.P. Putnam's, 1968.
An exploration of LSD and its effects on the lives of those who took it and who didn't. A collection of essays written between 1963 and 1967.

658. Leary, Timothy, Ralph Metzner, and Richard Alpert. *The Psychedelic Experience: A Manual Based on the Tibetan Book of the Dead.* New York: University Books, 1964.
The *Tibetan Book of the Dead* is a Buddhist book describing what one will feel at the moment of death. The authors use it as a way to prepare for a psychedelic experience to direct oneself to enlightenment.

659. Lee, Martin A., and Bruce Shlain. *Acid Dreams: The CIA, LSD, and the Sixties Rebellion.* New York: Grove Press, 1985.
A detailed history of LSD. Lee starts with its discovery in 1938, takes the reader through the government's testing of it as a "truth serum" and its testing by psychologists as a simulation of or cure for psychosis, and then through its use and effects in the 1960s.

660. Lennard, Henry L., et al. *Mystification and Drug Abuse: Hazards in Using Psychoactive Drugs*. San Francisco, Jossey-Bass 1971.
Psychoactive drugs are defined as stimulants, sedatives, tranquilizers, and antidepressants. The authors look at the use and misuse of both legal and illegal drugs.

661. Liberation News Service. *A Book for a Fighting Movement*. New York: Liberation News Service, 1969.
Alternately known as *The Bust Book*, this is a guide to what to do if one gets busted for drugs.

662. Lindesmith, Alfred R. *The Addict and the Law*. Bloomington: Indiana UP, 1965.
Issues which bear on the control of drug addiction within the U.S., both historical and contemporary. Focuses primarily on opiates. The author's thesis is that our present system of narcotic control is both unjust to the addict and intensifies the problem.

663. Louria, Donald B. *The Drug Scene*. New York: McGraw-Hill, 1968.
A somewhat alarmist view of the abuses of marijuana, LSD, opiate addiction, and the drug subculture. A glossary is included. Louria was an M.D.

664. ---. *Nightmare Drugs*. New York: Pocket Books, 1966.
An overview of the drug problem, including heroin, narcotics, and hallucinogens, in the U.S. in the early 1960s.

665. McLean, Gordon R., and Haskell Bowen. *High on the Campus: Student Drug Abuse, Is There an Answer?* Wheaton, IL: Tyndale House, 1970.
Using case studies, the authors try to convince readers of the extent of drug problems among youth and offer suggestions as to what can be done about them.

666. Marshall, William, and Gilbert W. Taylor. *The Art of Ecstasy*. [n.p.]: Burns & McEachern, 1967.
Includes sketches of people important in the psychedelic revolution, a discussion of the various psychedelic drugs, a drug glossary, the effects of psychedelics, a banned speech of Timothy Leary's, a description of the drug culture, pictures of a psychedelic exhibition, a debate on the use of psychedelics, and the future of the psychedelic revolution.

667. Masters, R.E.L., and Jean Houston. *The Varieties of Psychedelic Experience*. New York: Holt, Rinehart & Winston, 1966.
Early studies of what the use of psychedelic drugs can teach about the contents and processes of the mind. The viewpoint is positive.

668. Nowlis, Helen H. *Drugs on the College Campus*. Garden City, NY: Doubleday, 1969.

An examination of the types of drugs used, the types of students who might use them, the causes for their use, and institutional responses to drug use. Selected drugs are discussed thoroughly and a glossary is included.

669. Oursler, Will. *Marijuana: The Facts, the Truth.* New York: P.S. Eriksson, 1968.
A negative look at the use of marijuana in the 1960s. The author believed that use of marijuana was the first step to harder drugs and that frequent use would lead to the need for more and stronger doses.

670. Peterson, Mark E. *Drugs, Drinks, and Morals.* UT: Deseret, 1970.
A scare book on drugs, drinking, tobacco, and sex in the 1960s.

671. Pope, Harrison, Jr. *Voices from the Drug Culture.* Boston: Beacon Press, 1971.
Pope claims to have been involved with the drug culture and to have culled his description of drug use and users from personal experience. He deals with the causes for drug use and the magnitude of the problem.

672. Schaap, Dick. *Turned On.* New York: NAL, 1967.
Schaap covered the story of the drug death of Celeste Crenshaw, given an overdose of heroin by her boyfriend, Robert Friede. To Schaap, this incident was representative of the rise in hard drug abuse by middle- and upper-class youth and the resultant problems.

673. Smith, David E, ed. *The New Social Drug: Cultural, Medical and Legal Perspectives on Marijuana.* Englewood Cliffs, NJ: Prentice Hall, 1970.
An overview of marijuana and its use by medical doctors and scholars. Smith gives its pharmacology, cases of abuse, a look at its regulation, and analyses of its use as a social and a political issue. He favors more leniency in the laws for its use.

674. Solomon, David, ed. *LSD: The Consciousness Expanding Drug.* New York: G.P. Putnam's, 1964.
Essays from scientists and scholars who had used psychedelic drugs. Solomon explores the area of expanded consciousness. Contributors include T. Leary, A. Huxley, A. Watts, W.S. Burroughs, and others.

675. Solomon, David, ed. *The Marihuana Papers.* Indianapolis, IN: Bobbs-Merrill, 1966.
A selection of writings, including the La Guardia Report from 1944, on marijuana. The editor hoped that readers would be convinced by reading the book that marijuana should be legalized.

676. Stafford, Peter. *Psychedelic Baby Reaches Puberty.* New York: Praeger Publishers, 1971.

Reflections on the use of drugs in American society--primarily marijuana and LSD. Contributors range from doctors to kids on the streets.

677. Stevens, Jay. *Storming Heaven: LSD and the American Dream.* New York: Atlantic Monthly Press, 1987.
An account of the psychedelic movement in America starting with the discovery of LSD in 1943 and ending in 1983. A very readable book that covers all the people and events tied to this movement.

678. Surface, William. *The Poisoned Ivy.* New York: Coward-McCann, 1968.
On drugs on the college campuses. The author uses as examples Yale, Harvard, Columbia, Penn, Brown, Princeton, Dartmouth, and Cornell.

679. Tart, Charles, ed. *Altered States of Consciousness: A Book of Readings.* New York: Wiley, 1969.
Readings about altered states of consciousness, including the dream state, hypnosis, meditation, minor and major psychedelic drugs, and biofeedback.

680. Way, Walter, ed. *The Drug Scene: Help or Hangup.* Englewood Cliffs, NJ: Prentice Hall, 1969.
A textbook on drug use. Discussed are "Today's Drug Scene," "Why Do People Use Drugs," "Opinions About Drug Usage," and "What Should Be Done." Discussion questions follow most of the readings.

681. Yablonsky, Lewis. *The Tunnel Back: Synanon.* New York: Macmillan Publishing, 1965.
An early account of Synanon, the therapy program run by and for ex-drug addicts.

COMMUNAL LIVING, THE CONCEPT OF FAMILY AND SEXUAL FREEDOM

682. Atcheson, Richard. *The Bearded Lady: Going on the Commune Trip and Beyond.* New York: John Day, 1971.
Reflections on the communes existing in the late '60s - early '70-s. These communes were mostly countercultural, not religious.

683. Bell, Robert R. *Premarital Sex in a Changing Society.* Englewood Cliffs, NJ: Prentice Hall, 1966.
A sociological analysis of "premarital sexual values and behavior" in the U.S. in the 1960s. Bell found that although the adults did not verbally accept it, U.S. society was moving toward more sexual freedom.

684. Berger, Bennett M. *The Survival of the Counterculture: Ideological Work and Everyday Life Among Rural Communards.* Berkeley: U of California P, 1981.

The communards were the "hippies" of the 1960s. The writer reports as a participant observer. While focusing on childrearing practices of the communes, he also tries to touch on all aspects of the communal experience. The goal is to put the commune movement into a sociological framework.

685. Bernard, Jessie. *The Future of Marriage.* New York: Bantam Books, 1973.
A study of marriage and family relationships based on patterns emerging in the 1960s.

686. Brown, Joe David, ed. *Sex in the 60's: A Candid Look at the Age of Mini-Morals.* New York: Time-Life Books, 1968.
An overview from articles in *Time Magazine* of the changes in "manners, morals, and styles of living" in America in the 1960s, i.e., sexuality, relationships, and marriage.

687. Carr, Gwen B., ed. *Marriage and Family in a Decade of Change.* Reading, MA: Addison-Wesley Publishing, 1972.
Intended as a possible textbook for a course, this book is a selection of articles written in the 1960s and 1970 on love, relationships, sex, children, and alternatives to traditional marriages and families.

688. Case, John, and Rosemary C.R. Taylor, eds. *Co-ops, Communes & Collectives: Experiments in Social Change in the 1960s and 1970s.* New York: Pantheon Books, 1979.
Readings on alternative social styles. Subjects include underground media, free schools, law collectives, and food co-ops. Writers look at the background of the communal movement, the success of participatory democracy, the type of organizations, and their legacies.

689. Constantine, Larry L. and Joan M. *Treasures of the Island: Children in Alternative Families.* Beverly Hills, CA: Sage Publications, 1976.
Alternative families are considered either group marriages or communal families. A study of the literature that had been published to that date on the children of these families.

690. Cooper, David. *The Death of the Family.* New York: Random House-Pantheon Books, 1970.
An argument against the traditional nuclear family as being restrictive and violent.

691. Cuber, John F., and Peggy Harroff. *The Significant Americans: A Study of Sexual Behavior Among the Affluent.* New York: Appleton-Century-Crofts, 1965.
A study of the marriages, sexual relationships, and behaviors of successful middle-class people in the 1960s.

692. Fairfield, Richard. *Communes U.S.A.; A Personal Tour.* Baltimore: Penguin Books, 1972.

An historical survey of communes and a description of many that
existed in the 1960s, divided into the following groups: ideological,
religious, hip, group marriage, service, and youth. Photos included.

693. ---, ed. *Utopia, USA*. San Francisco: Alternatives Foundation,1972.
A study of communal life in the U.S. edited by a person who lived that
lifestyle and who had published a magazine on communes for several
years.

694. Fitzgerald, George R. *Communes: Their Goals, Hopes, Problems*. New York:
Paulist Press, 1971.
An overview of the commune movement in the United States with an
emphasis on religious communes.

695. Grier, George. *The Baby Bust*. Washington: The Washington Center for
Metropolitan Studies, 1971.
This is a report on the national fertility decline that occurred in the U.S.
in the 1960s, as America's child bearing population reached its highest
ever. The author sees this trend as alarming and offers his reasons for
alarm.

696. Hedgepeth, William. *The Alternative: Communal Life in New America*.
New York: Macmillan Publishing, 1970.
An investigation, in pictures and text, of the communal movement in
Californa, New Mexico, Colorado, and Georgia that developed in the
mid- to late-sixties.

697. Houriet, Robert. *Getting Back Together*. New York: Coward-McCann, 1971.
Houriet travelled to and wrote about communes in New England,
Oregon, New Mexico, Colorado, California, Virginia, and Vermont. He
also visited some communities of eastern religions. His style was New
Journalistic.

698. Kanter, Rosabeth Moss. *Commitment and Community: Communes and
Utopias in Sociological Perspective*. Cambridge: Harvard UP, 1972.
A history of utopian communities in America; description of selected
1960s communes with comparison and contrast to the historical
communes.

699. Otto, Herbert A., ed. *The Family in Search of a Future: Alternate Models for
Moderns*. New York: Appleton-Century-Crofts, 1970.
Readings that present a variety of alternatives to the traditional family,
e.g., tribal families, marriage as a non-legal, voluntary relation, serial
monogamy, temporary commitments and parental commitments,
group marriage, and polygamous marriage.

700. Packard, Vance. *The Sexual Wilderness: The Contemporary Upheaval in
Male-Female Relationships*. New York: David McKay, 1968.

An investigation of male-female relationships justified by the number of baby boomers reaching the 18-22 year age group, the changes in women's status, and the greater emphasis being placed on relationships in general.

701. Roberts, Ron E. *The New Communes: Coming Together in America.* Englewood Cliffs, NJ: Prentice Hall, 1971.
A look at 1960s communal experiments. Roberts looks at their antecedents in the U.S., and then looks at various contemporary types-- hip communes, religious communes, radical and women's communes, and even encounter groups.

702. Rothchild, John, and Susan Berns Wolf. *The Children of the Counter- Culture.* Garden City, NY: Doubleday, 1976.
The authors travel to several communes throughout the U.S. to explore how children of hippies were being raised.

703. Sundancer, Elaine. *Celery Wine: The Story of a Country Commune.* Yellow Springs, OH: Community Publications, 1973.
Sundancer writes about her experiences in a commune--how it got started, how she got involved, how it ran, how they decided on a spot, how they all got along together, how they made it work.

704. Veysey, Laurence. *The Communal Experience: Anarchist and Mystical Counter-Culture in America.* New York: Harper & Row, Publishers, 1973.
A study of communities in 20th century America--both anarchist and mystical--with the purpose of making comparisons between 1960s communes and their recent predecessors.

705. Wyden, Peter, and Barbara Wyden. *Growing Up Straight: What Every Thoughtful Parent Should Know About Homosexuality.* New York: Stein and Day, 1968.
An early guide to helping parents prevent homosexuality, considered a disorder, in their children.

706. Zicklin, Gilbert. *Countercultural Communes: A Sociological Perspective.* Westport, CT: Greenwood Press, 1983.
Research into communal life, mostly rural rather than urban. A research study, that offers many interesting theories and observations about the 1960s counterculture.

Radicalism, the New Left and the Far Right

GENERAL WORKS

707. Abcarian, Gilbert, ed. *American Political Radicalism: Contemporary Issues and Orientations*. Waltham, MA: Xerox College, 1971.
A selection of readings on radicalism--both right and left--in America. Abcarian deliberately did not use readings that mentioned opposition to the Vietnam war or campus protest. Writers include Robert Welch, Billy James Hargis, Mark Rudd, Carl Oglesby, Seymour M. Lipset, Irving Howe, Nathan Glazer, and many more.

708. Gregor, A. James. *The Fascist Persuasion in Radical Politics*. Princeton: Princeton UP, 1974.
Gregor has attempted to show what differentiated 1960s radicals from Marxism, and what similarities they shared with Fascism.

THE LEFT

709. Adelson, Alan. *SDS*. New York: Charles Scribner's Sons, 1972.
Not a history but an analysis of SDS as it was at the beginning of the 1970s. The author starts by distancing SDS from the Weathermen. His premise is that SDS was not losing ground, but that it was changing its goals and methods of effecting future change.

710. Ali, Tariq, ed. *The New Revolutionaries: A Handbook of the International Radical Left*. New York: William Morrow, 1969.
A gathering of readings from scholars and activists on the left. There are articles on socialism in Cuba, Japan, Zimbabwe, the Middle East, Italy, Poland, Czechoslovakia, China, and the United States.

711. Alinsky, Saul. *Rules for Radicals: A Practical Primer for Realistic Radicals*. New York: Random House, 1971.
"Rules for radicals who want to change the world." Focuses on communicating, working inside the system, and organizing to take power--to create a revolution.

712. Aya, Rod, and Norman Miller, eds. *The New American Revolution*. New York: Free Press, 1971.
Essays that examine whether or not revolution is possible in the U.S., how a revolution could occur, and who would lead it. Essayists include Christopher Lasch, Paul Kress, William Kornhauser, and Richard Flacks.

713. Bacciocco, Edward J., Jr. *The New Left in America: Reform to Revolution 1956-1970*. Stanford: Hoover Institution, 1974.
A history of the New Left from its beginnings to the breakdown of SDS in 1969. Focuses mainly on SDS. Also tries to assess the importance of the New Left in American society.

714. Baritz, Loren, ed. *The American Left: Radical Political Thought in the Twentieth Century*. New York: Basic Books, 1971.
Readings on American leftist movements throughout history. The last third focuses on 1960s issues--Black Liberation, the New Left, university movements, and women's liberation.

715. Bell, Daniel. *The Cultural Contradictions of Capitalism*. New York: Basic Books, 1976.
A theoretical analysis of society based on the author's division of contemporary society into three parts: 1) the techno-economic structure; 2) the polity; and 3) the culture. This book is indicative of the philosophical beliefs held by many of the intelligentsia of the 1960s. Bell refers to Marx, Nietzsche, Conrad, Paz, Weber, Arendt, Roszak, Marcuse, and other writers who were popular among students in the 1960s.

716. Benello, C. George, and Dimitri Roussopoulos, eds. *The Case for Participatory Democracy: Some Prospects for the Radical Society*. New York: Grossman Publishers, 1971.
An examination of participatory democracy, an organizational method used by SDS and encouraged by New Leftists as a means of counteracting the depersonalization of work, education, and society.

717. Berman, Ronald. *America in the Sixties: An Intellectual History*. New York: Free Press, 1968.
The author reviews the history of the New Left. He tries to transmit the tone of the decade. With his emphasis on the intellectual, he does spend some time defining what the 1960s intellectual was.

718. Bone, Christopher. *The Disinherited Children: A Study of the New Left and the Generation Gap*. Cambridge, MA: Schenkman Publishing, 1977.
Bone attempts to analyze both the New Left and the counterculture with a view to understanding the whole postwar generation. First he tells the histories of these groups, then he analyzes what was bothering them about society, and finally he attempts to explain their significance to America in the 20th century.

719. Breines, Paul, ed. *Critical Interruptions: New-Left Perspectives on Herbert Marcuse.* New York: Herder & Herder, 1970.
Six essays on Marcuse's influence on the New Left movements of the 1960s.

720. Breines, Wini. *Community & Organization in the New Left, 1962-1968: The Great Refusal.* South Hadley, MA: J.F. Bergin, 1982.
A study of the vision and organization of the New Left. Breines was a part of the New Left at Wisconsin and Cornell Universities and then went on to become a feminist, using much of what she had learned from the New Left.

721. Calvert, Greg, and Carol Neiman. *A Disrupted History: The New Left and the New Capitalism.* New York: Random House, 1971.
What was disrupted was the history of the New Left by the conservatism of the late '60s and early '70s. The authors explore this disruption to analyze the possibilities for a rejuvenation of the New Left.

722. Cantor, Milton. *The Divided Left: American Radicalism 1900-1975.* New York: Hill and Wang, 1978.
A history of leftism in America with two chapters on the New Left in the 1960s.

723. Chertoff, Mordecai S., ed. *The New Left and the Jews.* New York: Pitman, 1971.
The first section of this book focuses on the American New Left. Then the editor turns to the Jewish dimensions of this movement. There are several essays on Israel and its influence on the Jewish New Left.

724. Clecak, Peter. *Radical Paradoxes: Dilemmas of the American Left, 1945-1970.* New York: Harper & Row, Publishers, 1973.
A history of the American left focusing on the writings of C. Wright Mills, Paul Baran, Paul Sweezy, and Herbert Marcuse.

725. Cohen, Mitchell, and Dennis Hale, eds. *The New Student Left: An Anthology.* Boston: Beacon Press, 1966.
Readings from New Left activists which attempted to explain the movement and the discontent on which it grew. Writers include Tom Hayden, Jonathan Eisen, Todd Gitlin, Richard Flacks, Rennie Davis, Mario Savio, and others.

726. Cook, Terence E., and Patrick M. Morgan, eds. *Participatory Democracy.* San Francisco: Canfield Press, 1971.
An examination of the meaning and possibilities of participatory democracy, one of the cornerstones of SDS and the New Left.

727. Cranston, Maurice, ed. *The New Left: Six Critical Essays.* New York: Simon & Schuster, 1970.

Essays on six of the leading theorists of the New Left, i.e., Ché Guevara, Jean-Paul Sartre, Herbert Marcuse, Frantz Fanon, George Feaver, and R.D. Laing. Distinguishes between Marxism of the Old Left and Marxism of the New.

728. Diggins, John P. *The American Left in the Twentieth Century.* New York: Harcourt Brace Jovanovich, 1973.
Diggins posits that the American Left began in America with Emerson and Thoreau, not with Marx. He divides Left movements into three groups and analyzes each group.

729. Gerberding, William P., and Duane E. Smith, eds. *The Radical Left: The Abuse of Discontent.* Boston: Houghton Mifflin, 1970.
The editors are critical of the New Left. They gathered together readings on such issues as intellectuals and politics, students and the university, race, and the political system which looks at the New Left seriously but skeptically.

730. Gish, Arthur G. *The New Left and Christian Radicalism.* Grand Rapids, MI: Eerdmans, 1970.
A comparison of the New Left and 16th century Anabaptism. At the end of the book, Gish attempts to synthesize the two movements.

731. Goldwin, Robert A., ed. *How Democratic Is America? Responses to the New Left Challenge.* Chicago: Rand McNally, 1969.
An examination of the New Left from New Leftists like SDS, Howard Zinn, and others, Includes the Port Huron Statement.

732. Green, Gil. *The New Radicalism: Anarchist or Marxist.* New York: International Publishers, 1971.
Green argued that the new radicalism is valuable and that it has to move away from anarchism towards Marxism to remain viable.

733. Hamaliam, Leo, and Frederick R. Karl, eds. *The Radical Vision: Essays for the Seventies.* New York: Crowells, 1970.
Essays on radicalism and anti-authoritarianism from such people as Jerry Rubin, Gary Snyder, Alan Watts, Norman O. Brown, R.D. Laing, Sartre, Nat Hentoff, Leslie Fiedler, John Cage, and Theodore Roszak.

734. Harrington, Michael. *Toward a Democratic Left: A Radical Program for a New Majority.* New York: Macmillan Publishing, 1968.
A call for a democratic Left with a plan for change in American life. Harrington suggests solutions which will make it more natural to cooperate rather than compete with others.

735. Hobsbawm, E.J. *Revolutionaries: Contemporary Essays.* New York: Random House-Pantheon Books, 1973.
Hobsbawm is a scholar of the Old Left. This book gives a history of communism and then examines some 1960s issues, e.g., Vietnam, the

military, violence, revolution, and sex, from the perspective of one
from the Old Left.

736. Horowitz, David. *The Fate of Midas and Other Essays.* San Francisco:
Ramparts Press, 1973.
A group of theoretical essays on Marxism and political economy.
Addresses the New Left in the last part of the book.

737. Howe, Irving. *Steady Work: Essays in the Politics of Democratic Radicalism,
1953-1966.* New York: Harcourt Brace Jovanovich, 1966.
Essays examining radicalism in America, which were written between
1953 and 1966. Howe takes several looks at events and movements of
the 1960s.

738. ---, ed. *Beyond the New Left.* New York: McCall Publishing, 1970.
Analysis and criticism of the New Left by writers such as Howe, M.
Harrington, P. Goodman, R. Brustein, and T. Draper.

739. ---, ed. *Radical Imagination: An Anthology from "Dissent Magazine."* New
York: NAL, 1967.
Articles from the Left on American society, America, and the world, and
on radical people.

740. Isserman, Maurice. *If I Had a Hammer . . . The Death of the Old Left and the
Birth of the New Left.* New York: Basic Books, 1987.
Historical treatment of the Old Left, 1930s -1950s, and the sixties New
Left and an analysis of their linkages. A few photos included.

741. Jacobs, Harold. *The Personal and the Political: A Study of the Decline of the
New Left.* Dept. of Sociology, University of California, Berkeley, 1978
(Ph.D. dissertation)
Jacobs argues that the New Left did have a big impact on the United
States. Then he examines why it suddenly disappeared as a dominant
force.

742. Lader, Lawrence. *Power on the Left: American Radical Movements Since
1946.* New York: W.W. Norton, 1979.
Lader examined a far-ranging group of leftist organizations. He focused
on the 1960s groups (New Left, blacks, and women) to show how they
differed from the old systems of the Old Left. Lader also tried to show
how these newer leftist groups succeeded and failed.

743. Larner, Jeremy, and Irving Howe, eds. *Poverty, Views from the Left.* New
York: William Morrow, 1968.
A collection of essays from American leftists covering many faces of
poverty, such as the aged, blacks, grape pickers, children in Mississippi
and in Harlem schools, and Appalachians.

744. Lasch, Christopher. *The Agony of the American Left*. New York: Alfred A. Knopf, 1968.
     An analysis of why the American Left has previously failed and a look at movements of the 1960s and why they, too, ultimately failed.

745. Lens, Sidney. *Radicalism in America*. Rev. ed. New York: Crowell, 1969.
     A history of radicalism in the U.S. beginning with the Puritans and ending with the 1960s civil rights and peace protesters.

746. Lester, Julius. *Revolutionary Notes*. New York: R.W. Baron, 1969.
     A collection of weekly columns Lester wrote for *The Guardian*, a radical newspaper, from 1967-1969.

747. Levitt, Cyril. *Children of Privilege: Student Revolt in the Sixties: A Study of Student Movements in Canada, the United States, and West Germany*. Toronto: U of Toronto P, 1984.
     Levitt looks specifically at the New Left in these countries. He sees these movements having not so much of a basis in Communism as in the material conditions of the students and their ideologies.

748. Lindenfeld, Frank, ed. *Radical Perspectives on Social Problems: Readings in Critical Sociology*. 2d ed. New York: Macmillan Publishing, 1973.
     Readings critical of the American social structure from writers such as C. Wright Mills, David Riesman, Eldridge Cleaver, Michael Harrington, Stokely Carmichael, Ivan Illich, and others.

749. Long, Priscilla, ed. *The New Left: A Collection of Essays*. Boston: Porter Sargent, 1969.
     A brief history of the New Left by Staughton Lynd and essays by theorists and activists such as C. Wright Mills, Howard Zinn, Noam Chomsky, Daniel Berrigan, and Paul Goodman.

750. Lothstein, Arthur, ed. *"All We Are Saying...": The Philosophy of the New Left*. New York: G.P. Putnam's, 1970.
     Essays by radicals, all with different philosophical ideologies, but all against "advanced capitalist societies," both American and European. Writers include Murray Bookchin, David Horowitz, Herbert Marcuse, Jean-Paul Sartre, and Ché Guevara.

751. Luce, Phillip Abbott. *The New Left*. New York: David McKay, 1966.
     An account of the New Left by a person who was deeply involved in it and later became disenchanted with it. He concludes that most of the New Left groups were communist and that the communists used the alienated students as "pawns" in their game to overthrow the United States government.

752. ---. *The New Left Today: America's Trojan Horse*. Washington, DC: Capitol Hill Press, 1971.

Luce left the New Left in 1965, extremely disillusioned with it. In this book he examines New Left organizations and what it is that attracts alienated youth to these groups.

753. Maddox, Robert James. *The New Left and the Origins of the Cold War*. Princeton: Princeton UP, 1973.
   Maddox looks at seven New Left interpretations of the Cold War. His conclusion is that none of them used the evidence accurately and they were, thus, not to be believed.

754. Mairowitz, David Zane. *The Radical Soap Opera: The Roots of Failure in the American Left*. New York: Penguin Books, 1974.
   Mairowitz says this is not a history of the American Left, but an accounting of the mistakes made which have led to its malaise in the 1970s.

755. Miller, James. *Democracy Is in the Streets: From Port Huron to the Siege of Chicago*. New York: Simon & Schuster, 1970.
   Miller studies the New Left and specifically participatory democracy by taking a biographical approach, focusing on a few of the leaders of SDS in the 1960s. Photos included.

756. Myerson, Michael. *These Are the Good Old Days: Coming of Age as a Radical in America's Late, Late Years*. New York: Grossman Publishers, 1970.
   Myerson was an activist in the late 1950s and early 1960s at Berkeley. He was one of the leaders at the anti-HUAC demonstrations and the early beginnings of the New Left. Here is his account of the early activities, as well as his trip to Hanoi in 1965.

757. Newfield, Jack. *A Prophetic Minority*. New York: NAL, 1966.
   The "prophetic minority" is the New Left. Newfield analyzes this group and explores its relationship to the rest of American society. He believed they were going to have a noticeable, positive effect on history.

758. O'Brien, James. *A History of the New Left, 1960-68*. Boston: New England Free Press, [n.d.].
   This is a very short (26 pages) history of the New Left which starts with the southern sit-ins in 1960 and takes the reader through the Chicago Democratic Convention in 1968. Very good as a short introduction.

759. Oglesby, Carl, ed. *The New Left Reader*. New York: Grove Press, 1969.
   Selections from New Left writers internationally, e.g., C. Wright Mills, Herbert Marcuse, Louis Althusser, Frantz Fanon, Fidel Castro, Huey Newton, and Mark Rudd.

760. Oglesby, Carl, and Richard Shaull. *Containment and Change: Two Dissenting Views of American Foreign Policy*. New York: Macmillan Publishing, 1967.

Two essays which address the New Left and revolution in the United States and in third world countries.

761. Rothman, Stanley and S. Robert Lichter. *Roots of Radicalism: Jews, Christians, and the New Left.* New York: Oxford UP, 1982.
A study of why Jewish youth played such a large role in the American student New Left.

762. Sale, Kirkpatrick. *SDS.* New York: Random House, 1973.
The most quoted and referred to history of SDS. Sale looks at SDS almost yearly from 1960 to 1970 and then adds an epilogue of 1970-1972. He lists all the SDS organizations, and the officers, as well as printing the SDS Constitution and giving a brief history of SDS's roots.

763. Sargent, Lyman Tower. *New Left Thought: An Introduction.* Homewood, IL: Dorsey Press, 1972.
An introduction to the New Left focusing on the student movements of the 1960s, rather than on the intellectual theorists. Touches on such aspects as alienation, concept of community, equality, black radicalism, women's liberation, participatory democracy, hippies, activists, and the anti-war movement.

764. Teodori, Massimo, ed. *The New Left: A Documentary History.* Indianapolis: Bobbs-Merrill, 1969.
A history and an anthology. Teodori's historical notes come from his experiences in the New Left in Europe. He has also collected readings from the U.S. by Staughton Lynd, SLATE, Tom Hayden, Todd Gitlin, Mario Savio, SDS, Richard Flacks, David Dellinger, Bernardine Dohrn, Raymond Mungo, Rennie Davis, and many others.

765. Tucker, Robert W. *The Radical Left and American Foreign Policy.* Baltimore: Johns Hopkins UP, 1971.
Examines radical critiques of American foreign policy and the Vietnam war. What is central to these critiques is the belief that American capitalism is ultimately to blame for America's interventionist activities. Not an analysis of movements, but of thought.

766. Unger, Irwin. *The Movement: A History of the American New Left, 1959-1972.* New York: Harper & Row, Publishers, 1974.
Unger defines what he means by the New Left and then traces its history from 1960-1972, when, to him, it ceased to exist. He also distinguishes the New Left from leftist movements before and after this time period.

767. Waxman, C.I. *End of Ideology Debate.* New York: Simon & Schuster, 1968.
A debate among several writers as to whether the growth of the New Left means a rebirth of ideology or whether the U.S. really needs ideological politics. Writers include D. Bell, I. Kristol, C.W. Mills, S. Lipset, I.L. Horowitz, M. Harrington, and M. Novak.

768. Weinstein, James. *Ambiguous Legacy: The Left in American Politics.* New York: New Viewpoints, 1975.
A history of 20th century leftist movements. The last three chapters cover the leftist movements of the 1960s.

THE RIGHT

769. Bell, Daniel, ed. *The Radical Right.* Garden City, NY: Doubleday, 1963.
Although most of these essays were written before the sixties, this book is often cited by other writers in their analyses of 1960s rightist movements.

770. Cooper, John Charles. *The Turn Right.* Philadelphia: Westminster Press, 1970.
An examination of the American right--specifically extreme right. Includes a listing of left-wing and right-wing periodicals.

771. Epstein, Benjamin R., and Arnold Forster. *The Radical Right: Reports on the John Birch Society and Its Allies.* New York: Random House, 1966.
An overview of Radical Right groups in the 1960s. Epstein looks at their use of the media, their political activities, and their outlooks for the future. The second half of the book focuses on the John Birch Society.

772. Forster, Arnold, and Benjamin Epstein. *Danger on the Right.* New York: Random House, 1964.
Divided into essays on the Radical Right and on the extreme conservatives. Radical Right groups discussed include the John Birch Society, the Christian Anti-Communism Crusade, the National Education Program, the Manion Forum, the Church League of America, and the Conservative Society of America. Conservatives include Americans for Constitutional Action, Intercollegiate Society of Individualists, and the National Review.

773. Janson, Donald, and Bernard Eisman. *The Far Right.* New York: McGraw-Hill, 1963.
Introductions to such right-wing groups as the John Birch Society, Fred Schwarz and his Christian Anti-Communism Crusade, Billy James Hargis and his Christian Crusade, Harding College, Kent and Phoebe Courtney, the National Indignation Convention, the Minutemen, and many others.

774. Jones, J. Harry, Jr. *The Minutemen.* Garden City, NY: Doubleday, 1968.
A close examination of this militant right-wing organization that became well-known in the 1960s.

775. Lipset, Seymour Martin, and Earl Raab. *The Politics of Unreason: Right-Wing Extremism in America, 1790-1970.* Chicago: U of Chicago P, 1970.

A study of right-wing people and groups in the United States, including the John Birch Society and George Wallace.

776. McEvoy, James, III. *Radicals or Conservatives? The Contemporary American Right.* Chicago: Rand McNally, 1971.
An examination of the American right, specifically movements led by Barry Goldwater and by George Wallace.

777. Overstreet, Harry and Bonaro. *The Strange Tactics of Extremism.* New York: W.W. Norton, 1964.
Although warning of extremism of both right and left, the authors examine rightists--the John Birch Society, Dan Smoot, Carl McIntire, the Circuit Riders, and others.

778. Redekop, John Harold. *The American Far Right: A Case Study of Billy James Hargis and Christian Crusade.* Grand Rapids, MI: Eerdmans, 1968.
Hargis was the founder of the Christian Crusade. Redekop studies him as a representation of the far right Christian fundamentalist.

779. Rosenstone, Robert A., ed. *Protest from the Right.* Beverly Hills, CA: Glencoe Press, 1968.
An introduction to right-wing protest of the 1960s. The editors' main area of concern is the encroachment of Communism on America. Rosenstone has gathered together in this book readings from documents of these far right groups. Writers include Robert Welch, Paul Harvey, Billy James Hargis, William F. Buckley, Jr., J. Edgar Hoover, and others.

780. Schoenberger, Robert A., ed. *The American Right Wing: Readings in Political Behavior.* New York: Holt, Rinehart & Winston, 1969.
An exploration of rightist groups or movements which existed in the 1960s.

781. Welch, Robert. *The New Americanism and Other Speeches and Essays.* Boston: Western Islands, 1966.
Welch presents the position of the John Birch Society on civil rights, the war in Vietnam, and the insidiousness of Communism in the U.S.

The Military and
the Vietnam War

GENERAL WORKS

782. Ashmore, Harry S., and William C. Baggs, *Mission to Hanoi: A Chronicle of Double-Dealing in High Places.* New York: G.P. Putnam's, 1968.
"A special report from the Center for the Study of Democratic Institutions." The point of view is that Vietnam was only a symptom of the "corrosion of the nation's foreign policy-making process." This book is an analysis of the United States negotiation efforts in Vietnam, 1965-67.

783. Baritz, Loren. *Backfire: A History of How American Culture Led Us into Vietnam and Made Us Fight the Way We Did.* New York: Ballantine Books, 1985.
Baritz uses the ideals of "the city on the hill" and America as God's promised land as the bases for analysis of U.S. involvement in Vietnam.

784. Barnes, Peter. *Pawns: The Plight of the Citizen-Soldiers.* New York: Alfred A. Knopf, 1972.
An examination of the military from the point of view of a humanist. Barnes aims to do three things: 1) to analyze the power the military has over the lives of Americans; 2) to analyze the legitimacy of those powers, and 3) to search for responsible ways to limit those powers.

785. Berrigan, Daniel. *Night Flight to Hanoi: War Diary with Eleven Poems.* New York: Macmillan Publishing, 1968.
Berrigan's diary while he and Howard Zinn were in North Vietnam to retrieve three American fliers who had been prisoners of the North Vietnamese. They were there during the Tet offensive of 1968.

786. Bosch, Juan. *Pentagonism, A Substitute for Imperialism.* Translated by Helen Lane. New York: Grove Press, 1968.
Pentagonism is defined as the process in which, instead of exploiting colonial territories, pentagonist countries exploit their own people by sending its armies to make war on other countries with the purpose of increasing the profits to be made in the pentagonist country by constant mobilization for war. Bosch argues that imperialism is no longer; that it has been replaced by pentagonism.

787. Brown, Sam, and Len Ackland, eds. *Why Are We Still in Vietnam?* New York: Random House-Vintage Books, 1970.
      A collection of essays which focuse on the consequences of the Vietnam war and suggestions for getting out of it. It was written as a call to action for U.S. citizens.

788. Carper, Jean. *Bitter Greetings: The Scandal of the Military Draft.* New York: Grossman Publishers, 1967.
      An argument for abolishing the draft because of its unfairness.

789. Chapman, Bruce K. *The Wrong Man in Uniform: Our Unfair and Obsolete Draft--And How We Can Replace It.* New York: Trident Press, 1967.
      Chapman claims this is "the first careful and complete analysis of the draft since the 1951 House hearings" on it. He shows its inequities and proposes a volunteer army.

790. Charlton, Michael, and Anthony Moncrieff. *Many Reasons Why: The American Involvement in Vietnam.* New York: Farrar, Straus & Giroux, 1978.
      Based on a series of radio programs broadcast on BBC in 1977. Includes information on fighting the war, the role of television, and protest in the U.S. Nguyen Ky is interviewed, as well as General Westmoreland.

791. Chomsky, Noam. *For Reasons of State.* New York: Pantheon Books, 1973.
      A description of the Vietnam war. Chomsky first looks at the Pentagon Papers, then the wider war in Laos and Cambodia. He also looks at the U.S. goals in Indochina, civil disobedience, and the universities in this country. Finally, he examines the psychology and political ideology that was the basis for America's involvement in Vietnam.

792. Corson, William R. *The Betrayal.* New York: W.W. Norton, 1968.
      Corson writes about the "Other War" in Vietnam--the war to strengthen South Vietnam politically and economically. He says we are losing that war, but he offers suggestions, based on his own experiences, for winning it.

793. Donovan, Col. James A. *Militarism, U.S.A.* New York: Charles Scribner's Sons, 1970.
      An overview of the American military in the 1960s. Explains the trends of the military and some of the forces at work in American militarism, particularly with regard to U.S. involvement in Vietnam.

794. Draper, Theodore. *Abuse of Power.* New York: Viking Press, 1967.
      The power in the title is military power. This book is an analysis of the U.S. involvement in Vietnam. The author sees it as part of the pattern which began with the Cuban Missile Crisis and our intervention in the Dominican Republic.

795. Drinan, Robert F., S.J. *Vietnam and Armageddon: Peace, War, and the Christian Conscience.* New York: Sheed & Ward, 1970.
An examination of the arguments that Catholics, Protestants, and Buddhists have used to either justify or condemn the war in Vietnam.

796. Duncan, Donald. *The New Legions.* New York: Random House,1967.
A first-hand account of an inductee in the U.S. Army by a man who became a member of the Regular Army and went to Vietnam.

797. Enthoven, Alain C., and K. Wayne Smith. *How Much Is Enough? Shaping the Defense Program, 1961-1969.* New York: Harper & Row, Publishers, 1971.
Explores the role of the Secretary of Defense McNamara, the ways he exercised his power, and the planning of military strategy.

798. Felson, Henry Gregor. *To My Son in Uniform.* New York: Dodd, Mead, 1966.
Felson's reflections on war, the Army, draft card burners, a citizen's duty, and the enemy addressed to his son, who joined during the Vietnam war.

799. Fulbright, Senator J. William. *The Pentagon Propaganda Machine.* New York: Liveright, 1970.
Speeches given on the Senate floor in 1969. Fulbright argued that the military was using propaganda and public relations techniques to mold public and political opinion and to make the U.S. a militaristic state.

800. Galbraith, John Kenneth. *How to Get Out of Vietnam: A Workable Solution to the Worst Problem of Our Time.* New York: NAL-Signet Books, 1967.
Galbraith outlines what he says is a "practical way out" of the Vietnam war. His solutions are based on the needs of the U.S. and the South Vietnamese, and acceptance by North Vietnam.

801. Gardner, Fred. *The Unlawful Concert: An Account of the Presidio Mutiny Case.* New York: Viking Press, 1970.
In 1968 at the Presidio stockade, outside San Francisco, 27 inmates staged a sit-down strike in protest against the shooting of a fellow inmate and against terrible conditions. The military chose to prosecute those demonstrators as mutineers. This book is an account of the incident and of how the military mishandled it.

802. Halberstam, David. *The Best and the Brightest.* New York: Penguin Books, 1972.
An account of the people in power--Kennedy, McNamara, Bundy, Rusk, Johnson--and the way they led us into the Vietnam war and its resulting dissent in the U.S.

803. Hamilton, Michael, ed. *The Vietnam War: Christian Perspectives.* Grand Rapids, MI: Eerdmans, 1967.
     A collection of sermons preached at the National Cathedral on the Vietnam war--some supporting, some criticizing it.

804. Herman, Edward S., and Richard B. DuBoff. *America's Vietnam Policy: The Strategy of Deception.* New York: Public Affairs Press, 1966.
     The authors state that Americans are not hearing the truth about the U.S. involvement in Vietnam. In this book, they try to correct this problem. They discuss the aims of the U.S. escalation, diplomacy, aggression, and genocide.

805. Herring, George C. *America's Longest War: The United States and Vietnam, 1950-1975.* 2d ed. New York: Alfred A. Knopf, 1986.
     An account of the Vietnam war, emphasizing the American side of it and also exploring the antiwar protest in the U.S. and its impact on the conduct of the war.

806. Hersh, Seymour M. *Chemical and Biological Warfare: America's Hidden Arsenal.* Indianapolis, IN: Bobbs-Merrill, 1968.
     One of the first books to be written for the public on chemical and biological warfare. Includes a history of its use, the U.S. use of it in Vietnam, the research establishment responsible for its continuing development, and the problems of controlling it.

807. Herzog, Arthur. *The War-Peace Establishment.* New York: Harper & Row, Publishers, 1965.
     An analysis of three groups that make up the war-peace establishment: "deterrers" who believe that fear should be used to deter war; "experimentalists" who want eventually to dispense with all nuclear weapons; and the "peace movement."

808. Hull, Roger H., and John C. Novogrod. *Law and Vietnam.* Dobbs Ferry, NY: Oceana Publications, 1968.
     Hull's book questions the legality of the Vietnam war.

809. Johnson, Haynes, and George C. Wilson. *The Washington Post National Report: Army in Anguish.* New York: Pocket Books, 1971.
     A series of articles done by *Post* reporters suggesting that there was a crisis in morale and discipline in the Army. The major cause of this crisis was the means used to keep the Army going in Vietnam.

810. Knoll, Erwin, and Judith Nies McFadden. *American Militarism 1970.* New York: Viking Press, 1969.
     Readings based on a conference to determine what America's priorities should be, how to get out of Vietnam, and how to control the Pentagon.

811. Kraslow, David, and Stuart H. Loory. *The Secret Search for Peace in Vietnam.* New York: Random House-Vintage Books, 1968.

An account of American diplomacy to end the war in Vietnam. It is based on interviews with U.S. officials and other sources.

812. Lapp, Ralph E. *The Weapons Culture*. New York: W.W. Norton, 1968.
A look at the defense industry and the culture that tries to deter "war by threat of nuclear attack," from the end of the Eisenhower administration to 1967. Includes tables and charts.

813. Lens, Sidney. *The Military-Industrial Complex*. Philadelphia: Pilgrim Press, 1970.
An examination of how the military became such a hugely funded institution and what the implications are for Americans.

814. Long, Edward LeRoy, Jr. *War and Conscience in America*. Philadelphia: Westminster Press, 1968.
An examination of war and conscientious objection. The author classifies participants of war and those who refuse to go to war. Long also examines the laws for conscientious objection in the U.S.

815. Lynn, Conrad J. *How to Stay Out of the Army: A Guide to Your Rights Under the Draft Law*. New York: Monthly Review Press, 1968.
An explanation of the draft, including detailed descriptions of exemptions and alternatives. Lynn was a lawyer who was obviously anti-war.

816. McCarthy, Richard D. *The Ultimate Folly: War by Pestilence, Asphyxiation, and Defoliation*. New York: Random House-Vintage Books, 1969.
A collection of information on chemical and biological weapons of the U.S. with a view to educating the American public and encouraging discussion.

817. Manning, Robert, and Michael Janeway, eds. *Who Are We: An Atlantic Chronicle of the U.S. and Vietnam*. Boston: Little, Brown, 1969.
Articles on Vietnam and America's involvement in it, published in *Atlantic*, 1966-69. Writers include George McGovern, Frances Fitzgerald, Tom Wicker, Dan Wakefield, and Bill Moyers (an interview).

818. Mantell, David Mark. *True Americanism: Green Berets and War Resisters: A Study of Commitment*. New York: Teachers College, 1974.
A study of a group of green berets and a group of war resisters to determine how their interpretations of their roots led to differing interpretations of Americanism.

819. Marmion, Harry A. *Selective Service: Conflict and Compromise*. New York: Wiley, 1968.
An examination of the 1960s draft program. The author concludes that there is no viable alternative to the draft.

820. Melman, Seymour. *Pentagon Capitalism: The Political Economy of War.*
New York: McGraw-Hill, 1970.
Studies of the Department of Defense, which Melman says since
McNamara has become "a military-industry empire at home and an
instrument for building an empire abroad." Melman specifically tied it
to government waste and the Vietnam war.

821. ---, ed. *In the Name of America.* New York: Clergy and Laymen Concerned
about Vietnam, 1968.
Subtitled: "The Conduct of the War in Vietnam by the Armed Forces of
the United States as Shown by Published Reports." Various laws
governing the conduct of war are given. Included also are excerpts from
books, magazines, reports, and newspaper articles describing U.S. or
South Vietnam military actions which break these laws.

822. O'Brien, William V. *War and/or Survival.* Garden City, NY: Doubleday,
1969.
Argues not for the idealism of limiting war, but for the realism of
limiting it.

823. O'Connor, John. *A Chaplain Looks at Vietnam.* Cleveland, OH: World
Publishing, 1968.
A justification of U.S. involvement in Vietnam based on the moral
issue of the conflict. O'Connor was a chaplain in the U.S. Navy.

824. Pfeffer, Richard M., ed. *No More Vietnams? The War and the Future of
American Policy.* New York: Harper & Row, Publishers, 1968.
Essays and discussion from various foreign policy experts, including
Theodore Draper, Henry Kissinger, Hans Morgenthau, Arthur
Schlesinger, Jr., Adam Yarmolinsky, and others on what the Vietnam
war should teach the U.S., and what U.S. future foreign policy should
be.

825. Podhoretz, Norman. *Why We Were In Vietnam.* New York: Simon &
Schuster, 1982.
A reexamination of how and why the U.S. got involved in Vietnam and
an assessment of America's decision to get involved. Podhoretz argues
that the U.S. was not immoral because of its conduct of the war.

826. Proxmire, Senator William. *Report from Wasteland: America's Military
Industrial Complex.* New York: Praeger Publishers, 1970.
A study of cost overruns and waste in the military. Based on
investigations by the Economy in Government Subcommittee in the
U.S. Senate. Suggestions are made to bring the budget under control.

827. Pusey, Merlo J. *The Way We Go to War.* Boston: Houghton Mifflin, 1969.
An examination of the way in which the U.S. had drifted into war--in
Korea, Cuba, and Vietnam--without Congressional action. Pusey argues
that the power to go to war must be modernized and controlled.

828. Ramsey, Paul. *The Just War: Force and Political Responsibility.* New York: Charles Scribner's Sons, 1968.
A collection of writings that speaks to just-war theories. Ramsey examines the Vietnam war as it relates to his just-war description.

829. Reedy, George E. *Who Will Do Our Fighting For Us?* New York: World Publishing, 1969.
An analysis of the draft law in effect in 1969, and recommendations for making it more equitable.

830. Rodberg, Leonard S., and Derek Shearer. *The Pentagon Watchers: Students Report on the National Security State.* Garden City, NY: Doubleday, 1970.
Essays from student researchers on the operations of the "defense establishment." An appendix tells how to research the military.

831. Rohr, John A. *Prophets Without Honor: Public Policy and the Selective Conscientious Objector.* Nashville: Abingdon, 1971.
An examination of whether or not selective conscientious objection should be a law.

832. Rothenberg, Leslie S. *The Draft and You: A Handbook on the Selective Service System.* Garden City, NY: Doubleday, 1968.
Intended as a reference book on the draft. Rothenberg discusses the history of the draft, the physical examination, induction, appeals, deferments, conscientious objection, and resisting the draft. Examples of Selective Service forms are included.

833. Rovere, Richard. *Waist Deep in the Big Muddy: Personal Reflections on 1968.* New York: Little, Brown, 1968.
Mostly a discourse on U.S. involvement in Vietnam. Rovere argued very practically for the U.S. getting out, not so much because it would solve all the problems, but because to continue did not seem practical.

834. Sanders, Jacquin. *The Draft and the Vietnam War.* New York: Walker, 1966.
An examination and explanation of the draft during the Vietnam war. Neither pro nor con, it has sections on attitudes towards the war, draft boards, college protesters, the puzzlement of parents, legal and illegal draft dodging, the College Qualification test, the draftee, and the volunteer. Appendices contain classifications, pay scales, ROTC programs, and the GI Bill of Rights.

835. Schlesinger, Arthur M. *The Bitter Heritage: Vietnam and American Democracy, 1941-1966.* Boston: Houghton Mifflin, 1966.
An early essay on the problems of U.S. involvement in Vietnam. A well wrought rhetorical argument for the U.S. to take a middle ground-- not to increase bombing or to summarily withdraw all troops, but to hold firm until peace could be negotiated.

836. Stavins, Ralph, Richard J. Barnet, and Marcus G. Raskin *Washington Plans an Aggressive War*. New York: Random House, 1971.
A look at the planning of the war by U.S. authorities. First are discussions of why and how it happened. Finally, there is an examination of the weakening of Congressional power and a series of proposals to demilitarize the national security bureaucracy and place responsibility for the war on specific individuals.

837. Taylor, Maxwell. *Responsibility and Response*. New York: Harper & Row, Publishers, 1967.
Taylor defines the world as one of multipolar power, where many places could become the target of superpower intervention. He defends U.S. intervention in Vietnam as one of those multipolar situations in which the U.S. had to get involved so that South Vietnam could be free from Communism. He also makes suggestions for U.S. foreign policy to help counter such problems before they become as critical as Vietnam.

838. Taylor, Telford. *Nuremburg and Vietnam: An American Tragedy*. Chicago: Quadrangle Books, 1970.
Taylor describes in detail the laws of war and the Nuremburg and Tokyo tribunals. He then discusses the Vietnam war and the My Lai massacre in relation to the laws of war. He shows the complexity of the issues in both the Vietnam war and in My Lai.

839. *Three Documents of the National Liberation Front*. Boston: Beacon Press, 1970.
1) The Ten Points--Principles and Main Content of an Overall Solution to the South Viet Nam Problem; 2) Fundamental Resolutions of the South Viet Nam Congress of People's Representatives; and 3) Declaration of the Program of Action of the Provisional Revolutionary Government of the Republic of South Vietnam.

840. Walton, George H. *Let's End the Draft Mess*. New York: David McKay, 1967.
A discussion of the problems with the 1960s draft and suggestions for making it more equitable from an Army Colonel.

841. Williams, Reese, ed. *Unwinding the Vietnam War: From War into Peace*. Seattle: Real Comet Press, 1987.
Writings (fiction, nonfiction, poetry) on the war and its effects on America. Writers include John Balaban, Tran Van Dinh, Bobbie Ann Mason, Mark Gerzon, Robert Bly, Noam Chomsky, Adrienne Rich, Martin Luther King, Jr., and many others.

842. Woolf, Cecil, and John Bagguley. *Authors Take Sides on Vietnam: Two Questions on the War in Vietnam Answered by Authors of Several Nations*. New York: Simon & Schuster, 1967.
Questions: "Are you for or against the intervention of the U.S. in Vietnam?" "How. . . should the conflict in Vietnam be resolved?" Respondents include: H. Arendt, W.H. Auden, J. Baldwin, S. de

Beauvior, W. Burroughs, I. Calvino, J. Cheever, P. de Vries, D. du
Maurier, J. Pfeiffer, L. Ferlinghetti, J. Fowles, R. Graves, G. Greene, J.
Heller, J. Kosinski, D. Lessing, D. Levertov, J.A. Michener, H. Pinter, K.
Rexroth, P. Roth, I. Shaw, W. Styron, J. Updike, and many others.

AMERICANS FIGHTING IN VIETNAM

843. Baker, Mark. *Nam: The Vietnam War in the Words of the Men and
     Women Who Fought There.* New York: William Morrow, 1982.
     War stories from many of the men and women who fought in
     Vietnam. Interesting perspective. The editor does a good job of using
     the language as it was spoken in the interviews. He also includes a
     glossary of the vocabulary coined by the people who served in Vietnam.

844. Bryan, C.D.B. *Friendly Fire.* New York: G.P. Putnam's, 1976.
     A story of a family with one son killed in Vietnam by fire from friendly
     (U.S.) guns. Although the family was very patriotic before their son's
     death, the difficulties the Mullens had with the U.S. government,
     finding information about their son's death, led them into active
     organizing and protest against U.S. involvement in the Vietnam war.
     The writing was based on interviews.

845. *The Senator Gavel Edition: The Pentagon Papers.* 4 volumes. Boston:
     Beacon Press, 1971.
     The documents of the papers with extensive commentary. Coverage is
     from 1940-1968. This is the edition most often cited by others.

846. Denton, Jeremiah. *When Hell Was in Session.* Pleasantville, NY: Reader's
     Digest Press, 1976.
     The story of Denton's seven years of imprisonment as an American
     POW in Vietnam.

847. Greene, Felix. *Vietnam! Vietnam! In Photographs and Text.* Palo Alto:
     Fulton Publishing, 1966.
     A photodocumentary showing what the U.S. has done to Vietnam and
     to its people.

848. Hammer, Richard. *One Morning in the War: The Tragedy at Son My.* New
     York: Coward-McCann, 1970.
     A description of what happened at Son My (My Lai) and an attempt to
     figure out why it happened. Hammer believed that the army tried to
     cover-up the massacre. He also believed this massacre was not unique
     for U.S. soldiers in Vietnam.

849. Herman, Edward S. *Atrocities in Vietnam: Myths and Realities.*
     Philadelphia: Pilgrim Press, 1970.
     An explanation of the nature and scope of atrocities in Vietnam.
     Herman concludes by listing six atrocity myths and challenging each.

850. Herr, Michael. *Dispatches*. New York: Alfred A. Knopf, 1977.
Michael Herr was a free-lance writer covering the Vietnam war from the mid- to late-1960s. This book is his account of what he saw of American men fighting in Vietnam, before and during the Tet offensive in 1968.

851. Hersh, Seymour M. *Cover-Up: The Army's Secret Investigation of the Massacre at My Lai 4*. New York: Random House, 1970.
Not so much about the incident as about the Army, which, the author says, "made so much of My Lai 4 inevitable."

852. ---. *My Lai 4: A Report on the Massacre and Its Aftermath*. New York: Random House, 1970.
Based on interviews of the men who participated and transcripts from the government investigation of the attack on My Lai. The book was written before the trials took place.

853. Kovic, Ron. *Born On the Fourth of July*. New York: McGraw-Hill, 1976.
In the mid-1960s, Kovic joined with Marines and went to Vietnam, where he was wounded and paralyzed. This book is the story of his transformation from a trusting patriot into an active Vietnam Veteran Against the War.

854. Lang, Daniel. *Casualties of War*. New York: McGraw-Hill, 1969.
See Lang's *Incident on Hill 192*.

855. ---. *Incident on Hill 192*. London: Secker and Warburg, 1970.
The incident took place in 1966 in Vietnam. Four American men on a five-man mission kidnapped, raped, and murdered a Vietnamese girl. This book is an account of the incident and also of the difficulties the fifth man had in bringing the incident to light and the murderers to trial.

856. Lederer, William J. *Our Own Worst Enemy*. New York: W.W. Norton, 1968.
An argument for Lederer's theory that the U.S. and the South Vietnamese were actually aiding the North Vietnamese because of the way those in the South treated the land and the people.

857. Levy, Charles J. *Spoils of War*. Boston: Houghton Mifflin, 1974.
Levy looks at the violence of the Vietnam vet when he returned home. Many of them suffered from flashbacks, when they felt they were back in Vietnam and instinctively tried to kill or harm people around them.

858. Lifton, Robert. *Home from the War. Vietnam Veterans: Neither Victims nor Executioners*. New York: Simon & Schuster, 1973.
An analysis of why the American soldiers committed such atrocities as My Lai in Vietnam from a psychologist who has specialized in psychohistory and the Vietnam veteran.

859. MacPherson, Myra. *Long Time Passing: Vietnam and the Haunted Generation*. Garden City, NY: Doubleday, 1986.
Stories of those who went to Vietnam and those who did not. Balanced slightly on the side of those who went. MacPherson points to the lack of recognition of those who went and shows their problems with reintegrating into society. She also explores problems of traumatic stress syndrome and Agent Orange.

860. Novak, Marian Faye. *Lonely Girls with Burning Eyes: A Wife Recalls Her Husband's Journey Home from Vietnam*. Boston: Little, Brown, 1991.
Novak tells of her life in the military with her husband, of her life when he was in Vietnam, and of the many years it took for him to get over Vietnam and finally, really, return.

861. Russell, Bertrand. *War Crimes in Vietnam*. New York: Monthly Review Press, 1967.
The crimes included American lies about when Americans began to actually fight in Vietnam, and what kinds of chemical warfare the U.S. was using. Russell frequently compares the U.S. in Vietnam to Hitler's Germany during WWII.

862. Santoli, Al. *Everything We Had: An Oral History of the Vietnam War*. New York: Random House, 1981.
A personal view, or actually several personal views. The people interviewed were from different positions. Especially interesting is an interview with a prisoner of war.

863. Sevy, Grace, ed. *The American Experience in Vietnam: A Reader*. Norman: U of Oklahoma P, 1989.
A collection of readings on American involvement in Vietnam, including why we got in, why we stayed in so long, the role of the press, the antiwar movement, and the controversy still occurring over it.

864. Terry, Wallace. *Bloods: An Oral History of the Vietnam War by Black Veterans*. New York: Random House, 1984.
The stories from 20 black Vietnam vets about their war experiences and what happened to them after they returned home. Photos included.

865. Van Devanter, Lynda, with Christopher Morgan. *Home Before Morning: The Story of an Army Nurse in Vietnam*. New York: Warner Books, 1983.
Van Devanter served as a nurse in Vietnam in 1969-1970. This is her account of her experiences there and the difficulties she had readjusting to life when she got back.

866. Wheeler, John. *Touched with Fire: The Future of the Vietnam Generation*. New York: Franklin Watts, 1984.
An analysis of the Vietnam war by a West Pointer who served there and organized several veterans groups in this country, including the group

that was responsible for the building of the Vietnam War Memorial in Washington, D.C.

PROTEST AGAINST THE DRAFT AND THE WAR

867. American Civil Liberties Union. *Day of Protest, Night of Violence: The Century City Police March.* Los Angeles: Sawyer Press, 1967.
In June, 1967, Johnson attended a fundraising dinner in Los Angeles. This book presents a detailed account of a peace march to the hotel where the dinner was held and the violence that resulted from it.

868. American Friends Service Committee. *The Draft?* New York: Hill and Wang, 1968.
An attempt by a pacifist group to look at the influence of the draft on American society. The conclusions are understandably negative.

869. ---. *In Place of War: An Inquiry into Nonviolent National Defense.* New York: Grossman Publishers, 1967.
A study of the possibilities of maintaining independence without the use of arms in the hostile conflict.

870. Asinof, Eliot. *Craig and Joan: Two Lives for Peace.* New York: Viking Press, 1971.
A book about two young Americans who, together in 1969, committed suicide as a protest against the Vietnam war. Their full names were Craig Badiali and Joan Fox.

871. Bannan, John F., and Rosemary S. Bannan. *Law, Morality, and Vietnam: The Peace Militants and the Courts.* Bloomington: Indiana UP, 1974.
An examination of the major trials of the war resisters from 1965-1969, e.g., the Fort Hood Three, Dr. Benjamin Spock, the Oakland Seven, and the Catonsville Nine. The author explores the Courts' conflicts between their responsibility to society and the risk of conflicts with the President and Congress--over the legality versus the morality of the Vietnam war.

872. Baskir, Lawrence M., and William A. Strauss. *Chance and Circumstance: The Draft, the War and the Vietnam Generation.* New York: Random House-Vintage Books, 1986.
The author examines the draft-age men who did not fight in the Vietnam war--those who managed to avoid it, the deserters, and the exiles. Baskir also discusses the amnesty offered during Carter's administration.

873. Berrigan, Daniel. *The Trial of the Catonsville Nine.* Boston: Beacon Press, 1970.
In May, 1968, in Catonsville, MD, about 350 draft files were set afire in a parking lot. The trial of the nine people accused of this crime took place in October, 1968. This is the story of that trial by one of the accused.

874. Boettcher, Thomas D. *Vietnam: The Valor and the Sorrow*. Boston: Little, Brown, 1985.
Subtitled, "From the home front to the front line in words and pictures." Mostly this book is about Vietnam, but there is a chapter on protests. Photographs accompany the text. In addition, there are many insets with quotes, biographical sketches, and other bits of information.

875. Boulding, Kenneth E., ed. *Peace and the War Industry*. Chicago: Aldine Publishing, 1970.
Essays on the problems of international war and peace and considerations of ways to make the world peaceful. Essayists include Irving Horowitz, Marvin Kalkstein, Raoul Naroll, Milton Rosenberg, Henry S. Rowan, and Murray Weidenbaum.

876. Boyle, Kay. *The Long Walk at San Francisco State and Other Essays*. New York: Grove Press, 1970.
Reflections on the San Francisco State demonstrations in 1968 and on Black Panther leader Huey Newton--jury selection for his trial and his stay in prison.

877. Brown, Robert McAfee, Abraham Heschel, and Michael Novak. *Vietnam: Crisis of Conscience*. New York: Association Press, 1967.
Essays addressed to the churches and the synagogues to try to persuade religious leaders of how wrong it was for the United States to be in Vietnam and to work to protest the war.

878. Burchett, Wilfred. *At the Barricades: Forty Years at the Cutting Edge of History*. New York: Times Books, 1981.
Burchett is a journalist who favored the North Vietnam leadership during the Vietnam war and sided with the radicals all his life. In this, his autobiography, he writes of his experiences in 40 years of journalism, including coverage of the Vietnam war and American policy.

879. Chomsky, Noam. *American. Power and the New Mandarins*. New York: Random House-Pantheon Books, 1969.
Chomsky was a strong opponent of America's involvement in Vietnam. In these essays, he is critical of the role American intellectuals have played in their relationship to the war.

880. Cortright, David. *Soldiers in Revolt: The American Military Today*. Garden City, NY: Doubleday-Anchor Books, 1975.
A history of GI protest from 1968-1972. Not only did the GIs protest the Vietnam war; they also protested the authoritarianism of the military.

881. DeBenedetti, Charles. *An American Ordeal: The Antiwar Movement of the Vietnam Era*. Syracuse: Syracuse UP, 1990.
The story of the antiwar movement in the U.S. from its pre-Vietnam roots in 1955, until 1975. The author maintains that the war was more

over America and its future policies than it was over Vietnam. Photos included.

882. Dellinger, David. *More Power Than We Know: The People's Movement Toward Democracy*. Garden City, NY: Doubleday-Anchor Books, 1975. Mostly focused on protest of the Vietnam war. Dellinger makes a stand for nonviolence while at the same time encouraging revolution in the established forms of power.

883. Di Leo, David L. *George Ball, Vietnam, and the Rethinking of Containment*. Chapel Hill: U of North Carolina P, 1991. An examination of George Ball's dissent against the Vietnam war and the policy of containment that still guides U.S. public policy.

884. Duffett, John, ed. *Against the Crime of Silence: The Proceedings of the International War Crimes Tribunal*. New York: Simon & Schuster, 1968. Essays on the Vietnam war by Bertrand Russell and Noam Chomsky, and testimony by soldiers and reporters on atrocities committed in Vietnam by Americans.

885. Epp, Frank H., ed. *I Would Like to Dodge the Draft-Dodgers But. . . .* Waterloo: Conrad Press, 1970. Stories from draft dodgers, deserters, and counselors in Canada about why and how they got to Canada, and what can be done to help them.

886. Ferber, Michael, and Staughton Lynd. *The Resistance*. Boston: Beacon Press, 1971. An interesting and readable history of the Resistance--the anti-war resistance--that began in 1960 in the U.S.

887. Finn, James. *Protest, Pacifism and Politics: Some Passionate Views on War and Nonviolence*. New York: Random House, 1967. An exploration of 1960s protest in America. Based on interviews with such people as Philip Berrigan, Daniel Berrigan, A.J. Muste, Staughton Lynd, Julian Bond, Joan Baez, Denise Levertov, and many others.

888. ---, ed. *A Conflict of Loyalties: The Case for Selective Conscientious Objection*. New York: Pegasus, 1968. Selective conscientious objection, the objection to a particular war, was not grounds for release from induction into the Vietnam war. Finn gathers together essays which explore this idea and argue for its legitimacy.

889. Foner, Philip S. *American Labor and the Indochina War: The Growth of Union Opposition*. New York: International Publishers, 1971. This book dispels any ideas that the New York City hard hat rallies in 1970, which became famous for their violence to bystanders who supported peace, were representative of the attitudes of all unions.

Foner argues that many labor unions, including the United Auto Workers and the teamsters, publicly opposed the Vietnam war and joined with youth in protests against it.

890. Franks, Lucinda. *Waiting Out a War: The Exile of Private John Picciano.* New York: Coward-McCann, 1974.
The story of John Picciano, one of the first people to desert the Army in the Vietnam war years. He lived in Sweden after he left the Army, and eventually was followed by a sizeable colony of American Army deserters.

891. Gaylin, Willard. *In the Service of Their Country: War Resisters in Prison.* New York: Viking Press, 1970.
Gaylin did an intensive study of about 20 prisoners in two prisons in California. As he described these war resisters and the various psychological stages they went through in the imprisonment, one cannot help but wonder if they would not be as emotionally scarred as many of the vets returning from Vietnam.

892. Gettleman, Marvin E., *et al*, eds. *Vietnam and America: A Documented History.* New York: Grove Press, 1985.
A collection of readings which mainly focus on the war. However, there is a section on the movement against the war, mostly documents that are statements of resistance.

893. Gould, Donna, and David Dellinger. *In the Teeth of the War.* New York: Fifth Avenue Vietnam Peace Parade Committee, 1966.
A photodocumentary of the 1966 peace march in New York City. A group of veterans--both Vietnam and WWII--led the march, and from the photos it is obvious that opponents of the war came from all groups of Americans.

894. Hall, Mitchell K. *Because of Their Faith: CALCAV and Religious Opposition to the Vietnam War.* New York: Columbia UP, 1990
This book explores the Clergy and Laymen Concerned About Vietnam's resistance activities throughout the war.

895. Halstead, Fred. *GI's Speak out against the War: The Case of the Ft. Jackson 8.* New York: Pathfinder Press-Merit, 1970.
In 1969, an anti-war meeting was held by GIs at Fort Jackson. Eight men were later confined as a result of their participation in the meeting. This is the story of their anti-war activities and the formation of GIs United Against the War in Vietnam.

896. ---. *Out Now! A Participant's Account of the American Movement against the Vietnam War.* New York: Monad Press, 1978.
An account of the resistance to the war which covered events from 1960-1975. The writer was an active participant in the movement. Photographs included.

897.   Hayes, Thomas Lee. *American Deserters in Sweden: The Men and Their Challenge.* New York: Association Press, 1971.
       A close, sympathetic look at the deserters in Sweden from a minister of an American church there.

898.   Horowitz, Irving Louis. *The Struggle Is the Message: The Organization and Ideology of the Anti-War Movement.* Berkeley: Glendessary Press, 1970.
       An analysis of the anti-war movement. Horowitz argues that participation was more important than any long-range goals. He also felt that the end of the Vietnam war was not as important as an attack on the "war system" itself.

899.   Hurwitz, Ken. *Marching Nowhere.* New York: W.W. Norton, 1971.
       The author, a Harvard student at the time, worked for the Vietnam Moratorium Committee from June, 1969, to April, 1970. This is his story of that Committee's work until the April 15 rally in Boston, when Harvard Square was burned and looted. Hurwitz writes with a great deal of humor and humanness of his growth and awakenings.

900.   James, Allen, ed. *Stop the War.* Los Angeles: Stanyan Books and New York: Random House, 1970.
       Quotations on the negatives of war in general and specific wars, including Vietnam. Photographs accompany the quotes.

901.   Kerry, John, and Vietnam Veterans Against the War. *The New Soldier.* Edited by David Thorne and George Butler. New York: Macmillan, 1971.
       Photographs from the VVAW march on Washington, April 1971. Testimony from The Winter Soldier Investigation, February, 1971.

902.   Killmer, Richard L., Robert S. Lecky, and Deborah S. Wiley. *They Can't Go Home Again.* Philadelphia: Pilgrim Press, 1971.
       An examination of the immigration to Canada of war resisters and why they chose this method of resistance.

903.   Killmer, Richard L., and Charles P. Lutz. *The Draft and the Rest of Your Life.* Minneapolis: Augsberg, 1972.
       Describes the options available for those facing the draft and the ethical considerations for each.

904.   Kunen, James Simon. *Standard Operating Procedure: Notes of a Draft-Age American.* New York: Avon Books, 1971.
       An account of the National Veterans' Inquiry of December, 1970, in Washington, DC. In this inquiry many veterans testified to atrocities they had either witnessed or participated in in Vietnam. The Inquiry was not official, but was carried out by a group called the National Committee for a Citizen's Commission of Inquiry on U.S. War Crimes in Vietnam. All the witnesses volunteered their testimony.

905. Lang, Daniel. *Patriotism Without Flags*. New York: W.W. Norton,1974.
     Lang looks at patriotism in an unusual way by examining several
     typically non-patriotic cases: the conspiracy trial of Dr. Spock; a group of
     U.S. Army deserters in Sweden; a Vietnam Veteran Against the War;
     Pentagon officials who favored using nuclear weapons in Vietnam; a
     Navy man who went AWOL and stayed underground for two years; and
     a Rochester school teacher who refused to pledge the flag.

906. Lynd, Alice, compiler. *We Won't Go: Personal Accounts of War Objectors*.
     Boston: Beacon Press, 1968.
     Accounts by people who chose not to participate in the Vietnam war.
     Most were people who registered as conscientious objectors or who went
     to prison.

907. Lynd, Staughton, and Thomas Hayden. *The Other Side*. New York: NAL,
     1967.
     A diary of the authors' trip to North Vietnam in 1965. They also visited
     Czechoslovakia, Russia, and China. The authors believed, from what
     they saw and heard, that the U.S. was not really trying to negotiate peace
     with North Vietnam.

908. Mailer, Norman. *The Armies of the Night*. New York: NAL, 1968.
     A New Journalistic account of the 1967 march on the Pentagon from the
     point of view of the author, who was arrested in the march.

909. Mayer, Peter, ed. *The Pacifist Conscience*. New York: Holt, Rinehart &
     Winston, 1966.
     A history of pacificism as represented by writers throughout history.

910. Powers, Thomas. *The War At Home: Vietnam and the American People,
     1964-1968*. New York: Grossman Publishers, 1973.
     A history of opposition to the Vietnam war up to 1968, when Johnson
     announced he would not run for the presidency and that he was halting
     the bombing in North Vietnam. Powers argues that the opposition was
     responsible both for the deescalation of the war and the defeat of
     Johnson.

911. Quigley, Thomas E., ed. *American Catholics and Vietnam*. Grand Rapids,
     MI: Eerdmans, 1968.
     A collection of essays by Catholics in various fields which together serve
     as a protest to the Vietnam war.

912. Rosenberg, Milton J., Sidney Verba, and Philip F. Converse. *Vietnam and
     the Silent Majority: The Dove's Guide*. New York: Harper & Row,
     Publishers, 1970.
     A guide to reaching those whose attitudes need to be changed about U.S.
     involvement in Vietnam so that the government would be persuaded
     to get out of Vietnam.

913. Schlissel, Lillian, ed. *Conscience in America: A Documentary History of Conscientious Objection in America, 1757-1967.* New York: E.P. Dutton, 1968.
Contains records of cases, Congressional debate, and other documents chronicalling the history of conscientious objection, including to the Vietnam war.

914. Small, Melvin. *Johnson, Nixon, and the Doves.* New Brunswick, NJ: Rutgers UP, 1988.
A study of the impact of antiwar activities on Johnson and Nixon. Small's conclusion is that protest was a powerful influence on presidential decisionmaking about the war.

915. Sontag, Susan. *Trip to Hanoi.* New York: Farrar, Straus & Giroux, 1968.
An account of a two-week trip to North Vietnam that Sontag made in 1968.

916. Spock, Benjamin. *Dr. Spock on Vietnam.* New York: Dell Publishing, 1968.
A short book in which Spock justifies his objections to the Vietnam war, gives a brief historical sketch of how the U.S. got involved, discusses how and why the U.S. should simply withdraw from the war, and outlines how the U.S. is destroying Vietnam. The final chapter outlines suggestions for citizens who want to influence decisions to withdraw.

917. Stafford, Robert, et al. *How to End the Draft.* Washington, DC: National Press, 1967.
An examination of what steps could be taken to end the draft and instead have an all-volunteer armed forces. Stafford does not call for a reduction in the number of men. The authors were all members of the U.S. House of Representatives when the study was done.

918. Stapp, Andy. *Up Against the Brass.* New York: Simon & Schuster, 1970.
The story of one war resister who joined the Army in 1966 to organize rebellion from within the ranks. After his enlistment was ended, he started the American Serviceman's Union to help GIs fight for their rights within the military.

919. Stevens, Franklin. *If This Be Treason: Your Sons Tell Their Own Stories of Why They Won't Fight for Their Country.* New York: Peter H. Wyden, 1970.
An explanation of the draft, its history and operations. Includes interviews with men who managed to avoid the draft.

920. Taylor, Clyde, ed. *Vietnam and Black America: An Anthology of Protest and Resistance.* Garden City, NY: Doubleday-Anchor Books, 1973.
Taylor says that black opposition to the war was different from white. Whites wanted to end the war out of fatigue and frustration. Blacks were more concerned with human rights and racial justice. His selection of readings supports this view.

921. Uhl, Michael. *Vietnam: A Soldier's View*. Wellington, New Zealand: New Zealand UP, 1971.
The personal experiences of one of our American soldiers who came back and became active in VVAW. Also includes his justification for being against the war, and testimonies of others about American atrocities in Vietnam.

922. Useem, Michael. *Conscription, Protest, and Social Conflict: The Life and Death of a Draft Resistance Movement*. New York: Wiley, 1973.
A study of the draft resistance movement which was very active in 1966.

923. Vogelsang, Sandy. *The Long Dark Night of the Soul: The American Intellectual Left and the Vietnam War*. New York: Harper & Row, Publishers, 1974.
Vogelsang looked at four leftist periodicals to trace the development of leftist opposition to the Vietnam war. The opposition went through three stages: Vietnam was seen as a lapse in judgment; seen as an immoral exercise; seen as politically illegitimate. Vogelsang believed that the Vietman war coalesced fragmented dissent and led many to a personal "leftward odyssey."

924. Waterhouse, Larry G., and Marian G. Wizard. *Turning the Guns Around: Notes on the GI Movement*. New York: Praeger Publishers, 1971.
A book about the GI movement within the military to make the military more democratic and to protest the Vietnam war.

925. *We Accuse*. Berkeley: Diablo Press, 1965.
Speeches from "Vietnam Day" at Berkeley, May 21-22, 1965. Speakers included Norman Mailer, Mario Savio, Dr. Spock, Bertrand Russell, I.F. Stone, Dick Gregory, and many others against the war.

926. Windmiller, Marshall. *The Commentary of Marshall Windmiller*. Berkeley: TLD, 1966.
Radio broadcast scripts, September 1965 - May 1966, mainly focusing on the United States involvement in Vietnam. Windmiller was against the war, and his commentaries are persuasive editorials of protest.

927. Zaroulis, Nancy, and Gerald Sullivan. *Who Spoke Up? American Protest against the War in Vietnam, 1963-1975*. Garden City, NY: Doubleday, 1984.
Traces the history of the protest against the war in the U.S. from its beginnings in 1963 until the end of the war in 1975. Includes a glossary of acronyms for the various protest organizations.

1968: The Pivotal Year

928. Becker, Theodore L., ed. *Political Trials*. Indianapolis, IN: Bobbs-Merrill, 1971.
    A study which includes a long section on the Chicago Conspiracy Trial.

929. Berube, Maurice R., and Marilyn Gittell, eds. *Confrontation at Ocean-Hill-Brownsville: The New York School Strikes of 1968*. New York: Praeger Publishers, 1969.
    A history and analysis, through documents and interpretations, of the strikes that closed the New York City schools in 1968. The issues revolved around decentralization and community control. The editors felt that readers needed to do something about the failures of the educational systems in our urban areas.

930. Caute, David. *The Year of the Barricades: A Journey Through 1968* . New York: Harper & Row, Publishers, 1988.
    A description and analysis of the events of 1968 in the U.S., France, Czechoslovakia, Britain, Mexico, and Japan. Caute analyzes the relationship of the New Left to the counterculture and women's liberation. Photos and a chronology are included.

931. Chester, Lewis, Godfrey Hodgson, and Bruce Page. *An American Melodrama: The Presidential Campaign of 1968*. New York: Viking Press, 1969.
    A very comprehensive account of the campaign which, like many other 1968 happenings, was one of the most exciting in American history.

932. *The Chicago 8 Speak Out! Conspiracy*. New York: Dell Publishing, 1969.
    Pieces from each of the Chicago 8 on the nature of conspiracy and their part in the struggle to end the war and in the demonstrations at the Chicago Democratic Convention.

933. Clavir, Judy, and John Spitzer, eds. *The Conspiracy Trial*. Indianapolis, IN: Bobbs-Merrill, 1970.
    Complete report of the Chicago Conspiracy Trial. Includes transcripts of the trial, legal citations, and Bobby Seale's contempt proceedings.

934. Daniels, Robert V. *Year of the Heroic Guerrillas: World Revolution and Counter-Revolution in 1968*. New York: Basic Books, 1989.
A detailed account of national and world events in 1968 that still have an impact on us today. Daniels looks at Saigon, Haight-Ashbury, Washington, Paris, Peking, Prague, and Chicago.

935. English, David, and the Staff of the London *Daily Express*. *Divided They Stand*. Englewood Cliffs, NJ: Prentice Hall, 1969.
An account by a British journalist of the 1968 presidential campaign.

936. Epstein, Jason. *The Great Conspiracy Trial: An Essay on Law, Liberty and the Constitution*. New York: Random House, 1970.
This book is an account of the Chicago Seven conspiracy trial, focusing primarily on the conspiracy law and the application of that law in this case.

937. Fager, Charles S. *Uncertain Resurrection: The Poor People's Washington Campaign*. Grand Rapids: Eerdman's, 1969.
Martin Luther King was the driving force behind the Poor People's March and Resurrection City in Washington, D.C., in 1968. The idea was to demonstrate that there were thousands of people--both black and white--living in poverty in America. Even though King was assassinated before the campaign, it still went forward, led by Ralph Abernathy. This book details the campaign and offers an analysis of why it should be considered a failure.

938. Farber, David. *Chicago '68*. Chicago: U Chicago P, 1988.
Farber was too young to be involved in the riots in Chicago in 1968, so he explains that in this book he tries to make the scene alive for those who weren't there. He picked the Democratic convention because he feels it was representative of the conflicts that were splitting society at the time. He sees the various groups using speech to shape their worlds, so he uses their various speech patterns to show how the groups came into conflict.

939. Frank, Joseph, ed. *The New Look in American Politics: McCarthy's Campaign*. Albuquerque: U of New Mexico P, 1968.
A special issue of *New Mexico Quarterly*. The articles were written about the campaign in the various states and follow it to the Democratic convention. Includes some of McCarthy's poetry.

940. Frost, David, ed. *The Presidential Debate*. New York: Stein and Day, 1968.
Conversations with Nixon, Eugene McCarthy, Reagan, Humphrey, Harold Stassen, George Wallace, John Lindsay, Nelson Rockefeller, and Robert Kennedy before the 1968 elections.

941. Gleason, Bill. *Daley of Chicago: The Man, the Mayor, and the Limits of Conventional Politics*. New York: Simon & Schuster, 1970.

An account of Daley's handling of the Chicago race riots and of the Democratic National Convention.

942. Halberstam, David. *The Unfinished Odyssey of Robert Kennedy*. New York: Random House, 1968.
A first-hand account of Robert Kennedy's campaign for the presidency in 1968.

943. Hastings, Max. *The Fire This Time: America's Year of Crisis*. New York: Taplinger Publishing, 1969.
This British journalist gives his impressions (based on his stay in the U.S.) of 1968. He covers the election, the rioting in Chicago in April, civil rights, university rebellions, middle-class America, and the media.

944. Hayden, Tom. *Trial*. New York: Holt, Rinehart & Winston, 1970.
Hayden's account of the Chicago conspiracy trial and his reflections on the meaning and importance of what happened during it.

945. Hoeh, David C. *The Biography of a Campaign: McCarthy In New Hampshire*. University of Massachusetts, Ph.D. Dissertation, 1973.
Hoeh was an organizer and participant in McCarthy's campaign. This is a case study of the strategies used in this campaign.

946. Kaiser, Charles. *1968 in America: Music, Politics, Chaos, Counterculture, and the Shaping of a Generation*. New York: Weidenfeld & Nicolson, 1988.
Kaiser adds to the history of that pivotal year. His account is very readable and adds a new perspective to the wide range of 1968 events. Photos included.

947. Koning, Hans. *Nineteen Sixty-Eight: A Personal Report*. New York: W.W. Norton, 1987.
Koning relates his experiences of 1968 as a participant in most of the events. He sees 1968 as a year when "people power" meant something.

948. Larner, Jeremy. *Nobody Knows: Reflections on the McCarthy Campaign of 1968*. New York: Macmillan Publishing, 1970.
Larner was one of McCarthy's speech writers during the campaign. He says he has written this book to try to show what happened--why McCarthy was such a hopeful choice, but ultimately failed in the election.

949. Levine, Mark L., George C. McNamee, and Daniel Greenberg, eds. *Tales of Hoffman*. New York: Bantam Books, 1969.
An edited version of the transcripts of the Chicago Conspiracy Trial.

950. Lukas, J. Anthony. *The Barnyard Epithet and Other Obscenities: Notes on the Chicago Conspiracy Trial*. New York: Harper & Row, Publishers, 1970.

Lukas covered the Chicago conspiracy trial of 1969-70 for the *New York Times*. He does not consider this book to be the definitive book on the trial, but his firsthand observations of what occurred.

951. Mailer, Norman. *Miami and the Siege of Chicago.* New York: NAL,1968.
Mailer's account of the Republican national convention in Miami and the Chicago Democratic convention in 1968. As a participant, Mailer used New Journalistic techniques as he did in *Armies of the Night.*

952. Mayer, Martin. *The Teachers' Strike; New York, 1968.* New York: Harper & Row, Publishers, 1969.
A narrative account of the New York City teachers' strike in 1968.

953. *Rights In Conflict: Convention Week in Chicago, August 25-29, 1968.* (The Walker Report) New York: Bantam Books, 1968.
This report was done for the National Commission of the Causes and Prevention of Violence. The conclusions reached blamed the police for the rioting.

954. Schneir, Walter, ed. *Telling It Like It Was: The Chicago Riots.* New York: NAL-Signet Books, 1969.
A documentation of the 1968 Democratic convention and its accompanying riots by those who experienced them--Abbie Hoffman, Paul Krassner, Carl Oglesby, William Styron, Arthur Miller, Tom Wicker, Jimmy Breslin, Jack Newfield, Tom Hayden, David Dellinger, and others.

955. Schultz, John. *No One Was Killed: Documentation and Meditation: Convention Week, Chicago--August 1968.* Chicago: Big Table Publishing, 1969.
Schultz was reporting on the convention for *Evergreen Review.* He tells the story from the point of view of a participant.

956. St. John, Jeffrey. *Countdown to Chaos: Chicago, 1968, Turning Point in American Politics.* Los Angeles: Nash Publishing, 1969.
St. John believed that the violent confrontations in Chicago constituted a premeditated assault on the American political system and individual rights. In this book he describes the week of the Democratic National Convention from that point of view.

957. Stavis, Ben. *We Were the Campaign. New Hampshire to Chicago for McCarthy.* Boston: Beacon Press, 1969.
Stavis was a graduate student at Columbia when McCarthy decided to run for the presidency. He started working for McCarthy's campaign about four weeks before the New Hampshire primary and followed it to its end.

958. Stein, David Lewis. *Living the Revolution: The Yippies in Chicago.* Indianapolis, IN: Bobbs-Merrill, 1969.

Stein gives a history of the Yippies and then reconstructs a day-by-day history of what was happening on the streets at the 1968 Chicago Democratic convention.

959. Unger, Irwin, and Debi Unger. *Turning Point: 1968.* New York: Charles Scribner's Sons, 1988.
The authors discuss the divisions that occurred during 1968--between Black Power and other civil rights movements; division in the Democratic party; division in the New Left. It was also the year of new alliances for homosexuals and feminists. It was the year America started swinging back to the right. It was a pivotal year. Photos included.

960. White, Theodore. *The Making of the President, 1968.* New York: Atheneum Publishers, 1969.
Again White describes a campaign and a campaign year. The year starts with Tet, moves through Johnson's renunciation and Robert Kennedy's death, to the victory of Richard Nixon at year's end.

The Environment, Overpopulation and Consumer Issues

961. Appleman, Philip. *The Silent Explosion*. Boston: Beacon Press, 1965.
A study of the problems of international overpopulation and an argument that the U.S. should take the lead in dealing with the problem.

962. Borgstrom, Georg. *Hungry Planet*. New York: Macmillan Publishing, 1965.
A description of the problems of overpopulation and hunger in the world.

963. Carr, Donald E. *Death of the Sweet Waters*. New York: W.W. Norton, 1966.
A book on the dangers to the earth's water supply and recommendations for how to correct it.

964. Carson, Rachel. *Silent Spring*. Boston: Houghton Mifflin, 1962.
One of the most famous books on the damage that humans are doing to the planet.

965. Commoner, Barry. *Science and Survival*. New York: Viking Press, 1967.
An argument that people are not in control of the powers science has given us and that humanity may be in danger from their own creations.

966. Day, Lincoln H., and Alice Taylor Day. *Too Many Americans*. New York: Houghton Mifflin, 1964.
An exploration of the benefits of limiting population growth in the United States. The authors look at religious beliefs and values, and also at how the U.S. population increase could affect the rest of the world.

967. de Bell, Garrett, ed. *The Environmental Handbook*. New York: Ballantine Books, 1970.
A collection of writings on the ecological crisis compiled for the First National Environmental Teach-In. Includes lists of environmental groups and suggestions for organizing.

968. Ehrlich, Paul R. *The Population Bomb*. New York: Ballantine Books, 1968.
A call for a control of population growth so that the earth can continue
to support its inhabitants. One of the most widely read of such calls.

969. Ehrlich, Paul R., and Anne H. Ehrlich. *Population, Resources, Environment:
Issues in Human Ecology*. San Francisco: Freeman, 1970.
A survey of issues in ecology, including overpopulation, the limits of
the earth (water, energy, food, minerals), environmental threats, and
ecosystems. A positive program is recommended to alleviate some of
these problems.

970. Ferkiss, Victor C. *Technological Man: The Myth and the Reality*. New York:
George Braziller, 1969.
An examination of the pluses and minuses of the new age of technology
in which man has total control over himself and his environment.

971. Gofman, John W., and Arthur R. Tamplin. *Poisoned Power*. Emmaus, PA:
Rodale Press, 1971.
A discussion of nuclear power used to generate electricity and its threat
to life. Written to generate citizen action against it.

972. Graham, Frank, Jr. *Disaster by Default: Politics and Water Pollution*. New
York: M. Evans, 1966.
An early look at water pollution and sewage treatment in the U.S.

973. Laycock, George. *The Diligent Destroyers*. Garden City, NY: Doubleday, 1970.
An examination of the Army Corps of Engineers and the Bureau of
Reclamation and of the irreparable damage done to the earth's
environment.

974. League of Women Voters of the U.S. Education Fund. *The Big Water Fight:
Trials and Triumphs in Citizen Action on Problems of Supply,
Pollution, Floods, and Planning across the U.S.A.* Brattleboro, VT: S.
Greene Press, 1966.
An examination of water-resource problems.

975. Lewis, Howard R. *With Every Breath You Take: The Poisons of Air
Pollution, How They Are Injuring Our Health, and What We Must Do
About Them*. New York: Crown Publishers, 1965.
An extensive discussion of the dangers of air pollution in the U.S.
Lewis also makes recommendations for how the problems could be
alleviated.

976. Marine, Gene. *America the Raped: The Engineering Mentality and the
Devastation of a Continent*. New York: Simon & Schuster, 1969.
Marine blames America's environmental problems on the engineering
mentality which wants to build and destroy, justifying only with:

"Who needs swamps? Who needs salt marshes? Let's use them for better purposes."

977. Marx, Wesley. *The Frail Ocean.* New York: Coward-McCann, 1967.
       A look at the oceans and their ecosystems. According to Marx, the oceans can be a major resource, but they must be guarded carefully. The U.S. must play a leading role in taking care of the oceans.

978. Meadows, Dennis, et al. *The Limits to Growth.* New York: NAL, 1974.
       Using a statistical world model, the authors have analyzed the effects of "accelerating trends" in industrialization, population growth, malnutrition, and deterioration of the envrionment. They conclude that if these trends are not checked, the world will reach its limit of growth within the next 100 years.

979. Nader, Ralph. *Unsafe at Any Speed: The Designed-In Dangers of the American Automobile.* New York: Bantam Books, 1972. Originally published in 1965.
       One of Nader's first books, this one took on the automobile industry in an effort to improve the safety of driving. The 1972 version has an updated chapter.

980. Ng, Larry K.Y., and Stuart Mudd, eds. *The Population Crisis: Implications and Plans for Action.* Bloomington: Indiana UP, 1965.
       A collection of essays on the popoulation explosion and its dangers, including the facts of the growth, resources, psychological considerations, genetic considerations, and public health.

981. Paddock, William, and Paul Paddock. *Famine--1975!* Boston: Little, Brown, 1967.
       An early look at the problems of food supply worldwide and specific suggestions for how the U.S. could help avert famine in the future.

982. Reinow, Robert, and Leona Train Reinow. *Moment in the Sun: A Report on the Deteriorating Quality of the American Environment.* New York: Dial Press, 1967.
       A report on the human influence on the environment due to overpopulation, overuse of resources, pollution, and destruction of wildlife.

983. Ridgeway, James. *The Politics of Ecology.* New York: E.P. Dutton, 1970.
       A look at the politics of ecology. Ridgeway argues that large corporations are really behind the ecology movement to ensure their control of policies.

984. Rudd, Robert L. *Pesticides and the Living Landscape.* Madison: U of Wisconsin P, 1964.
       A study of the effects of chemicals as pest controls on the environment.

985. Snyder, Gary. *Earth House Hold*. New York: New Directions Publishing, 1969.

    Reflections from the fifties and sixties on Snyder's involvement in Eastern religions and his feelings about the ecology of the earth and the environmental crisis.

The Arts

986. Adair, Gilbert. *Hollywood's Vietnam: From the Green Berets to Apocalypse Now*. New York: Proteus, 1981.
The author says this book is not about how the war was covered, but how it was represented by filmmakers. He only deals with those movies that are centered on the war and American society during the war--not with movies about men who were also veterans of Vietnam (i.e., *Taxi Driver*). Included is a filmography of the movies discussed.

987. Aldridge, John W. *The Devil in the Fire: Retrospective Essays On American Literature and Culture, 1951-1971*. New York: Harper's Magazine, 1972.
Of the 1960s writers, Aldridge focuses on Norman Mailer, John Updike, William Styron, Mary McCarthy, Saul Bellow, John Cheever, James Jones, Wright Morris, Donald Barthelme, and Jerzy Kosinski.

988. Altieri, Charles. *Enlarging the Temple: New Directions in American Poetry During the 1960's*. Lewisburg, PA: Bucknell UP, 1979.
A study of post-modern poetry which focuses on such poets as Robert Lowell, Robert Bly, Charles Olson, Frank O'Hara, Gary Snyder, Robert Duncan, Robert Creeley, and Denise Levertov.

989. *Astronauts of Inner-Space*. San Francisco: Stolen Paper Review Editions, 1966.
A selection of essays and poetry from some of the 1960s most influential writers--Allen Ginsberg, Marshall McLuhan, W. Burroughs, and others--giving a view of how the artists of the day perceived the arts.

990. Averson, Richard. *Electronic Drama: Television Plays of the Sixties*. Boston: Beacon Press, 1971.
Scripts of TV dramas done in the 1960s. The introduction and preface offer explanations for the rarity of good drama on TV. A brief history of TV drama is also given.

991. Baxandall, Lee, ed. *Radical Perspectives in the Arts*. Baltimore: Penguin Books, 1972.
A selection of readings on the arts and capitalism, the arts and socialism, and the future of culture. Writers include C. Oglesby, H. Marcuse, C. Fuentes, F. Castro, and others.

992. Baxter, John. *Hollywood in the Sixties*. London: Tantivy Press, 1972.
A chronicle of movie-making in the U.S. in the 1960s. This was the time when movies began to suffer from the competition from television. It was also the time when many old greats lost their drawing power and many died. The author believes that quality diminished as more movie makers made Grade-B movies.

993. Bender, Marylin. *The Beautiful People*. New York: Coward-McCann, 1967.
Analyzes the fashion trends of the 1960s. Her theory is that clothes are becoming minimalist and that fashion has become a part of Pop art. According to Bender, the fashion industry will never regain the quality workmanship that has been lost.

994. Bernard, Barbara. *Fashion in the 60s*. New York: St. Martin's Press, 1978.
A photodocumentary of the fashions, mostly for women, of the 1960s.

995. Berthoff, W. "Witness and Testament: Two Contemporary Classics, excerpts from 'Fiction and Events.'" In Berthoff, W., *Fictions and Events: Essays in Criticism and Literary History* (New York: E.P Dutton, 1971), pp. 288-308 or in Miller, J.H., ed., *Aspects of Narrative*, pp. 173-98.
Analysis of *The Autobiography of Malcolm X* (Alex Haley, ed.) and *Armies of the Night* (Norman Mailer).

996. Brode, Douglas. *The Films of the Sixties*. Secaucus, NJ: Citadel Press, 1980.
Divided by years, this book gives all the important information for significant films of the 1960s. Plot summaries with commentary on special aspects of the films and evaluations are included. Photos accompany the text. Unfortunately, there are no references to other materials.

997. Calas, Nicholas and Elena. *Icons & Images of the Sixties*. NY: E.P. Dutton, 1971.
According to the authors, sixties art was a reaction to Abstract Expressionism. This book is an analysis of the most famous artists of the time, as well as various types of art, e.g. pop art, kinetics, artificial realism, lettrism. The book is divided into 2-10 page essays of the artist and his work. Includes sculpture. Photos accompany analyses for many works.

998. Carroll, Paul. *The Poem and Its Skin*. Chicago: Follett Publishing, 1968.
Using various types of criticism, Carroll offers readings of various poets of the 1960s and before, e.g., James Dickey, Isabella Gardner, and Allen Ginsberg. Photos included.

999. Clor, Harry M. *Obscenity and Public Morality: Censorship in a Liberal Society*. Chicago: U of Chicago P, 1969.
Clor argues for controlled censorship to be enforced to promote public morality but to also protest artistic integrity.

1000. Cohen, John, ed. *The Essential Lenny Bruce.* New York: Ballantine Books, 1967.
Material Lenny Bruce used on stage concerning racism, politics, drugs, sex, obscenity, and the law.

1001. Davidson, Michael. *The San Francisco Renaissance: Poetics and Community at Midcentury.* Cambridge: Cambridge UP, 1989.
Analysis of the San Francisco poets between 1955 and 1965. Includes a history of the influences that produced them. Poets discussed are Gary Snyder, Philip Whalen, Robert Duncan, Jack Spicer, Michael McClure, Allen Ginsberg, Jack Kerouac, Helen Adam, Joanne Kyger, and Judy Grahn.

1002. De Grazia, Edward, and Roger K. Newman. *Banned Films: Movies, Censors, and the First Amendment.* New York: R.R. Bowker, 1982.
A history of film censorship. The banned movies are discussed individually by decade.

1003. Fernandez, Benedict J. *In Opposition: Images of American Dissent in the Sixties.* New York: Da Capo Press, 1968.
Photographs of dissent and protest. Fernandez says he has tried to capture people as they have "stepped out" to protest, because when they do, they have changed internally.

1004. Gilman, Richard. *The Confusion of Realms.* New York: Random House, 1969.
Essays and critical reviews on Afro-American writing, Marshall McLuhan, Susan Sontag, Donald Barthelme, John Rechy, John Updike, Norman Mailer, the theater, Macbird!, and the Living Theater.

1005. Ginsberg, Allen. *Allen Verbatim: Lectures on Poetry, Politics, and Consciousness.* Edited by Gordon Ball. New York: McGraw-Hill, 1974.
Transcripts of informal lectures and conversations of Ginsberg on a national tour he made in the spring of 1971.

1006. Gottfried, Martin. *Opening Nights: Theater Criticism of the Sixties.* New York: G.P. Putnam's, 1969.
Criticism of the theatre from 1963-1969.

1007. Hewison, Robert. *Too Much: Art and Society in the Sixties, 1960 - 1975.* London: Methuen, 1986.
British art and literature and the society which produced it. Includes visual arts, music, theatre, poetry, and films.

1008. Hopper, Dennis. *Dennis Hopper: Out of the Sixties.* Pasadena, CA: Twelvetrees Press, 1986.
A collection of photographs by Dennis Hopper, the actor and director, 1966-1967. His association with the world of the famous make these photographs documents of who and what were "in" during these years.

1009. Hunt, Tim. *Kerouac's Crooked Road*. Hamden, CT: Shoe String Press, 1981.
A critical analysis of *On the Road* and *Visions of Cody*. Hunt felt Kerouac's writing had been taken too superficially by literary critics.

1010. Jason, Philip K., ed. *Fourteen Landing Zones: Approaches to Vietnam War Literature*. Iowa City: U of Iowa P, 1991.,
Jason explains that the Vietnam literature that will endure will be that literature that confronts American myths and tell us about American society in the 1960s and 1970s. The writers analyzed in this collection of essays include Bobbie Ann Mason, Joseph Heller, John Clark Pratt, Joan Didion, and several others.

1011. Kherdian, David. *Six Poets of the San Francisco Renaissance: Portraits and Checklists*. Fresno, CA: Giligia Press, 1967.
Essays on poets of the 1950s and 1960s. Included are Lawrence Ferlinghetti, Gary Snyder, Philip Whalen, David Meltzer, Michael McClure, and Brother Antoninus.

1012. Kirby, Michael, *Happenings: An Illustrated Anthology*. New York: E.P. Dutton, 1965.
Kirby defines "Happenings," a distinctly 1960s art form which combined theater, sculpture, and other media. Then happenings from five artists are presented, with statements from each artist. Artists include Allan Kaprow, Red Grooms, Robert Whitman, Jim Dine, and Claus Oldenberg. Photos included.

1013. Klinkowitz, Jerome. *The American 1960s: Imaginative Acts in a Decade of Change*. Ames, IA: Iowa State UP, 1980.
A look at literature of the 1960s, including authors such as Richard Brautigan, James Kunen, Donald Barthelme, Hunter Thompson, as well as an exploration of what that literature tells about the 1960s.

1014. Kostelanetz, Richard. *The Theatre of Mixed Means: An Introduction to Happenings, Kinetic Environments, and Other Mixed-Means Performances*. New York: Dial Press, 1968.
Kostelanetz defines the new theater forms which burgeoned in the 1960s. Artists discussed include John Cage, Robert Rauschenberg, Usco, Ann Halprin, and others.

1015. ---, ed. *The New American Arts*. Horizon Press, 1965.
Readings which attempt to point out new trends in the arts, to identify and discuss new artists, and to place new works in their historical context. Arts included are film, theatre, painting, poetry, dance, fiction, and music.

1016. Kuh, Richard H. *Foolish Figleaves? Pornography in and out of Court*. New York: Macmillan Publishing, 1967.

An overview of censorship and obscenity issues as they were viewed in the 1960s.

1017. Lippard, Lucy R. et al. *Pop Art*. New York: Praeger Publishers, 1967.
A definition and description of Pop Art, a major art movement of the 1960s. Focused on British Pop, New York Pop, California, European, and Canadian Pop.

1018. Lobenthal, Joel. *Radical Rags: Fashions of the Sixties*. New York: Abbeville Press, 1990.
A fairly comprehensive book, with photos and text, of the fashion world of the 1960s.

1019. Masters, Robert E.L., and Jean Houston. *Psychedelic Art*. New York: Grove Press, 1968.
Examples and analyses of psychedelic art, i.e., art that attempted to portray the psychedelic experience. Includes photo and many color plates.

1020. Mersmann, James F. *Out of the Vietnam Vortex: A Study of Poets and Poetry Against the War*. Lawrence, KA: The UP of Kansas, 1974.
A study of the poetry of Denise Levertov, Allen Ginsberg, Robert Bly, and Robert Duncan as it relates to artists' attempts to deal with this particular war.

1021. Mordden, Ethan. *Medium Cool: The Movies of the 1960s*. New York: Alfred A. Knopf, 1990.
Mordden believes the films of the 1960s ushered in a new era of independent, nonconformist films and film-makers. He examined films like *Psycho, The Manchurian Candidate, The Graduate, Dr. Strangelove, The Wild Bunch*, and many others.

1022. *The Obscenity Report. Pornography and Obscenity in America*. London: MacGibbon & Kee, 1970.
A report which argues strongly against obscenity and pornography, including the banning of many works which were allowed in the U.S. during the 1960s.

1023. Randall, Richard S. *Censorship of the Movies: The Social and Political Control of a Mass Medium*. Madison: U of Wisconsin P, 1970.
Primarily concerned with film censorship, this book is a thorough examination of governmental and nongovernmental censorship in the 1960s.

1024. Rembar, Charles. *The End of Obscenity: The Trials of Lady Chatterley, Tropic of Cancer and Fanny Hill*. New York: Random House, 1968.
While this book is primarily about the three books mentioned, it is also about the liberalism of the Supreme Court and society in the 1960s.

1025. Rexroth, Kenneth. *The Alternative Society: Essays from the Other World.* New York: Herder & Herder, 1970.
Essays mostly on art and artists of the era, both national and international, and their relation to America's cultural turmoil.

1026. Rosenthal, M.L. *The New Poets: American and British Poetry Since World War II.* New York: Oxford UP, 1967.
Rosenthal begins with an introduction to modern poetry, commenting on such characteristics as its focus on the self, its alienation, and its constant reference to war. He writes about many poets, including Robert Lowell, Allen Ginsberg, Denise Levertov, and LeRoi Jones.

1027. Sanders, Ed. *Investigative Poetry.* San Francisco: City Lights, 1976.
A lecture in which Sanders argues that poetry can be political and he shows how it can be done.

1028. Sontag, Susan. *Against Interpretation.* New York: Farrar, Straus & Giroux, 1966.
A prime example of criticism of literature, film, plays and the arts culture in general in the 1960s.

1029. Ultra Violet. *Famous for Fifteen Minutes: My Years with Andy Warhol.* New York: Avon Books, 1988.
Ultra Violet was one of Andy Warhol's superstars, She tells her story of life with Andy Warhol from 1964 until his death. Photos included.

1030. Weber, Ronald. *The Literature of Fact: Literary Nonfiction In American Writing.* Athens, OH: Ohio UP, 1980.
Weber includes New Journalism in his definition of literary nonfiction. He gives a history of the genre, which he says is a long and distinguished one, and also discusses literary nonfiction of the 1960s and 1970s, including writers such as Norman Mailer, Tom Wolfe, Gay Talese, George Plimpton, and others.

1031. White, George Abbott, and Charles Newman, eds. *Literature in Revolution.* New York: Holt, Rinehart & Winston-TriQuarterly, 1972.
An examination of literature and its relationship to the social and political upheavals of the time. Writers examined include T.S. Eliot, Herman Melville, W.B.Yeats, Blake, Shakespeare, Milton, Hermann Hesse, and Solzhenitsyn.

Music of the Period

1032. Belz, Carl. *The Story of Rock*. New York: Oxford UP, 1969.
    An historical study of the art of rock, not its sociological, political, or economic aspects. Focuses on rock in the U.S. Divided into three periods: 1954-1956, 1957-1963, 1964-1968. Selected discography included.

1033. Boeckman, Charles. *And the Beat Goes On: A Survey of Pop Music in America*. Washington, DC: R.B. Luce, 1972.
    A history of popular music as well as a look at the revolution in pop music in the 1960s.

1034. Brown, Len, and Gary Friedrich. *Encyclopedia of Rock & Roll*. New York: Tower Publications, 1970.
    An encyclopedia of rock-n-roll stars in America up to 1963.

1035. Brown, Peter, and Steven Gaines. *The Love You Make: An Insider's Story of the Beatles*. New York: McGraw-Hill, 1983.
    A very detailed story of the Beatles with what are said to be many facts never before revealed. Important because it takes the reader a decade beyond their break-up and past J. Lennon's death.

1036. Budds, Michael J. *Jazz in the Sixties: The Expansion of Musical Resources and Techniques*. Iowa City: U of Iowa P, 1978.
    A scholarly study of the innovative elements of jazz in the sixties.

1037. Busnar, Eugene. *The Superstars of Rock: Their Lives and Their Music*. New York: Messner, 1980.
    Sketches with photos of rock stars. Those from the 1960s include the Beatles, the Stones, Eric Clapton, Jimi Hendrix, the Bee Gees, and Janis Joplin. For each, there is a listing of their albums and singles by year.

1038. Carr, Roy, and Tony Tyler. *The Beatles: An Illustrated Record*. New York: Harmony Books, 1975.
    A survey of the Beatles' recordings accompanied by photographs and other graphics surveying their individual and collective lives.

1039. Castleman, Harry, and Walter J. Podrazik. *The Beatles Again.* Ann Arbor, MI: Pierian, 1977.
A reference work on the Beatles, covering principally 1975-1977, but also including information on the early Beatles.

1040. Christgau, Robert. *Any Old Way You Choose It: Rock and Other Pop Music, 1967-1973.* Baltimore: Penguin Books, 1973.
These are articles on rock published in *Esquire* and *The Village Voice.* Christgau writes using some New Journalism techniques and his articles touch on everyone in rock music during that time period.

1041. Cohn, Nik. *Rock from the Beginning.* New York: Stein and Day, 1969.
A history of rock from Bill Haley through the groups of the late 1960s. Includes essays on the Who, the Monkees, folk rock, P.J. Proby, and the California groups.

1042. Cook, Bruce. *The Beat Generation.* New York: Scribner's Sons, 1971.
Mostly about the beats of the '50s, although the writer does give some unusual reflections on the Woodstock concert in the last chapter.

1043. Dalton, David. *Rolling Stones.* New York: Amsco Music Publishing, 1972.
An unauthorized photodocumentary of the Stones and scores for some of the songs. Also includes record reviews and a discography.

1044. Damsker, Matt. *Rock Voices: The Best Lyrics of an Era.* New York: St. Martin's Press, 1980.
The lyrics for what Damsker feels are the best rock songs. Sixties songs come from Bob Dylan, Paul Simon, the Beatles, Leonard Cohen, the Mamas and the Papas, Neil Young, Stephen Stills, Janis Ian, Grateful Dead, the Doors, Laura Nyro, Joni Mitchell, the Band, Randy Newman, Van Morrison, and James Taylor.

1045. Davies, Hunter. *The Beatles: The Authorized Biography.* New York: McGraw-Hill, 1968.
This biography takes the Beatles up to their *White Album* and just a little past the death of Brian Epstein, their manager, who exerted a great influence on their music and their lives. At the time the author stops, the Beatles were involved with the Maharaji, although at the end Davies says their feelings were already starting to change about him. Very interesting, as far as it goes, but something more analytical and more recent would do better.

1046. Davis, Stephen. *Hammer of the Gods: The Led Zeppelin Saga.* New York: Ballantine Books, 1985.
A biography of the very popular British rock group, another 1960s legendary band. Photos included.

1047. Dean, Robert, and David Howells, comps. *The Ultimate Album Cover Album.* New York: Prentice Hall, 1987.

A collection of album covers from the '60s, '70s, and '80s from various rock, jazz, and folk albums.

1048. Denisoff, R. Serge. *Sing a Song of Social Significance.* 2d ed. Bowling Green, OH: Bowling Green State University Popular Press, 1983. A look at what is a protest song in any given time or place, who sings these songs, how they are used, and how they affect their constituencies. Primarily, Denisoff focuses on 1960s protest music.

1049. ---. *Solid Gold: The Pop Record Industry.* New Brunswick, NJ: Transaction Books, 1975. An analysis of the recording industry and what it took to be a success in the business.

1050. Denisoff, R. Serge and Richard A. Peterson, eds. *The Sounds of Social Change: Studies in Popular Culture.* Chicago: Rand McNally, 1972. Scholarly essays on the uses of music as an "opiate, weapon, and/or harbinger of social change." This is, according to the editors, the first such book to treat social music seriously.

1051. DeTurk, David, and A. Puolin, Jr.. *The American Folk Scene: Dimensions of the Folksong Revival.* New York: Dell Publishing, 1967. Essays that examine folk music and musicians as a cultural phenomenon, reflecting the needs of its audiences.

1052. Dilello, Richard. *The Longest Cocktail Party: A Personal History of Apple.* Chicago: Playboy Press, 1972. Subtitled "An Insider's Diary of the Beatles, Their Million-Dollar Empire and Its Wild Rise and Fall." Dilello was the House Hippie at Apple Records and most of this book is about Apple and the people involved with the company. Photos included.

1053. Dunson, Josh. *Freedom in the Air: Song Movements of the Sixties.* New York: International Publishers, 1965. Dunson divides the socially conscious songs of the sixties into two groups: the freedom songs of the South, and the topical songs of the North. In this book, he examines the background and development of these song types in the U.S.

1054. Eisen, Jonathan, ed. *The Age of Rock.* 2 volumes. New York: Random House, 1969, 1970. Collections of writings on rock from all over the U.S. and all over the cultural landscape. Photos included.

1055. Epstein, Brian. *A Cellarful of Noise.* London: Souvenir Press, 1964. Brian Epstein tells his own history. This book is mainly about the Beatles, but he also wrote about other groups he managed. Photos included.

1056. Fawcett, Anthony. *John Lennon: One Day at a Time.* Rev. ed. New York: Grove Press, 1980.
A study of Lennon and his music, 1970-1980. Fawcett presents a positive picture of both John and Yoko. Many photos included.

1057. Fong-Torres, Ben, ed. *What's That Sound? The Contemporary Music Scene from the Pages of Rolling Stone.* Garden City, NY: Doubleday-Anchor Books, 1976.
Although most of these pieces were done in the 1970s, they are about many people who became famous in the 1960s. Included are interviews with Paul McCartney, George Harrison, John Lennon, Peter Townshend, David Bowie, Dylan, the Band, Paul Simon, Sly Stone, Eric Clapton, and Led Zeppelin.

1058. Frame, Pete. *Rock Group Family Trees.* London: Quick Fox, 1979.
An interesting series of family trees of many rock groups. Each tree also includes an historical narrative. There is an index of individual and group names.

1059. Frith, Simon. *The Sociology of Rock.* London: Constable, 1978.
A discussion of rock's place in society in the 1960s. Frith considers youth, leisure, radio, records, the music press, mass culture, and musicians.

1060. Garland, Phyl. *The Sound of Soul.* Chicago: Regnery, 1969.
A history of soul music and a look at the attitudes of blacks and the black mood. Includes comments from the musicians. Jazz music is treated. Photos included.

1061. Gillett, Charlie. *Making Tracks: Atlantic Records and the Growth of a Multi-Billion-Dollar Industry.* New York: E.P. Dutton, 1974.
A history of Atlantic records from the late 1940s through the 1960s. Photos included.

1062. ---. *The Sound of the City: The Rise of Rock and Roll.* New York: Outerbridge & Dienstfrey, 1970.
A history of rock which focuses more on the sociological, cultural aspects than on the artistic.

1063. Gleason, Ralph. *The Jefferson Airplane and the San Francisco Sound.* New York: Ballantine Books, 1969.
Gleason begins with a look at the rock scene in San Francisco, beginning in 1965. Next he looks closely at the Jefferson Airplane. He concludes with a look at Jerry Garcia (Grateful Dead) and a list of the survivors from the San Francisco rock scene. Photos included.

1064. Goldstein, Richard. *Goldstein's Greatest Hits: A Book Mostly About Rock 'n' Roll.* Englewood Cliffs, NJ: Prentice Hall, 1970.

Many of these essays on music and the teen culture that followed the stars were published in the *The Village Voice*, all between 1966 and 1968.

1065. Gray, Andy. *Great Pop Stars.* New York: Hamlyn, 1973.
An almanac of rock, with a year-by-year chronology of rock happenings and many photos. Starts in 1955 and goes through 1974. No index.

1066. Greenfield, Robert. *S.T.P.: A Journey Through America with the Rolling Stones.* New York: E.P. Dutton, 1974.
A detailed account of the Rolling Stones U.S. tour in 1972. Photos included.

1067. Hamm, Charles. *Yesterdays: Popular Song in America.* New York: W.W. Norton, 1979.
A comprehensive historical treatment of popular songs. The last two chapters focus on the rise and rule of rock. Photos included.

1068. Hendler, Herb. *Year By Year in the Rock Era.* New York: Praeger Publishers, 1987.
From 1954-1981, gives such information as popular artists, juke box hits, rock news, news that influenced rock, fashion, fads, and alternative life styles. Also gives information such as the cost of living, tuition fees for colleges, and comics and comic strips.

1069. Herman, Gary. *The Who.* New York: Macmillan Publishing, 1972.
A history of the group, which started in 1964. There is some analysis of their music and lyrics. Includes interviews, photos, and a discography.

1070. Hirsch, Abby. *Photography of Rock.* Indianapolis, IN: Bobbs-Merrill, 1972.
A selection of rock photos of the 1960s from a selection of rock photographers.

1071. Hopkins, Jerry. *Festival!* New York: Macmillan Publishing, 1970.
A photodocumentary of the important rock festivals in the 1960s, including Newport Folk Festival, Woodstock, Monterey Jazz Festival, and the Berkeley Folk Festival.

1072. ---. *The Rock Story.* New York: NAL-Signet Books, 1970.
A short history of rock, ending before Woodstock. Also essays on the money-making aspects of the rock business, AM radio stations' top forties, rock fans, rock idols, and the lifespan of a rock group. Ends with a discography of each chapter.

1073. Hotchner, A.E. *Blown Away: The Rolling Stones and the Death of the Sixties.* New York: Simon & Schuster, 1990.
A biography of the Rolling Stones which focuses on Brian Jones. His death and the murder at the Altamont concert in 1969 paralleled the death of the youth and energy of the 1960s.

1074. Jahn, Mike. *Jim Morrison and the Doors: An Unauthorized Book.* New York: Grosset & Dunlap, 1969.
      This book reads like an extended magazine article on the Doors. Morrison got the most attention, but there was no great depth to the study of him or the group. Many photos included.

1075. Kooper, Al, with Ben Edmonds. *Backstage Passes: Rock 'n' Roll Life in the Sixties.* New York: Stein and Day, 1977.
      Kooper played in several groups that were famous in the sixties--with early Dylan and the Blues Project, for example. He also produced a number of groups and records. This is his story of rock.

1076. Laing, David. *Buddy Holly.* New York: Macmillan Publishing, 1970.
      Although Holly is considered a fifties person, he is included here because of the great influence he had on the sixties rock world. Laing claims this book is not about Buddy Holly, but about his music, which Laing feels was the best of rock 'n' roll. Includes photos and a discography.

1077. ---. *The Sound of Our Time.* Chicago: Quadrangle Books, 1970.
      An analysis of pop music which focuses on the media, the audience, and the music itself. A chapter each is devoted to the Beatles, the Who, and Bob Dylan.

1078. Laing, David, et al. *The Electric Muse: The Story of Folk into Rock.* London: Methuen, 1975.
      A study of the different forms of folk music and the ways it influenced rock music of the time. Includes discographies.

1079. Landau, Jon. *It's Too Late to Stop Now: A Rock and Roll Journal.* San Francisco: Straight Arrow Press, 1972.
      A selection of essays on various artists of the 1960s, including Bob Dylan, the Rolling Stones, the Beach Boys, Blood, Sweat and Tears, Three Dog Night, Grateful Dead, Joni Mitchell, Carole King, Van Morrison, the Band, Paul Simon, Otis Redding, Wilson Pickett, B.B. King, Muddy Waters, Aretha Franklin, and Janis Joplin. The author was a rock critic for *Rolling Stone* and *Phoenix*. A discography concludes the book.

1080. Leaf, David. *The Beach Boys and the California Myth.* New York: Grosset & Dunlap, 1978.
      A book about Brian Wilson, the "leader" of the Beach Boys. Leaf believes that Wilson started the process which made California a state of mind for American teens, not just a state. Photos included.

1081. London, Herbert I. *Closing the Circle: A Cultural History of the Rock Revolution.* Chicago: Nelson-Hall, 1984.
      An exploration of the relationship between rock music and the society in which it thrives. London points to the revolutions in music that paralleled the revolutionary nature of the times.

1082. Lydon, Michael, and Ellen Mandel. *Boogie Lightning.* New York: Dial
Press, 1974.
An exploration of the union of music and electricity. Lydon starts by
describing older blues singers--John Lee Hooker and Bo Didley--then
moves into the 1960s with the Chiffons, the Action, and Aretha
Franklin. He includes a chapter on the electric guitar.

1083. McCabe, Peter, and Robert D. Schonfeld. *Apple to the Core: The Unmaking
of the Beatles.* New York: Pocket Books, 1972.
A short history of the Beatles and a detailed description of their break-
up. Photos included.

1084. McGregor, Craig, ed. *Bob Dylan: A Retrospective.* New York: William
Morrow, 1972.
A critical anthology of Dylan from 1961 to 1972. Essays from many well-
known rock critics.

1085. Macken, Bob, Peter Fornatale, and Bill Ayres. *The Rock Music Source Book.*
New York: Doubleday, 1980.
A reference book for rock in the '50s, '60s, and '70s. The first section has
themes listed alphabetically with lists of songs on those themes. Next is
a section on a basic rock library, rock films, rock history, record
companies, and rock magazines.

1086. Makower, Joel. *Woodstock: The Oral History.* New York: Doubleday, 1989.
A story of this famous festival, told in interviews in 1988 with the
people who "made it happen." Two things emerge from the interviews:
1) hardly anyone remembers the music; and 2) those who were
involved tend to date their lives around the festival. Includes many
photos.

1087. Marchbank, Pearce, and Barry Miles. *The Illustrated Rock Almanac.*
London: Paddington, 1977.
Day-by-day, a listing of significant events in the rock world, births,
deaths, releases, gigs. Includes the birth dates of other celebrities not tied
to the rock world. Photos included. Unfortunately, the book is not
indexed.

1088. Marcus, Greil. *Mystery Train: Images of America in Rock 'n' Roll.* New
York: E.P. Dutton, 1976.
A look at rock 'n' roll and what it says about American culture. Only a
few artists are explored--the Band, Sly Stone, Randy Newman, Elvis--as
symbolic Americans.

1089. ---, ed. *Stranded: Rock and Roll for a Desert Island.* New York: Alfred A.
Knopf, 1979.
In this book, 20 rock critics explain their choices of what album they
would most like to have with them on a desert island. Choices include
several 1960s artists: the Rolling Stones, the Ronettes, Captain

Beefheart, the Velvet Underground, the Kinks, Neil Young, and Van Morrison. Discography included.

1090. Marks, J., and Linda Eastman. *Rock and Other Four Letter Words: Music of the Electric Generation.* New York: Bantam Books, 1968.
A photographic montage of sixties rock, including individuals, groups, and the culture itself. Some text; mostly quotes from the artists.

1091. Marsh, Dave, and Kevin Stein. *The Book of Rock Lists.* New York: Dell Publishing, 1981.
Like the regular *Book of Lists*, this is a compilation of all sorts of lists having to do with rock up to 1980. Fascinating if you are interested in the rock world.

1092. Miller, Jim, ed. *The Rolling Stone Illustrated History of Rock & Roll.* New York: Random House-Rolling Stone Press, 1976.
A comprehensive overview of the history of rock music. The essays were written by various people associated with *Rolling Stone Magazine*. Each essay concludes with a discography that represents a sample of the primary work of an artist, genre, or locale from the essay.

1093. Mitchell, Mitch, with John Platt. *Jimi Hendrix: Inside the Experience.* New York: Harmony Books, 1990.
A photodocumentary/biography of Jimi Hendrix and his band, the Experience.

1094. Murray, Charles Shaar. *Crosstown Traffic: Jimi Hendrix and the Post-War Rock 'n' Roll Revolution.* New York: St. Martin's Press, 1989.
Murray analyses Jimi Hendrix's music as black music. He feels that to divorce him from his black culture is to do a disservice to his music and to black music in general. He also feels Hendrix was a great artist. Photos included.

1095. Myra, Harold, and Dean Merrill. *Rock, Bach, and Superschlock.* Nashville, TN: Holman, 1972.
The authors were Christians who tried to write a Christian book for youth on rock music.

1096. Nanry, Charles, ed. *American Music: From Storyville to Woodstock.* Brunswick, NJ: Trans-action Books, 1972.
Through analysis of jazz and rock, these selections focus on the relationship of their development to the development of urbanism and technology.

1097. Norman, Philip. *The Life and Good Times of the Rolling Stones.* New York: Harmony Books, 1989.
A photo-documentary of the Stones up to 1989.

1098. ---. *Shout! The Beatles in Their Generation.* New York: Simon & Schuster, 1981.
A history of the Beatles. Includes an epilogue written in 1980, right after Lennon's death. Many photos are also included.

1099. ---. *Symphony for the Devil: The Rolling Stones Story.* New York: Simon & Schuster-Linden, 1984.
A biography of the group up to their 1981 American and European tour.

1100. Peck, Ira, ed. *The New Sound.* New York: Scholastic Book Services, 1966.
A collection of essays on rock, including the California sound, the songwriters, the Supremes, deejays, the Beatles, Elvis, and Bob Dylan. Authors include James Michener, Tom Wolfe, Murray the K, and others. Photos included.

1101. Pichaske, David R. *Generation in Motion: Popular Music & Culture in the Sixties.* NY: Schirmer Books, 1979.
The one thing that differentiated the '60s from the '50s or the '70s was change--motion. Music was a reflection of this motion; it was a record of the decade. Pichaske puts together a history of the '60s and a history of the music and ties each of the various strains together with songs and artists. Photographs.

1102. Pollack, Bruce, and John Wagman. *The Face of Rock & Roll: Images of a Generation.* New York: Holt, Rinehart & Winston, 1978.
A photohistory of rock. Includes a lot of the covers from the albums of the 1960s

1103. Rivelli, Pauline, and Bob Levin, eds. *Rock Giants.* New York: World Publishing, 1970.
Articles on John and Yoko, Frank Zappa, Paul McCartney, the Chambers Brothers, Jefferson Airplane, the Beatles, the Stones, Donovan, Canned Heat, Cream, and others. Photos included.

1104. Rodnitzky, Jerome L. *Minstrals of the Dawn: The Folk-Protest Singer as a Cultural Hero.* Chicago: Nelson-Hall, 1976.
Rodnitzky argues that folk-protest singers and songs were "the most vivid symbols" of the protest of the 1960s and that the musicians became cultural heroes. Music had never before been so important as a generational symbol. Photos included.

1105. Sander, Ellen. *Trips: Rock Life in the Sixties.* New York: Charles Scribner's Sons, 1973.
A cultural history of the rock scene from 1960 through Altamont. In the process, Sander at least mentions nearly every rock star to make it--from east to west coast. She concludes with a rock taxonomy of just about anyone who contributed to the rock scene in the 1960s.

1106. Schafer, William J. *Rock Music; Where It's Been, What It Means, Where It's Going.* Minneapolis: Augsberg, 1972.
A look at rock music--its past, present, and future. Schafer also tries to show how rock has affected all of American culture.

1107. Schaffner, Nicholas. *The Beatles Forever.* Harrisburg, PA: Stackpole, 1977.
The Beatles as popular culture in America. Schaffner looks at the history of the Beatles and their impact on America. Many photos, especially of merchandise developed and sold using pictures of the Beatles.

1108. Schmidt, Eric von, and Jim Rooney. *Baby Let Me Follow You Down: The Illustrated Story of the Cambridge Folk Years.* Garden City, NY: Doubleday-Anchor Books, 1979.
Photographs and text on the various people involved in the folk movement of the late fifties/early sixties.

1109. Schultheiss, Tom. *A Day in the Life: The Beatles Day-by-Day, 1960-1970.* Ann Arbor, MI: Pierian Press, 1980.
Schultheiss argued that there was so far no accurate history of the Beatles. His chronology was intended as a "backbone of history" and he called for the Beatles to be taken seriously. The chronology is very detailed and does include an index. A few photos.

1110. Shaw, Arnold. *The World of Soul: Black America's Contribution to the Pop Music Scene.* New York: Cowles Books, 1970.
Shaw traces the development of soul music from its roots in blues to Jimi Hendrix and Aretha Franklin. There is a heavy emphasis on pre-1960s artists. Photos included.

1111. Shelton, Robert. Photographs by David Gahr. *The Face of Folk Music.* New York: Citadel Press, 1968.
A photodocumentary of the folk music world, concentrating mainly on the 1960s in the U.S., but going back to the history and considering other nations' folk music.

1112. Spitz, Robert. *Barefoot in Babylon: The Creation of the Woodstock Music Festival.* 1969. New York: Viking Press, 1979.
An interesting account of what went on behind the scenes in preparation for the Festival. Though we may have all heard about the glory of Woodstock, it is amazing how much work and money went into its presentation.

1113. ---. *The Making of Superstars: The Artists and Executives of the Rock Music World.* Garden City, NY: Doubleday, 1978.
A book about some of the people in the rock business. Spitz says it is a "behind-the-scenes view" of how they got interested in music and how they progressed in the music world. Sixties people include Janis Ian, Grace Slick, Jerry Wexler, and others.

1114. Stambler, Irwin. *Encyclopedia of Pop, Rock and Soul.* Rev. ed. New York:
St. Martin's Press, 1989.
An alphabetical listing by person or group name. Although it covers
most people, there are some important people missing, e.g., Barry
McGuire, Karla Bonoff. Also includes listings of gold and platinum
record award winners, Oscar winners, and photos.

1115. Szatmary, David P. *Rockin' in Time: A Social History of Rock and Roll.*
Englewood Cliffs, NJ: Prentice Hall, 1987.
Szatmary explores the history through the blues, Elvis and rockabilly,
Dick Clark, Bob Dylan, the British invasion, acid rock, black rock,
Woodstock, corporate rock, and on into the 1970s and 1980s. He looks at
the effect of technology, the economy and American business, and
politics on rock.

1116. Vassal, Jacques. *Electric Children: Roots and Branches of Modern Folk
Rock.* New York: Taplinger Publishing, 1976.
The history of folk-rock from a Frenchman's point of view.

1117. Ward, Ed, Geoffrey Stokes, and Ken Tucker. *Rock of Ages: The Rolling
Stone History of Rock & Roll.* New York: Rolling Stone Press, 1986.
Divided by decade from the 1950s to the 1980s, this is a comprehensive,
entertaining history of rock music. Photos included.

1118. Weiner, Rex and Deanne Stillman. *Woodstock Census: The Nationwide
Survey of the Sixties Generation.* New York: Viking Press, 1979.
The results of a survey taken of over 1000 sixties people on all kinds of
questions about their experiences and ideas. The survey questionnaire
is included.

1119. Yorke, Ritchie. *The History of Rock 'n' Roll.* London: Methuen, 1976.
A photohistory, with text, of rock from 1955 to 1975. Also included is a
brief chronology of the development of popular music.

Media Bring the Message

1120. Agee, Warren K., ed. *Mass Media in a Free Society*. Lawrence: UP of
      Kansas, 1969.
      Several famous journalists look at their trade in the 1960s. There are
      essays on the press and government, the press as a voice of change,
      television, and movies.

1121. Arlen, Michael J. *Living-Room War*. New York: Viking Press, 1966.
      A series of articles that appeared in *The New Yorker*. Some are about
      television coverage of the Vietnam war, but many of them are
      comments on the various types of programs that were on the air in the
      1960s.

1122. Aronson, James. *Deadline for the Media: Today's Challenges to Press, TV,
      Radio*. Indianapolis, IN: Bobbs-Merrill, 1972.
      The communication industry's upheavals paralleled the upheavals in
      the country during the 1960s in several ways: the government
      administration began putting pressure on them to curtail their
      investigations while much of the country was asking for greater
      honesty; the rise of the underground press challenged the established
      press to modify their own style; black journalists became regulars on
      staffs; women began to organize and demand equality in the
      newsrooms; the communication industry was making great
      technological changes. The publication of the Pentagon Papers in 1971
      brought to the fore the questions of First Amendment rights. This
      books examines the communications fortress which stands in the way of
      opening up the communication industry and broadening its scope and
      responsibilities.

1123. ---. *Packaging the News, A Critical Survey of Press, Radio and TV*. New
      York: International, 1971.
      Aronson argues that the media has become an arm of the government--
      it is managed by the administration in power. The author cites many
      instances which support this view, mostly taken from the first term of
      the Nixon administration.

1124. Braestrup, Peter. *Big Story: How the American Press and Television Reported and Interpreted the Crisis of Tet 1968 in Vietnam and Washington.* Boulder, CO: Westview Press, 1977.
Braestrup studied the Associated Press, the *New York Times, Time, Newsweek,* and the news shows of ABC, CBS, and NBC for their coverage of Tet. He found that the journalists did not distort the news but were overwhelmed by the events, so that any distortion of news was influenced more by the complexity rather than by ideology. Photos included.

1125. Dennis, Everette E. *The Magic Writing Machine: Student Probes of the New Journalism.* Eugene: School of Journalism, U of Oregon, 1971.
Student papers on New Journalism covering such areas and people as Esquire's nonfiction, Tom Wolfe, Norman Mailer, Gloria Steinem, underground newspapers, the military underground press, and precision journalism.

1126. Dennis, Everette, and William L. Rivers. *Other Voices: The New Journalism in America.* San Francisco: Canfield Press, 1974.
New journalism without the capital letters. Describes seven types of new journalism: new nonfiction, alternative journalism, journalism reviews, advocacy journalism, counterculture journalism, alternative broadcasting, and precision journalism. Each type is defined and explained. This is a much broader view of what New Journalism is than Tom Wolfe's.

1127. Divoky, Diane, ed. *How Old Will You Be in 1984? Expressions of Student Outrage from the High School Free Press.* New York: Avon Books-Discus, 1969.
Articles from high school underground papers on the schools, the students, and society, with a revolutionary bent.

1128. Dobrow, Larry. *When Advertising Tried Harder: The Sixties, the Golden Age of American Advertising.* New York: Friendly Press, 1984.
An overview of advertising in the 1960s, considered revolutionary and ingenious even today.

1129. Draper, Robert. *Rolling Stone Magazine: The Uncensored History.* Garden City, NY: Doubleday, 1990.
The story of *Rolling Stone Magazine,* which started as a music magazine in 1967 and still thrives today as a magazine of American culture and music. Through its years it has contributed for the fame of Hunter Thompson, Greil Marcus, Annie Liebovitz, and many others.

1130. Felton, David. *Shots: Photographs from the Underground Press.* New York: Douglas, 1971.
Photographs taken by photographers of the underground press. Subjects are Vietnam, Berkeley, Columbia, marches in Washington, New Haven

and Chicago, the Black Panthers, communes, People's Park, and the Chicago Democratic Convention.

1131. Forcade, Thomas King, ed. *Underground Press Anthology*. New York: Ace Books, 1972.
A collection of articles from the underground presses by such writers as Leary, Ed Sanders, Huey Newton, Dick Gregory, Todd Gitlin, Robin Morgan, Jean Genet, Bernadine Dohrn, and others.

1132. Friendly, Fred W. *Due to Circumstances Beyond Our Control*. New York: Random House-Vintage Books, 1967.
An examination of broadcast journalism--especially CBS. Friendly criticizes the directions television was moving in during the 1960s and offers suggestions for improving it.

1133. Gans, Herbert J. *Deciding What's News: A Study of CBS Evening News, NBC Nightly News, Newsweek, and Time*. New York: Pantheon Books, 1979.
Most of this study was done between 1965 and 1969. Gans discusses coverage of war protesters, the Vietnam war, and other 1960s issues.

1134. Gitlin, Todd. *The Whole World Is Watching: Mass Media in the Making and Unmaking of the New Left*. Berkeley: U of California P, 1980.
The relationship of the mass media to the New Left in the 1960s. Gitlin feels mass media both hurt and helped the various movements.

1135. Glessing, Robert J. *The Underground Press in America*. Bloomington: Indiana UP, 1970.
A detailed look at the underground newspapers in the 1960s. Includes a list of papers, a glossary, and some sample pages from papers.

1136. Gross, Gerald, ed. *The Responsibility of the Press*. New York: Fleet Publishing, 1966.
Essays offering viewpoints as to the responsibilities of the press-- newspapers, magazines, television, TV shows about lawyers, educational television, and book publishers and reviewers. Specific cases looked at are reporting of the Vietnam war and the responsibility of the press during the John F.K. assassination.

1137. Hallin, Daniel C. *The "Uncensored War": The Media and Vietnam*. New York: Oxford UP, 1986.
Hallin studies television and *New York Times* coverage of the Vietnam war and concludes that 1) the U.S. press was not consistently anti-U.S. policy, and 2) that the U.S. press did not significantly affect public opinion towards the war.

1138. Hopkins, Jerry, ed. *The Hippie Papers: Notes from the Underground Press.*
New York: NAL-Signet Books, 1968.
Selections from underground papers all over the country on all subjects.
Also includes cartoons and illustrations. Most are from 1967.

1139. Howard, Mel, and Thomas King Forcade, eds. *The Underground Reader.*
New York: NAL, 1972.
Writings printed in many of the underground papers of the 1960s.
Writers include James Baldwin, William S. Burroughs, Tim Leary,
Allen Ginsberg, John Sinclair, Huey Newton, Dick Gregory,
Buckminster Fuller, Eldridge Cleaver, and many more.

1140. Johnson, Michael L. *The New Journalism: The Underground Press, the
Artists of Nonfiction, and Changes in the Established Media.* Lawrence:
UP of Kansas, 1971.
Johnson defines New Journalism as including the underground press.
He had a positive attitude towards New Journalism, calling it fresh and
creative. In this book, he explored all types of New Journalism and the
writers who produced it.

1141. Knightley, Philip. *The First Casualty.* New York: Harcourt Brace
Jovanovich-Harvest, 1975.
A history of war journalism. Two chapters are on journalism in
Vietnam.

1142. Kornbluth, Jessie, ed. *Notes From the New Underground: An Anthology.*
New York: Viking Press, 1968.
Articles published in the underground presses by writers such as Allen
Katzman, Paul Goodman, Michael McClure, Allen Ginsberg, Tom
Robbins, William Burroughs, and many others.

1143. Krassner, Paul. *How a Satirical Editor Became a Yippie Conspirator.* New
York: G.P. Putnam's, 1971.
A collection of writings from *The Realist,* one of the most popular,
iconoclastic magazines of the 1960s, from 1950-1968 by the editor, .

1144. ---, ed. *Best of the Realist.* New York: Running Press, 1984.
An anthology. Includes articles by Lenny Bruce, Kurt Vonnegut, Terry
Southern, Viva, Richard Pryor, and many others.

1145. Krock, Arthur. *In the Nation: 1932-1966.* New York: McGraw-Hill, 1966.
Articles from Krock's *New York Times* column of the same name. He
was close to both Kennedy and Johnson, but yet was able to see the
weaknesses of each.

1146. Ladd, Jim. *Radio Waves: Life and Revolution on the FM Dial.* New York:
St. Martin's Press, 1991.

A story of what it was like to work for FM rock stations since they began in 1967. Although most of the book covers the '70s and '80s, there are a few good chapters in the beginning on the '60s.

1147. Leamer, Lawrence. *The Paper Revolutionaries: The Rise of the Underground Press*. New York: Simon & Schuster, 1972
Leamer says that the underground press was the one unifying institution produced by the counterculture. He traces the development of the underground press as a part of the "radical-youth culture."

1148. Lewis, Roger. *Outlaws of America: The Underground Press and Its Context*. New York: Penguin Books, 1972.
An examination of the various underground presses of the 1960s in terms of the groups that produced them--"street people, Chicanos, artists, commune makers, hippies, and many others" Photos included.

1149. McGaffin, William, and Erwin Knoll. *Anything But the Truth: The Credibility Gap--How the News Is Managed in Washington*. New York: G.P. Putnam's, 1968.
The authors examine problems "of government secrecy, deception and distortion of the news" particularly in relation to the U2 affair, the Bay of Pigs, and Johnson's presidency.

1150. Minor, Dale. *The Information War*. New York: Hawthorn Books, 1970.
An exploration of the forces that were acting to restrict the flow of information and the ability of the press to act against those forces.

1151. Paul, Jon, and Charlotte. *Fire! Reports from the Underground Press*. New York: E.P. Dutton, 1970.
Writings, graphics, and photographs from underground presses all over the country.

1152. Reston, James. *The Artillery of the Press: Its Influence on American Foreign Policy*. New York: Harper & Row, Publishers, 1967.
An exploration of the relationship of the press and American foreign relations, and how the freedom of the press can sometimes complicate foreign relations.

1153. Rips, Geoffrey. *The Campaign Against the Underground Press*. San Francisco: City Lights, 1981.
A report on government harassment of the underground press movement. Includes essays by Allen Ginsberg, Todd Gitlin, Aryeh Neier, and Angus Mackenzie. Also includes copies of documents and examples of underground press pages.

1154. Romm, Ethel Grodzins. *The Open Conspiracy: What America's Angry Generation Is Saying*. Harrisburg, PA: Stackpole, 1970.

Excerpts from the underground and movement presses to represent
what youth's dissent is all about. Romm chose articles to show the
cultural scene and the political movement.

1155. Rosenthal, Raymond, ed. *McLuhan Pro and Con.* New York: Funk &
Wagnalls, 1968.
A short biography of McLuhan followed by several essays defending or
rejecting his ideas about mass media and their effects on society.

1156. Rosset, Barney, ed. *Evergreen Review Reader, 1957-1967: A Ten-Year
Anthology.* New York: Grove Press, 1969.
The Evergreen Review was an experimental magazine, leftist in point of
view. These selections, from a host of famous people, give a
representative overview of American culture of the times.

1157. Schoenfeld, Eugene, M.S.. *Dear Doctor Hip Pocrates.* New York: Grove
Press, 1968.
Schoenfeld did an advice column that was used in many underground
newspapers. Most of the questions he answered were related to sex and
drugs.

1158. Stansill, Peter, and David Zane Mairowitz, eds. *BAMN (By Any Means
Necessary): Outlaw Manifestos and Ephemera 1965-70.*
Harmondsworth, England: Penguin Press, 1971.
Materials from the United States, England, and Holland. Manifestos,
pamphlets, posters, and other ephemera which indicate the cultural and
political climate of the times.

1159. Stearn, Gerald Emanuel, ed. *McLuhan: Hot and Cool.* New York: Dial
Press, 1967.
A collection of essays, reviews, and interviews on McLuhan, as well as
materials by him and a dialog with him. Contributors include Tom
Wolfe, Kenneth Boulding, Frank Kermode, Dwight Macdonald, Susan
Sontag, and many others.

1160. Talese, Gay. *Fame and Obscurity.* New York: World Publishing, 1970.
Talese's definition of New Journalism follows closely that of Tom
Wolfe. This book is a collection of New Journalism pieces on such
subjects as Frank Sinatra, Joe Louis, and bridge builders, all written
during the 1960s.

1161. Ungar, Sanford J. *The Papers and the Papers: An Account of the Legal and
Political Battle over the Pentagon Papers.* New York: E.P. Dutton, 1972.
A detailed account of the decisionmaking that led up to the publication
of the Pentagon Papers, as well as the effects of their publication on the
government and the press.

1162. Watson, Mary Ann. *The Expanding Vista: American Television in the Kennedy Years.* New York: Oxford UP, 1990.
A study of how television was used in the Kennedy years as a governing tool, probably for the first time. Watson also examines how television added richness to the record of his administration.

1163. Wolfe, Tom, ed. *The New Journalism.* New York: Harper & Row, Publishers, 1973.
This is a fine collection of New Journalism pieces from the 1960s. This book is also important because it contains Wolfe's definition of New Journalism, the one most accepted as definitive.

The New Enlightenment
of Women

1164. Allen, Mary. *The Necessary Blankness: Women in Major Fiction of the Sixties*. Urbana: U of Illinois P, 1976.
Allen finds writers' views of women during the rise of women's liberation to be reactionary; she feels women's roles should be expanding. The most notable quality of women in literature is their blankness--their lack of character. To back up her claims she analyzes Barth, Pynchon, Purdy, Kesey, Philip Roth, Updike, Oates, and Plath.

1165. Bernard, Jessie. *The Sex Game*. Englewood Cliffs, NJ: Prentice Hall, 1968.
An analysis of how communication differs between the sexes.

1166. ---. *Women and the Public Interest: An Essay on Policy and Protest*. Chicago: Aldine Publishing, 1971.
An examination of the issues policymakers must face in relation to the place of women in society.

1167. Bird, Caroline. *Born Female: The High Cost of Keeping Women Down*. New York: David McKay, 1969.
The author writes from the assumption that we are entering an age that will be more androgynous than sexist. Things are changing, but not fast enough. She examines the countercultural lifestyles as examples of new relationships, new families.

1168. Brenton, Myron. *The American Male*. New York: Coward-McCann, 1966.
An examination of gender stereotypes and how they constrain men as much as women.

1169. Carden, Maren Lockwood. *The New Feminist Movement*. New York: Russell Sage Foundation, 1974.
A study of women who were involved either in Women's Liberation (e.g., consciousness raising) and Women's Rights (e.g., NOW) groups during the mid-1960s and early 1970s.

1170. Chafe, William Henry. *The American Woman: Her Changing Social, Economic and Political Roles, 1920-1970*. New York: Oxford UP, 1972.

A history of feminism in the United States from the 1920s, with a chapter on the '60s movement. Good overview and interesting in that it was written by a man.

1171. Cohen, Marcia. *The Sisterhood: The Inside Story of the Women's Movement and the Leaders Who Made It Happen.* New York: Simon & Schuster, 1988.
Focuses on four 1960s leaders of the Women's Liberation Movement: Betty Friedan, Gloria Steinem, Germaine Greer, and Kate Millett. Photos included.

1172. Daly, Mary. *The Church and the Second Sex.* New York: Harper & Row, Publishers, 1968.
An early examination of discrimination against women in the Catholic Church.

1173. Davidson, Sara. *Loose Change: Three Women of the Sixties.* Garden City, NJ: Doubleday, 1977
A chronicle of the lives of three women, including the author, who graduated from the University of California at Berkeley in the mid-1960s. Each of them followed different paths--one a radical protester, one a follower of the art culture, and the last a noted journalist. A New Journalism style of writing.

1174. Doely, Sarah Bentley, ed. *Women's Liberation and the Church: The New Demand for Freedom in the Life of the Christian Church.* New York: Association Press, 1970.
Women write about their experiences in and concerns about women's "place" in the church. They mostly express dissatisfaction with the church's refusal to take them seriously.

1175. Ellis, Julie. *Revolt of the Second Sex.* New York: Lancer, 1970.
A history of women's liberation and a look at the organizations and activities popular in the 1960s.

1176. Ellmann, Mary. *Thinking About Women.* New York: Harcourt Brace Jovanovich, 1968.
An early survey of literature and language to reveal perceptions of women by men and by other women.

1177. Elshtain, Jean Bethke. *Women and War.* New York: Basic Books, 1987.
A thorough discussion of the place of the feelings towards war by women. There are some very good sections on women in the Vietnam war.

1178. Evans, Sara. *Personal Politics: The Roots of Women's Liberation in the Movement and the New Left.* New York: Random House-Vintage Books, 1979.

A history of the women's liberation movement as coming from civil rights activism and from the New Left. Evans' analysis comes from interviews with many women who were also beginning the movement that eventually broke many women away from the male-dominated Vietnam protest work.

1179. Ferguson, Charles W. *The Male Attitude.* Boston: Little, Brown, 1966.
An examination of the "cult of masculinity."

1180. Firestone, Shulamith. *The Dialectic of Sex: The Case for Feminist Revolution.* New York: William Morrow, 1970.
Basing feminism in its historical context, Firestone does one of the first Marxist analyses of feminism. She expands on Engels' dialectical materialism, substituting sex for class.

1181. Firestone, Shulamith, and Anne Koedt, eds. *Notes from the Second Year: Major Writings of the Radical Feminists.* New York: Radical Feminism, 1970.
A very important collection documenting the seminal issues of the Women's Liberation Movement.

1182. Freeman, Jo. *The Politics of Women's Liberation: A Case Study of an Emerging Social Movement and Its Relation to the Policy Process.* New York: David McKay, 1975.
A study, through participant observation, of the burgeoning women's liberation movement. The author participated in the organization of the first independent women's liberation group in the country. She discusses the roots of the movement as well as NOW, small groups, and policy.

1183. Gornick, Vivian, and Barbara K. Moran, eds. *Woman in Sexist Society: Studies in Power and Powerlessness.* New York: Basic Books, 1971.
A collection of readings gathered together to demonstrate that women's positions have been culturally defined solely as child bearers and companions to men. Writers include Jessie Bernard, Phyllis Chesler, Shulamith Firestone, Kate Millett, Cynthia Ozick, Elaine Showalter, and many others.

1184. Gruberg, Martin. *Women in American Politics: An Assessment and Sourcebook.* Oshkosh, WI: Academia Press, 1968.
A history of women in politics since 1920, and a sourcebook of the women's organizations in the U.S. at the time the author wrote. Gruberg argues that women have been forced into their political obscurity.

1185. Hole, Judith, and Ellen Levine. *Rebirth of Feminism.* New York: Quadrangle Books, 1971.
An analysis of the resurgence of feminism in the U.S. in the 1960s. Includes a history of U.S. feminism, a discussion of the "biological

differences" argument, "feminist social critique," and resistance to feminism. Section III delineates areas of action within the feminist movement. There is a chronology of feminist activities 1961-1971, and several feminist documents are included.

1186. Kanowitz, Leo. *Women and the Law: The Unfinished Revolution.* Albuquerque: U of New Mexico P, 1969.
An examination of the way the U.S. laws discriminate against women. Kanowitz looks at such aspects as single women, married women, civil rights, equal pay, and political rights.

1187. Lader, Lawrence. *Abortion.* Indianapolis: Bobbs-Merrill, 1966.
An examination of the abortion issue from a pro-abortion point of view.

1188. Lifton, Robert J. *The Woman in America.* Boston: Houghton Mifflin, 1965.
Early essays on women by such writers as Erik Erikson, Diana Trilling, David Riesman, and Alice Rossi.

1189. Marshall, Kathryn. *In the Combat Zone: An Oral History of American Women in Vietnam, 1966-1975.* Boston: Little, Brown, 1987.
Interviews with twenty women, some who were nurses in Vietnam, some who were not.

1190. Mattfield, Jacqueline A., and Carol G. Van Aken, eds. *Women and the Scientific Professions: The M.I.T. Symposium on Women in Science and Engineering.* Cambridge, MA: MIT, 1965.
One of the first serious looks at women in the scientific disciplines.

1191. Merriam, Eve. *After Nora Slammed the Door; American Women in the 1960's: The Unfinished Revolution.* Cleveland: World Publishing, 1964.
Merriam's book is rather like Friedan's *The Feminine Mystique* (see entry 1228) in that she is trying to wake women up to the facts of their subordination. One of her premises, though, is that men do not have such a great life either and that there needs to be a total revolution for both sexes.

1192. Solanas, Valerie. *S C U M Manifesto.* New York: Olympia Press, 1968.
SCUM stands for Society for Cutting Up Men. Solanas has written a manifesto against men in which she says she wants to eliminate them and then gives her reasons. An early, extremist women's liberation tract. Solanas was the woman who later shot Andy Warhol.

1193. Tanner, Leslie B., ed. *Voices from Women's Liberation.* New York: NAL-Mentor, 1970.
A collection of essays from women. Some are Voices from the Past, e.g., Abigail Adams, Mary Wollstonecraft, Sarah Grimke, Susan Cady Stanton, and Susan B. Anthony, but most were written in the 1960s when the Women's Liberation Movement began to flourish again.

1194. Thompson, Mary Lou, ed. *Voices of the New Feminism.* Boston: Beacon Press, 1970.

 Several essays which point out the inequities women of the 1960s believed they were struggling under.

Religion and Its Alternatives

1195. Adams, John P. *At the Heart of the Whirlwind.* New York: Harper & Row, Publishers, 1976.
   The author presents several specific events of the '60s and '70s, e.g., the Poor People's Campaign and Kent State, and tells of some ways in which Christian ministries were attempted in the midst of these events.

1196. Altizer, Thomas J.J. *The Descent into Hell: A Study of the Radical Reversal of Christian Consciousness.* Philadelphia: J.B. Lippincott, 1970.
   Altizer takes the example of the revolutions which negate the past and look to the future and applies such thinking to theology. He shows that this model must be one for modern theologians to use.

1197. Baba Ram Dass. *Be Here Now.* San Cristobel, NM: Lama Foundation, 1971.
   Baba Ram Dass was Richard Alpert, the psychologist who with Timothy Leary experimented with hallucinogens, especially LSD, from the early 1960s. Later he travelled to India and studied Eastern religion with an Indian guru. This book tells of his experiences and presents, in an unusual format, his interpretation of Eastern philosophy.

1198. Beck, Hubert F. *The Age of Technology.* St. Louis: Concordia Publishing House, 1970.
   Beck theorizes about how the Christian faith should look at and respond to the new technological age. He looks at power, community, and life's tensions.

1199. Benson, Dennis C. *The Now Generation.* Richmond, VA: John Knox Press, 1969.
   An examination of rock music, youth, and Christianity. Benson focuses on the Beatles, Bob Dylan, Simon and Garfunkle, Arlo Guthrie, and Janis Ian.

1200. Berrigan, Daniel. *No Bars to Manhood.* Garden City, NY: Doubleday, 1970.
   A group of essays in which Berrigan relates religion and religious stories to the people and politics of the 1960s. Closes with two modern parables. Also includes a few poems.

1201. Berrigan, Philip. *Prison Journals of a Priest Revolutionary.* New York: Holt, Rinehart & Winston, 1967.
Reflections on freedom, war, religion, revolutionaries, and human life and relationships.

1202. Casteneda, Carlos. *The Teachings of Don Juan: A Yaqui Way of Knowledge.* Berkeley: U of California P, 1968.
Don Juan was a Yaqui Indian allegedly with powers of a sorcerer. Casteneda spent several years with him as an apprentice. In this book he describes Don Juan's teachings and use of drugs, and he analyzes don Juan's methodology.

1203. Clouse, Robert G., Robert D. Linder, and Richard V. Pierard, eds. *Protest and Politics: Christianity and Contemporary Affairs.* Greenwood, SC: Attic Press, 1968.
Essays on the Christian's responsibilities in dealing with such political issues as voting, the radical right, war, the welfare state, civil rights, and the population explosion.

1204. Colaianni, James. *The Catholic Left: The Crisis of Radicalism within the Church.* Philadelphia: Chilton Books, 1967.
Analyzes the Catholic Left in the church in the 1960s. Colaianni was himself a Catholic Leftist who loved his religion but felt that the church needed to change. He explores the crises of change--in authoritarianism, birth control, Catholic education, poverty, divorce, liturgy, and several other areas.

1205. Cooper, John Charles. *Religion in the Age of Aquarius.* Philadelphia: Westminster Press, 1971.
A book about the rise of interest in astrology and the occult in the 1960s American culture. Cooper ascribes this rise to the inability of religion to meet the new needs of youth.

1206. Ellwood, Robert S. *One Way: The Jesus Movement and Its Meaning.* Englewood Cliffs, NJ: Prentice-Hall,1973.
A description of the Jesus movement, as well as a look at it in the context of American culture. In addition, Ellwood looks at parallel phenomena in other times to compare them to the Jesus movement.

1207. Enroth, Ronald M., Edward E. Ericcson, Jr., and C. Breckinridge Peters. *The Jesus People: Old-Time Religion in the Age of Aquarius.* Grand Rapids, MI: Eerdmans, 1972.
An exploration of the various Jesus movements and an examination of them as social movements and Christian alternatives.

1208. Freedland, Nat. *The Occult Explosion.* New York: G.P. Putnam's, 1972.
An examination of occult groups that were springing up in the 1960s based on astrology, space travel (and extraterrestrials), and ESP. Forerunners to the New Age of the 1980s and 1990s.

1209. Gerlach, Luther P., and Virginia H. Hine. *People, Power, Change: Movements of Social Transformation*. Indianapolis, IN: Bobbs-Merrill, 1970.
Definitions and study of movements and radical change which specifically focus on Pentecostalism and Black Power.

1210. Gustafson, James M. *Sixties: Radical Change in American Religion*. Philadelphia: American Academy of Political and Social Science, 1970.
A special issue of *The Annals of the American Academy of Political and Social Science* focusing on religion in the 1960s, which the editor claims was in a state of "crisis." Articles cover such topics as Jewish theology, Catholicism in America, black churches, fundamentalism, Easter religions, and the Vietnam war.

1211. Gustaitis, Rasa. *Turning On*. New York: Macmillan Publishing, 1969.
Gustaitis is referring to turning on without drugs, or making oneself more aware and responsive. This book explores several sites where people went to learn to be more "turned on," e.g., Esalen, Tassajara, Morningstar Ranch, and people who were gurus, spreading their knowledge, e.g., Maharishi Mahesh Yogi, Timothy Leary, Fritz Perls.

1212. Howard, Jane. *Please Touch: A Guided Tour of the Human Potential Movement*. New York: McGraw-Hill, 1970.
Howard writes about her experiences in encounter groups all over the world to describe and analyze the human potential movement.

1213. Kleps, Art. *The Boohoo Bible*. San Cristobal, NM: Toad, 1971.
The handbook for the New American Church, the religion established by Leary and Kleps stressing enlightenment through the use of LSD.

1214. McFadden, Michael. *The Jesus Revolution*. New York: Harper & Row, Publishers-Harrow, 1972.
An overview of the turn to Christianity that many young people took in the late 1960s. McFadden wrote about several communes and spoke with many individuals.

1215. Mowry, Charles E. *The Church and the New Generation*. Nashville: Abingdon, 1969.
A call for churches to change so that they could reach and help the youth of the times.

1216. Novak, Michael. *Theology for Radical Politics*. New York: Herder & Herder, 1969.
Novak believed that a Christian had to be anti-American in the 1960s-- that the "American way of life" had become sacrilegious. In this book, he shows why he sides with the New Left and why he feels that radicals are leading America to a new sense of community, of theology.

1217. Raines, John C., and Thomas Dean. *Marxism and Radical Religion: Essays toward a Revolutionary Humanism.* Philadelphia: Temple UP, 1970.
A collection of essays which attempt to link Marxism, radical theology, and revolutionary humanitarianism.

1218. Ruether, Rosemary Radford. *The Radical Kingdom: The Western Experience of Messianic Hope.* New York: Paulist Press, 1970.
An historical examination of the religious motifs which operate in movements for radical social change. In the last section, Ruether looks at youth movements and the New Left of the 1960s.

1219. Schutz, William C. *Joy: Expanding Human Awareness.* New York: Grove Press, 1967.
A very popular self-help book of the 1960s to be used for attaining more joy and expanding human potential.

1220. Shinn, Roger Lincoln. *Man: The New Humanism.* Philadelphia: Westminster Press, 1968.
An examination of the rise of humanism in society and religion.

1221. Streiker, Lowell D. *The Jesus Trip: Advent of the Jesus Freaks.* Nashville: Abingdon, 1971.
An analysis of the Jesus movement by a highly qualified scholar. He interviewed youth and leaders and lived with a few of these groups for a while.

1222. Struchen, Jeanette. *Zapped by Jesus.* Philadelphia: J.B. Lippincott, 1972.
Quotes from the *Bible* and "hip" responses designed to appeal to youth and to attract them to the Jesus movement. Photos included.

1223. Tipton, Steven, M. *Getting Saved from the Sixties: Moral Meaning in Conversion and Cultural Change.* Berkeley: U of California P, 1982.
A study of the conversion of 1960s youth to alternative religious movements to find moral meanings in their lives.

1224. Ward, Hiley H. *The Far-Out Saints of the Jesus Communes.* New York: Association Press,1972.
The author travelled to several Jesus People communes and reported on such things as integration, sex, social action, links with the occult, their finances, and their leadership. He generally seems positive about all of them except the Children of God.

Major Influential Literature

1225. Brown, Norman. *Love's Body*. New York: Random House, 1966.
An influential philosophical work that defines man's state as one of
alienation. Much of the book is a series of quotes from other writers and
philosophers.

1226. Drucker, Peter F. *The Age of Discontinuity: Guidelines to Our Changing
Society*. New York: Harper & Row, Publishers, 1969.
Drucker believed that the transition from this century to the next would
be marked by drastic changes in society. He looks at these changes in
relation to the new industries and economics, the growth of
organizations and concern for the individual, and the importance of
knowledge.

1227. Erikson, Erik H.. *Identity: Youth and Crisis*. New York: W.W. Norton,
1968.
This writer was popular in the 1960's. Most of the essays, which attempt
to explain youth and its problems, were written in the 1950's.

1228. Friedan, Betty. *The Feminine Mystique*. New York: W.W. Norton, 1963.
This is one of the seminal works which triggered the '60s Women's
Liberation Movement. The "mystique" Friedan refers to is the idea that
women should find complete fulfillment in the home as wives and
mothers.

1229. Galbraith, John Kenneth. *The New Industrial State*. Boston: Houghton
Mifflin, 1967.
An interpretation of current (1960s) economics. It is Galbraith's theory
that power resides in large corporations. They fix the prices and then
accommodate the consumers to their needs. This idea closely fit the
radicals' belief that America had become a huge military-industrial
complex and that this complex was unresponsive to individuals.

1230. Goodman, Paul. *Growing Up Absurd: Problems of Youth in the Organized Society.* New York: Random House-Vintage Books, 1960.
An influential book on the problems of growing up in technological society and the reasons that made youth reject becoming part of the Establishment.

1231. Greer, Germaine. *The Female Eunuch.* New York: McGraw-Hill, 1970.
One of the more famous manifestos of the women's liberation movement. Greer argues that in a sense women have been castrated-- that they have been educated to be ineffective and that they should know themselves to become more powerful.

1232. Huxley, Aldous. *The Doors of Perception.* New York: Harper & Row, 1963.
Published first in 1954, this is a classic for the hippies in the 1960s. It is Huxley's description of an incident during which he had taken mescaline, and it is beautifully descriptive of the hallucinogenic drug "trip."

1233. Laing, R.D. *The Politics of Experience.* New York: Pantheon Books, 1967.
A form of psychology based on man's alienation from man-- existentialist psychology. All behavior is based on experience. Schizophrenia may be a way of healing our alienation.

1234. Lavan, George, ed.. *Ché Guevara Speaks: Selected Speeches and Writings.* New York: Grove Press, 1967.
Speeches, articles, interviews, and letters from Ché, a hero to American 1960s activist youth. The period covered was 1959 to Ché's death in Bolivia in 1967.

1235. McLuhan, Marshall. *The Gutenberg Galaxy: The Making of Typographic Society.* Toronto: U of Toronto P, 1962.
A powerful argument for the ways in which print closed society and now (or in the 1960s) the new technology, especially television, forces man into a more open, global community.

1236. ---. *Understanding Media: The Extensions of Man.* New York: NAL-Signet Books, 1964.
A look at the media that man was using as an extension of himself. McLuhan looks at the spoken word, the written word, clothing, housing, money, comics, the press, games, advertisements, the telephone, movies, radio, and many more things.

1237. McLuhan, Marshall, and Quentin Fiore. *The Medium Is the Massage.* Bantam Books, 1967.
McLuhan shows how the medium--technology specifically--is reshaping our relationships and every other pattern of our personal lives. The book itself is an example of mixed medium, very nonlinear, with graphics done by Fiore.

1238. Mao Tse Tung. *Quotations from Chairman Mao Tse-Tung*. Edited by Stuart R. Schram. New York: Praeger Publishers, 1967.
The *Little Red Book* read by Chinese and Americans, Mao's quotations became a Bible for 1960s revolutionaries.

1239. Marcuse, Herbert. *Counterrevolution and Revolt*. Boston: Beacon Press, 1972.
In this book, Marcuse argues that the Establishment won over the revolutionary forces in the country, but only temporarily. He also explains his "new aesthetics."

1240. ---. *An Essay on Liberation*. Boston: Beacon Press, 1969.
Marcuse believed that advanced technology could end any physical blocks to utopian society. But society cannot improve until it changes drastically so that the world can host an environment of liberation. The establishment, he felt, was oppressive.

1241. ---. *One Dimensional Man: Studies in the Ideology of Advanced Industrial Society*. Boston: Beacon Press, 1964.
Very influential. An analysis of advanced technological societies which suppress individuality and encourage the growth of the societal corporation. Though man may be becoming free from want, he may be losing his autonomy.

1242. Masters, William H., and Virginia E. Johnson. *Human Sexual Response*. Boston: Little, Brown, 1966.
A classic. A study of the physiologic aspects of sexual response with a view to bettering the sexual relationships by educating about the differences between male and female responsiveness.

1243. Millett, Kate. *Sexual Politics*. Garden City, NY: Doubleday, 1970.
A classic of the feminist movement. Millett's book is an analysis of patriarchy as a political institution. She offered a history of the institution and an analysis of four writers who, to her, exemplified her theories. The writers are D.H. Lawrence, Henry Miller, Norman Mailer, and Jean Genet.

1244. Reich, Charles. *The Greening of America*. New York: Random House, 1970.
The influence of Reich's book is attested to by its frequent citation in many books about the 1960s. In it, Reich discusses the new revolution brought about by a new consciousness in youth. Very optimistic and idealistic.

1245. Roszak, Theodore. *The Making of a Counter Culture: Reflections on the Technocratic Society and Its Youthful Opposition*. New York: Doubleday, 1969.
Roszak thought that the counterculture had the potential to free our society from the objective confines of technocracy. He explored different

political theorists (i.e., Marcuse, Norman Brown, Marx, and Freud), mysticism, the use of drugs, and theories of utopia. This book was a major influence on scholars and students of the time.

1246. Sartre, Jean-Paul. *Search for a Method*. New York: Alfred A. Knopf, 1963. In the early 1960s, Sartre, one of the leading existential philosophers, began to espouse Marxism, two philosophies that were accepted as being opposed to each other. In this book, Sartre shows how Marxism can work with existentialism.

The People Who Made
the Times

1247. Allen, Ivan Jr., with Paul Hemphill. *Mayor: Notes on the Sixties*. New
    York: Simon & Schuster, 1971.
    Memoirs of the man who was mayor of Atlanta during the 1960s. He
    was considered to be a liberal and he took Atlanta through its years of
    desegregation. He was mayor when Martin Luther King, Jr., was buried
    in Atlanta

1248. Alpert, Jane. *Growing Up Underground*. New York: William Morrow,
    1981.
    An autobiography of one women who was arrested for bombing several
    government buildings. She pleaded guilty and then went underground
    for more than four years.

1249. Aptheker, Bettina. *Morning Breaks: The Trial of Angela Davis*. New York:
    International Publishers, 1975.
    Aptheker was active in the movement to free Angela Davis. Both were
    Communist, so they shared ideologies and aims. In addition, they had
    known each other since the beginning of the civil rights movement.

1250. Baez, Joan. *And a Voice to Sing With: A Memoir*. New York: Summit
    Books, 1987.
    Her autobiography written just before she did her first new album in six
    years. She says she is writing for three reasons: 1) because she has lived
    a unique, exciting life and wants to share it; 2) because she still feels
    young and active and does not want to be relegated to nostalgia; and 3)
    she wants to take stock of the past before she faces the future.
    Photographs included.

1251. ---. *Daybreak*. New York: Dial Press, 1968.
    More of a mental autobiography than one which gives times, places, and
    names. Baez draws on her feelings and reactions to her growing up
    rather than actual incidents.

1252. Bennett, Lerone, Jr. *What Manner of Man: A Biography of Martin Luther
    King*. Chicago: Johnson Publishing, 1968.

The author was a schoolmate of King's at Morehouse College. The book was written when King was 35, just after he had been given the Nobel Prize for peace.

1253. Bloom, Lynn Z. *Doctor Spock: Biography of a Conservative Radical.* Indianapolis, IN: Bobbs-Merrill, 1972.
A biography of the famous baby-care expert and peace movement activist. Bloom concentrates on the public Spock and thus on his activities such as his writing of *Baby and Child Care* and his efforts in the peace movement of the 1960s.

1254. Bremser, Bonnie. *Troioa: Mexican Memoirs.* New York: Croton Press, 1969.
An autobiographical account of beat poet Ray Bremser and his wife's travels through Mexico in the 1960s, told from his wife's point of view. They had no money and Bonnie often worked as a prostitute to support them. In the end, they both returned to New York.

1255. Bruce, Lenny. *How to Talk Dirty and Influence People.* Chicago: Playboy Press,1965.
The autobiography of this comic who became a cult hero to many '60s people. His treatment of his early years reflects his comedic wit. However, his later years were plagued by arrests for obscenity and drugs and his tone becomes more somber and obsessive.

1256. Caserta, Peggy, as told to Dan Knapp. *Going Down with Janis.* New York: Dell Publishing, 1973.
A rather sensationalized account of Joplin's life written by a woman who owned a clothing boutique in San Francisco and who claims to have been a favorite lover of Joplin's. She dwells more than Friedman (see entry 1272) on Joplin's sex life and drug life. According to Caserta, Joplin was to blame for her own (Caserta's) addiction to heroin and eventual disintegration.

1257. Casey, William Van Etten, and Philip Nobile, eds. *The Berrigans.* New York: Praeger Publishers, 1971.
Essays which attempt to assess the significance of the Berrigan brothers. Also includes some documents on the Berrigans' trial, the indictment, and, from D. Berrigan, a "Letter to the Weathermen."

1258. Cassady, Carolyn. *Off the Road: My Years with Cassady, Kerouac, and Ginsberg.* New York: Penguin Books, 1990.
Although this begins before the 1950s, there is a significant portion devoted to the lives of these beat/hippie writers in the 1960s. Both Cassady and Kerouac died in the late 1960s. Photos included.

1259. Charters, Ann. *Kerouac: A Biography.* New York: Straight Arrow Press, 1973.

Kerouac's biography includes much information on other writers he
was close to--Ginsberg, Corso, Burroughs, and many others.
Photographs included.

1260. Chisholm, Shirley. *Unbought and Unbossed*. Boston: Houghton Mifflin,
1970.
Chisholm was the first black woman to be elected to Congress. In this
autobiography she gives her views on several issues, e.g., black
politicians, women's liberation, youth, the Vietnam war, and abortion.

1261. Clark, Dick, and Richard Robinson. *Rock, Roll & Remember*. New York:
Crowell, 1976.
Dick Clark's autobiography, mainly focusing on American Bandstand
music and music people of the late 1950s and early 1960s.

1262. Clark, Tom. *Jack Kerouac*. San Diego: Harcourt Brace Jovanovich, 1984.
A biography of Jack Kerouac. Photographs included.

1263. Cummings, Richard. *The Pied Piper: Allard K. Lowenstein and the Liberal
Dream*. New York: Grove Press, 1985.
A biography of Allard Lowenstein, who was a student leader, a civil
rights organizer, an anti-war activist, but who was also very anti-
Communist and worked for the CIA for a time.

1264. Dalton, David. *James Dean: The Mutant King*. New York: St. Martin's
Press, 1974.
Although James Dean died in 1955, he became a cultural hero who has
influenced many of the rock stars of the '60s, as well as youth in every
decade since. This biography captures the idol and the idolatry that
followed his death.

1265. ---. *Janis*. New York: Simon & Schuster, 1971.
Joplin's biography told through interviews, newspaper articles, and
photographs. Includes scores to some of her songs.

1266. Douglas, William O. *The Court Years, 1939-1975*. New York: Random
House-Vintage Books, 1980.
Douglas was a U.S. Supreme Court Justice during the sixties. He was
one of the few liberals on the court, and he championed civil rights and
questioned the constitutionality of the President to control the Vietnam
war. This book is the second volume of his autobiography.

1267. Dowley, Tim, and Barry Dunnage. *Bob Dylan: From a Hard Rain to a Slow
Train*. Tunbridge Wells, Eng: Midas Books, 1982.
A short biography of Dylan that focuses on the changes Dylan went
through. A discography and a few pictures are included.

1268. Eisele, Albert. *Almost to the Presidency: A Biography of Two American
Politicians*. Blue Earth, MN: Piper, 1972.

Biographies of Eugene McCarthy and Hubert Humphrey, whom the author says were "representative American politicians." Both were from Minnesota, as was the author.

1269. Farber, Tom. *Tales for the Son of My Unborn Child,* Berkeley, 1966-1969. New York: E.P. Dutton, 1971.
Sketches of people who were activists or hippies in Berkeley at the time.

1270. Fiedler, Leslie. *Being Busted.* New York: Stein and Day, 1969.
An autobiography which focuses on the author as dissenter, his struggles with society, and society's attempto to stifle dissent. Fiedler was arrested in 1967 for drug charges and most of the book is about the aftermath of this bust on his life and on his world view.

1271. Frady, Marshall. *Wallace.* New York: NAL-World, 1968.
An exploration of George Wallace during the time he was running for President in the 1968 campaign. Some early biographical information, but mainly a focus on his activities in the 1960s.

1272. Friedman, Myra. *Buried Alive: The Biography of Janis Joplin.* New York: Bantam Books, 1973.
Written by the woman who worked closely with Janis Joplin managing press relations for Albert Grossman, Joplin's manager. Friedman often accompanied Joplin to concerts and other events. She spends a great deal of time on Joplin's life before she became famous, as a young woman in Texas. This book is much more balanced than the one by Caserta (see entry 1256). Friedman does discuss Joplin's addictions, to speed (amphetamines), heroin, and alcohol, and her crazy breakneck life. Some photographs.

1273. Gambaccini, Paul. *Paul McCartney in His Own Words.* New York: Flash, 1976.
Paul McCartney tells his life story through interviews. He also talks about his music. Many photos included.

1274. Garbarini, Vic, and Brian Cullman, with Barbara Graustark. *Strawberry Fields Forever: John Lennon Remembered.* New York: Bantam Books, 1980.
Written right after Lennon's death, this book is a biography, but it focuses on his death. Includes a *Newsweek* interview, a chronological biography, and photos.

1275. Garry, Charles, and Art Goldberg. *Streetfighter in the Courtroom: The People's Advocate.* New York: E.P. Dutton, 1977.
The autobiography of a leftist lawyer. He fought against the death penalty, and HUAC and McCarthyism in the 1950s. In the 1960s, he defended Huey Newton, the Oakland Seven, and Bobby Seale.

1276. Ginsberg, Allen. *Journals: Early Fifties, Early Sixties*. NY: Grove Press, 1977.
A selection of Ginsberg's journal entries, including poetry and many
dream descriptions, from 1952 to 1962.

1277. Goldman, Albert. *The Lives of John Lennon*. New York: Bantam Books,
1988.
A very unflattering portrait of Lennon. Although Goldman shows
some sympathy for Lennon, admitting to his musical genius, he
obviously sees Yoko Ono as a driven, half-crazy, domineering woman.
Photos included.

1278. Grogan, Emmett. *Ringolevio: A Life Played for Keeps*. Boston: Little,
Brown, 1972.
Grogan was the main force behind the Diggers, a loosely organized
group who provided free food and other goods to the hippies of the
Haight-Ashbury. This is his autobiography, though it is hard to tell
what is fact and what fiction.

1279. Guevara, Ché. *Ché: Selected Works of Ernesto Guevara*. Edited by Rolando
Bonachea and Nelson P. Valdes. Cambridge, MA: MIT, 1970.
Guevara's writings spanning the years from 1958 to 1967--letters,
speeches, interviews. Biographical information included.

1280. Guiles, Fred Lawrence. *Jane Fonda: An Actress in Her Time*. New York:
Pinnacle Books, 1981.
An unauthorized biography that dwells more on her movie-making
than on her political activities.

1281. Guthman, Edwin. *We Band of Brothers*. New York: Harper & Row,
Publishers, 1971.
The author says he is writing of his experiences with Robert Kennedy
from 1956 until his death. He argues that Kennedy did not experience a
great transformation in his later years--that he was always as full of
concern for his country and its people with regard to the Vietnam war
and civil rights.

1282. Halpert, Stephen, and Tom Murray, eds. *Witness of the Berrigans*. Garden
City, NY: Doubleday, 1972.
A collection of essays on the Berrigans and their activities. Not
autobiographical, these essays reflect how various people felt about the
Berrigans as resisters, as fugitives, and as leaders.

1283. Hayden, Tom. *Reunion: A Memoir*. New York: Random House, 1988.
Tom Hayden, one of the most famous leaders of SDS, Jane Fonda's
former husband, California politician, here records his autobiography.
Includes photos.

1284. Henderson, David. *'Scuse Me While I Kiss the Sky: The Life of Jimi
Hendrix*. New York: Bantam Books, 1983.

A biography of Jimi Hendrix, one of the three famous 1960s rock stars who died before the end of the decade. Photos included.

1285. Hentoff, Nat. *Peace Agitator: The Story of A.J. Muste*. New York: Macmillan Publishing, 1963.
The biography of A.J. Muste, a peace activist for many years. In the '60s, Muste was in his seventies. Many of the serious '60s peace leaders of the 1960s cite him as one of their major influences.

1286. ---, ed. *The Essays of A. J. Muste*. Indianapolis, IN: Bobbs-Merrill, 1967.
An autobiographical sketch and a selection of this champion of nonviolence's writings from 1905-1966.

1287. Heylin, Clinton. *Bob Dylan: Behind the Shades*. New York: Summit Books, 1991.
Heylin says Dylan did not exert any influence on this biography, which means it is unauthorized. The uniqueness of this biography is that it is primarily concerned with Dylan after his motorcycle accident in 1966.

1288. Hoffman, Abbie. *Soon to Be a Major Motion Picture*. New York: G.P. Putnam's, 1980.
An autobiography written while Hoffman was still underground. Focuses mainly on his '60s activities. Does describe his early manic-depressive experiences which started while he was in hiding.

1289. Hopkins, Jerry, and Danny Sugarman. *No One Here Gets Out Alive*. New York: Warner Books, 1981.
The biography of Jim Morrison, of the Doors, with reference to much that was happening in the music world in the 1960s.

1290. Horwitt, Sanford D. *Let Them Call Me Rebel: Saul Alinsky--His Life and Legacy*. New York: Alfred A. Knopf, 1989.
A biography of this activist who began in the 1940s starting "People's Organizations" in Chicago and was active in the civil rights and war protests of the 1960s. Photos included.

1291. Hunt, E. Howard. *Undercover: Memoirs of an American Secret Agent*. New York: Berkley Publishing, 1974.
Hunt's autobiography. He was a CIA operative for most of his life and was jailed for his participation in the Watergate break-in.

1292. James, Daniel. *Ché Guevara: A Biography*. New York: Stein and Day, 1969.
Guevara, who died in Bolivia in 1967, was a leftist guerrilla leader who made his mark all over South America, but is most known for his Cuban adventures. He was a hero to leftists in America during the 1960s.

1293. Jarvis, Charles E. *Visions of Kerouac*. Lowell, MA: Ithaca Press, 1974.
       A biography of Jack Kerouac. Jarvis focuses on the rebelliousness of
       Kerouac. Photos included.

1294. Keats, John. *Howard Hughes*. New York: Random House, 1966.
       A biography of this elusive, powerful man.

1295. Kerouac, Jan. *Baby Driver*. New York: Holt, Rinehart & Winston, 1981.
       The autobiography of Jack Kerouac's daughter. Although he did not
       play a big part in her life, she lived the same kind of crazy lifestyle that
       he did, in a decade when that style became the way of life for many
       American youth.

1296. Kesey, Ken. *Kesey's Garage Sale*. New York: Viking Press, 1973.
       A collection of Kesey's writings and drawings. Some are fiction, but
       there are also reflections on him and his times. The book is like a giant
       scrapbook.

1297. Kiernan, Thomas. *Jane Fonda: Heroine for Our Time*. New York: G.P.
       Putnam's-Delilah, 1982.
       Much more on the political life than in Guiles (see entry 1280). Takes
       Fonda up to 1979, when she played in *The China Syndrome*.

1298. Koch, Thilo. *Fighters for a New World*. New York: G.P. Putnam's, 1968.
       Photographic essays which pay tribute to John F. Kennedy, Martin
       Luther King, and Robert F. Kennedy.

1299. Kostelanetz, Richard. *Master Minds: Portraits of Contemporary American
       Artists and Intellectuals*. New York: Macmillan Publishing, 1969.
       All are men who have created at least one "masterpiece." The fourteen
       portraits are of Glenn Gould, Ralph Ellison, John R. Pierce, Marshall
       McLuhan, John Cage, Bernard Muller-Thym, Richard Hofstadter, Allen
       Ginsberg, Milton Babbitt, Reinhold Niebuhr, Robert Rauschenberg, Paul
       Goodman, Elliott Carter, and Herman Kahn.

1300. Kramer, Daniel. *Bob Dylan*. New York: Citadel Press, 1967.
       Dylan between 1963 and 1965, at the time Dylan was beginning to
       capture fame in the music world. Kramer was a photographer, so
       mostly this book is photos, with a very little bit of text, of these two
       years.

1301. Leary, Timothy. *Confessions of a Hope Fiend*. New York: Bantam Books,
       1973.
       Leary's own account of his escape from prison in 1970 (with the help of
       the Weatherman), his flight to Algeria, his treatment by the Panthers,
       and his subsequent flight to Switzerland.

1302. ---. *Flashbacks: An Autobiography*. Los Angeles: J.P. Tarcher, 1982.
The flashbacks are of Leary's younger days before the death of his first wife. Photographs included.

1303. ---. *High Priest*. New York: World Publishing, 1968.
A sort of autobiographical account of Leary's and his friends' mystical experiences of the early 1960s.

1304. ---. *Jail Notes*. New York: Douglas Books, 1970.
Notes taken when Leary was in jail for drug use in 1970. Introduction by Allen Ginsberg.

1305. Lens, Sidney. *An American Activist's Account of Five Turbulent Decade: Unrepentant Radical*. Boston: Beacon Press, 1980.
Sidney Lens was a peace activist during the 1920s through the 1970s. His account included a long section on activism in the 1960s; he seemed to be in the middle of all the peace activity.

1306. McMillan, Priscilla Johnson. *Marina and Lee*. New York: Bantam Books, 1977.
Based on Marina Oswald's reminiscences, the story of Marina's and Lee Oswald's life together. Photos included.

1307. Miles, Barry. *Bob Dylan: In His Own Words*. New York: Omnibus, 1978.
This book is a collection of quotes from 1960 to 1978. They are grouped together under such topics as Biographical Fragments, the Music, the Albums, the Rock 'n' Roll Lifestyle. Includes many photos.

1308. ---. *Ginsberg: A Biography*. New York: Simon & Schuster, 1989.
Ginsberg is one of the most famous poets of this generation. He was at the forefront of all the 1960s movements and made friends with the cultural and political youth leaders.

1309. Miller, William Robert. *Martin Luther King, Jr: His Life, Martyrdom, and Meaning for the World*. New York: Weybright & Talley, 1968.
A biography of King, mainly his public persona.

1310. Peck, James. *Underdogs Vs. Upperdogs*. NY: AMP&R, 1980.
An autobiography. Peck was a conscientious objector in WWII, and in the sixties he was an activist for civil rights and for an end to the Vietnam war.

1311. Plimpton, George, ed. *American Journey: The Times of Robert Kennedy*. New York: Harcourt Brace Jovanovich, 1970.
A biography of RFK put together as an oral history or narrative. The whole book comes from interviews with people on or standing by Kennedy's funeral train.

1312. Raskin, Jonah. *Out of the Whale: Growing Up in the American Left.* New York: Links, 1974.
Raskin was one of the Red Diaper Babies of the 1960s radicals and in his autobiography he was able to show what it was these kids went through in the 1950s and how they easily moved into the radicalism of the 1960s.

1313. Ribakove, Sy and Barbara. *Folk-Rock: The Bob Dylan Story.* New York: Dell Publishing, 1966.
An early biography of Dylan and critical analysis of his music. Photographs included.

1314. Rojo, Ricardo. *My Friend Ché.* Trans. Julian Casart. New York: Grove Press, 1968.
Rojo knew Guevara for 14 years as a friend and co-revolutionary. This book tells his story about Ché's life. Photos included.

1315. Scaduto, Anthony. *Bob Dylan.* New York: Grosset & Dunlap, 1971.
A biography up to 1970 and Dylan's release of the album New Morning. Dylan reviewed the manuscript for this book and made some suggestions for it.

1316. Scheer, Robert, ed. *The Diary of Ché Guevara.* Bolivia: November 7, 1966 - October 7, 1967. New York: Bantam Books, 1968.
Made public by Cuba and with an introduction by Castro, this is the last accounting of Ché's life, his Bolivian campaign. Photos and photos of pages from Ché's diary included.

1317. Schlesinger, Arthur M. *Robert Kennedy and His Times.* New York: Ballantine Books, 1978.
A thorough, detailed biography of Robert Kennedy.

1318. Shelton, Robert. *No Direction Home: The Life and Music of Bob Dylan.* New York: William Morrow, 1986.
A thorough biography that takes Dylan from his childhood in Minnesota to the Live Aid concert in 1985. Includes a discography and song index.

1319. Sherrill, Robert, and Harry W. Ernst. *The Drugstore Liberal.* New York: Grossman Publishers, 1968.
A political biography of Hubert Humphrey.

1320. Solberg, Carl. *Hubert Humphrey: A Biography.* New York: W.W. Norton, 1984.
This biography ends with Humphrey's defeat in the 1968 presidential election. Well documented.

1321. Stein, Jean, edited with George Plimpton. *Edie: An American Biography.* New York: Alfred A. Knopf, 1982.

Edie is Edie Sedgwick, one of Andy Warhol's superstars. She was a rich girl from one of America's best families, and she was also eccentric. For a while she had the limelight as Warhol's favorite, but later she lost her popularity. She finally died as a result of a drug overdose. Her biography does a good job of showing the whole art/culture scene, of which Andy Warhol was a leader, of New York in the 1960s.

1322. Thompson, Toby. *Positively Main Street: An Unorthodox View of Bob Dylan.* New York: Coward-McCann, 1971.
A strange sort of biography of Dylan constructed out of a trip Thompson made to Minnesota and his encounters and interviews with all the people in Dylan's past.

1323. Tinnan, David B. *Just About Everybody vs. Howard Hughes.* Garden City, NY: Doubleday, 1973.
The case between Howard Hughes and TWA. A lot of biographical information is included.

1324. Viorst, Milton. *Hustlers and Heroes: An American Panorama.* New York: Simon & Schuster, 1971.
Profiles of political personages of the 1960s. Includes Dean Rusk, Richard Daley, Robert F. Kennedy, McGeorge Bundy, John Mitchell, William O. Douglas, Jacob Javits, Everett Dirkson, and others.

1325. Welch, Chris. *Hendrix.* New York: Delilah-G.P. Putnam's, 1978.
A photo-biography of Jimi Hendrix. Welch felt that Hendrix was at his best when he reached stardom in 1967, but that by 1970 he had gotten weaker and lost his spark.

1326. Wenner, Jann. *Lennon Remembers: The Rolling Stone Interviews.* New York: Rolling Stone Press, 1971.
An extensive interview with Lennon and Yoko Ono, December, 1970. Photos included.

1327. Williams, Don. *Bob Dylan: The Man, the Music, the Message.* Old Tappan, NJ: F.H. Revell, 1985.
A short biography of Dylan focusing on what led him to his conversion to Christianity in the early 1980s.

1328. Williams, Richard. *Out of His Head: The Sound of Phil Spector.* New York: Outerbridge & Dienstfrey, 1972.
This is a biography of Phil Spector, the rock producer noted for his "wall of sound." He produced such rock stars as the Ronettes, the Righteous Brothers, Ike and Tina Turner, and John Lennon.

Retrospectives on the Era

1329. Bonior, David, Steven M. Champlin, and Timothy S. Kolly. *The Vietnam Veteran: A History of Neglect*. New York: Praeger Publishers, 1984.
An analysis of how the returning Vietnam veteran was treated by our society. He was totally isolated, with little support for reintegrating from the Veterans Administration or other government agencies. The author looks at media coverage, failed leadership, and the actions of Congress and the Veterans Administration on behalf of veterans.

1330. Broyles, William, Jr. *Brothers in Arms: A Journey from War to Peace*. New York: Alfred A. Knopf, 1986.
Broyles served in Vietnam in 1969. In 1983, he went back to Vietnam; he talked to many Vietnamese, including a girl who had lived through My Lai, soldiers and generals of North Vietnam. He visited Hanoi and Saigon, as well as sites where he had fought. His story is a mixture of past and present, of anger and sorrow and guilt.

1331. Capps, Walter. *The Unfinished War: Vietnam and the American Conscience*. Boston: Beacon Press, 1982.
Ties the experience of the Vietnam war to the "revitalization of conservative religion" and the "new spirituality."

1332. Casale, Anthony M., and Philip Lerman. *Where Have All the Flowers Gone? The Fall and Rise of the Woodstock Generation*. New York: Andrews and McMeel, 1989.
From 1969 to 1988, the authors analyze what happened to the Woodstock generation. They saw a reawakening of the activism in such issues as the environment, AIDS activism, and several other issues that affect the generation as it ages.

1333. Collier, Peter and David Horowitz. *Destructive Generation: Second Thoughts About the Sixties*. New York: Summit Books, 1989.
Part political analysis and part memoir, the authors look back at the people and events of the 1960s. They assess the times and reject them as both dangerous and immature.

1334. ---. *Second Thoughts: Former Radicals Look Back at the Sixties.* New York: Madison Books, 1989.
A collection of essays from a conference of former 1960s radicals in which the common theme was that the 1960s turned out to be a failure personally and a disaster for the U.S.

1335. Conlin, Joseph Robert. *Troubles: A Jaundiced Glance Back at the Movement of the Sixties.* New York: Watts, 1982.
A book of reflections on the happenings of the 1960s. The author feels that not only were the 1960s not humanistic, not selfless, not radical, but they were not even important.

1336. Emerson, Gloria. *Winners and Losers: Battles, Retreats, Gains, Losses, and Ruins from a Long War.* New York: Random House, 1976.
Emerson was assigned to Vietnam in 1970 by the *New York Times.* In this book, she goes back and forth between then and now, sharing hers and others' experiences in Vietnam and in the United States as a result of Vietnam.

1337. Ericson, Edward E., Jr. *Radicals in the University.* Stanford: Hoover Institution Press, 1975.
A retrospective study of SDS and the old guard New Leftists' impact on academia and academic research in the 1970s.

1338. Gelb, Leslie H., with Richard K. Betts. *The Irony of Vietnam: The System Worked.* Washington: Brookings Institution, 1979.
An investigation into the decision-making that went on during the Vietnam war. It is the author's contention that, though the policies failed, the "domestic decisionmaking system" worked.

1339. Gottlieb, Annie. *Do You Believe in Magic? Bringing the Sixties Back Home.* New York: Simon & Schuster, 1987.
Gottlieb recounts the 1960s through interviews with the people born between 1945-1955. She feels that there is a new interest among these people in reflecting on what happened during the 1960s and a new stirring of energy in the ones she talked to.

1340. Horne, A.D., ed. *The Wounded Generation: America After Vietnam.* Englewood Cliffs, NJ: Prentice Hall, 1981.
A retrospective look at Americans and the generation of people who fought in Vietnam and whose lives are still being affected by the war.

1341. Jeffords, Susan. *The Remasculinization of America: Gender and the Vietnam War.* Bloomington: Indiana UP, 1989.
Jeffords defends her argument that current interest in the Vietnam war is based on relations of gender and a reinforcement of masculinity and patriarchy.

1342. Kessler, Lauren. *After All These Years: Sixties Ideals in a Different World.* New York: Thunder's Mouth Press, 1990.
Kessler follows up on the subsequent lives of 50 people important in the 1960s counterculture to show how they have integrated their earlier commitments into their present lifestyles.

1343. *Rolling Stone* Editors. *The Age of Paranoia: How the Sixties Ended.* New York: Pocket Books, 1972.
Journalism pieces written between November, 1967, and October, 1970. Documentation of the end of the 1960s spirit.

1344. Schafer, D. Michael, ed. *The Legacy: The Vietnam War in the American Imagination.* Boston: Beacon Press, 1990.
Essays that explore the ways that the Vietnam war is still affecting America today. The writers explore issues such as the veterans, the media, blacks, women, domestic policy, and the Vietnamese now living in America.

1345. Whalen, Jack and Richard Flacks. *Beyond the Barricades: The Sixties Generation Grows Up.* Philadelphia: Temple UP, 1989.
The authors have identified a group of 1960s activists and analyzed how their youth affected their adult lives. Their conclusions are that 1960s activists did not follow the paths of normal adult lives and that those 1960s activists are still being affected by their idealism.

Subject Index

Numbers used in the indexes refer to entry numbers, not page numbers.

Toys, 5

U-2 incident, 100, 142
Ultra-Resistance, 460
Ultra Violet, 1029
Underground press, 69, 1127, 1130-31, 1135, 1138-40, 1142, 1147-48, 1151, 1153-54, 1157
United States: Congress, 126, 141; foreign relations, 106, 121, 124, 126, 131, 134, 143, 170, 265, 269, 760, 765, 824, 837; history, 6, 55, 67; post WW II, 14, 66, 125
United States-Soviet relations, 100
Universities, 322, 330, 348, 352, 360, 362-65, 368-73, 375-87, 391, 395-98, 400, 403-4, 406-8, 540, 1337. See also Students
Updike, John, 1164
Upper class, 110
U.S.S. Pueblo incident, 9, 47

Vanderbilt University, 375
Vietnam Moratorium Committee, 899
Vietnam Summer, 519
Vietnam Veterans Against the War, 901, 921
Vietnam war, 4, 46, 51, 53, 62, 65, 73, 77-78, 117, 121, 124, 126, 133-34, 153, 157-58, 227, 229, 239, 242, 254, 265, 277, 291, 765, 782-84, 787, 790-92, 794-95, 800, 802-3, 806, 809-11, 817, 821, 823-25, 828, 833-39, 842, 843, 874, 892, 1121, 1137, 1141, 1330-31, 1336, 1338, 1341, 1344; atrocities, 849, 855, 858-66, 884, 904; friendly fire, 844; legality, 808, 821, 861, 871; My Lai, 838, 848, 851-52; prisoners of war, 846; protest and protesters, 120, 790-91, 805, 818, 867-927; Tet, 784, 1124; veterans, 7, 857, 859, 864-65, 1329, 1340; women, 1189. See also Anti-war movement; Peace

movement; Protest; Soldiers; War
Violence, 51, 93, 114, 123, 150, 409, 415, 423, 442, 444, 453, 457

Wall Street, 104
Wallace, George, 47, 70, 207, 776, 1271
War, 40, 124, 396, 798, 806-7, 814, 822, 827-28, 875, 900, 1177
Warhol, Andy, 1029
Warren Commission, 192, 196, 201, 205, 208, 216-217, 223-25
Washington, D.C., 226
Watergate, 10, 40, 133, 137, 155, 157, 188, 219, 262, 292-309
Watts riots, 70
Wayne, John, 20
Weatherman, 2, 25, 583-85, 587-88, 1248
West coast, 20, 23
White Panthers, 586
The Who, 1069, 1077
Wisconsin, University of, 503
Wofford, Harris, 181
Women, 1164-94, 1228, 1231, 1243
Women in the Movement, 2, 1178
Women's liberation, 9, 83, 1169-71, 1174-75, 1178. 1180-82, 1185, 1192-94, 1231, 1243
Woodstock, 601, 1042, 1086, 1112, 1118
Wooster College, 375
Working class, 94, 889

Yale University, 513
Yippies, 958
Youth, 28, 46, 50, 77, 310-408, 464-576, 1118, 1199, 1227, 1230, 1244-45, 1332; generation gap, 331, 334, 340-41, 347, 349, 452, 554, 718; adolescents, 326; legal rights, 351. See also Students

Zappa, Frank, 1103

Author Index

Boulding, Kenneth E.,   875
Bowen, Haskell, 665
Bowers, John Waite,   418
Boyd, Malcolm, 7
Boyle, Kay, 876
Braden, William,   8, 636
Braestrup, Peter, 1124
Brauer, Carl M.,   164
Breines, Paul, 719
Breines, Wini, 720
Bremser, Bonnie, 1254
Brenton, Myron,   103, 1168
Breslin, Jimmy, 292
Brickman, William W.,   476
Brode, Douglas, 996
Brooks, John, 104
Brown, Joe David,   598, 686
Brown, Len, 1034
Brown, Michael, 477
Brown, Norman, 1225
Brown, Peter, 1035
Brown, Robert McAfee,   877
Brown, Sam, 787
Broyles, William, Jr.,   1330
Bruce, Lenny, 1255
Bruno, Jerry, 152
Brustein, Robert, 419
Bryan, C.D.B., 844
Bryant, Barbara E., 317
Buchanan, James M.,   368
Buchanon, Thomas G.,   187
Buchwald, Art, 9
Buckhout, Robert, 420
Buckley, William F., Jr.,   10-11
Buckman, Peter, 421
Budds, Michael J.,   1036
Bugliosi, Vincent, 590
Bullock, Charles S., III,   30
Burchett, Wilfred, 878
Burke, John P., 153
Burner, David,   12, 165
Busnar, Eugene, 1037
Butler, Ed, 422
Butler, George, 901
Butz, Otto, 318

Cain, Arthur H.,   478
Calas, Elena, 997
Calas, Nicholas, 997
Califano, Joseph A., Jr.,   479
Calvert, Greg, 721
Campbell, James S.,   423
Canfield, Michael, 188
Canning, Jeremiah W.,   424
Cantelon, John E.,   369
Cantor, Milton, 722
Cantor, Norman F.,   425
Capaldi, Nicholas, 370
Capps, Walter, 1331
Carden, Maren Lockwood, 1169
Carey, James T., 637
Carling, Francis, 480
Carnegie Commission on Higher
    Education, 481
Carper, Jean, 788
Carr, Donald E., 963
Carr, Gwen B., 687
Carr, Roy, 1038
Carroll, Maurice C.,   185
Carroll, Paul, 998
Carson, Rachel, 964
Casale, Anthony M., 1332
Casale, Ottavio M.,   564
Case, John, 688
Caserta, Peggy, 1256
Casey, William Van Etten,   1257
Cashman, John, 638
Cassady, Carolyn, 1258
Castellucci, John, 583
Casteneda, Carlos, 1202
Castleman, Harry, 1039
Caute, David, 930
Cavan, Sherri, 622
Center for the Study of Democratic
    Institutions,   13
Chafe, William Henry,   14, 1170
Chalmers, David, 15
Champlin, Steven M.,   1329
Chapman, Bruce K., 789
Charlton, Michael, 790
Charters, Ann, 1259
Chertoff, Mordecai S., 723

Goheen, Robert, 378
Gold, Alice Ross, 506
Gold, Gerald, 296
Gold, Robert S., 437
Goldberg, Art, 1275
Goldman, Albert, 1277
Goldman, Eric F., 236
Goldstein, Richard, 29, 648, 1064
Goldwater, Senator Barry, 237
Goldwin, Robert A., 731
Golembiewski, Robert T., 30
Goode, Erich, 649
Goodman, Mitchell, 438
Goodman, Paul, 31, 1230
Goodman, Walter, 119
Goodwin, Richard N., 32
Gordon, Kermit, 267
Gordon, William A., 567
Gornick, Vivian, 1183
Gottfried, Martin, 1006
Gottlieb, Annie, 1339
Gould, Donna, 893
Goulden, Joseph C., 238
Graff, Henry, 239
Graham, Frank, Jr., 972
Graham, Hugh Davis, 442
Grant, Edward J., 568
Grant, Joanne, 507
Graubard, Stephen R., 379
Graustark, Barbara, 1274
Gray, Andy, 1065
Green, Gil, 732
Greenberg, Bradley, 199
Greenberg, Daniel, 949
Greene, Bob, 328
Greene, Felix, 847
Greene, Thayer A., 329
Greenfield, Jeff, 33, 152
Greenfield, Robert, 1066
Greenstein, Fred I., 153
Greer, Germaine, 1231
Gregor, A. James, 708
Grier, George, 695
Grinspoon, Lester, 650
Grogan, Emmett, 1278
Gross, Bertram M., 34

Gross, Gerald, 1136
Gruberg, Martin, 1184
Gruen, John, 597
Guevara, Ché, 1279
Guiles, Fred Lawrence, 1280
Gulley, Bill, 154
Gurr, Ted Robert, 442
Gustafson, James M., 1210
Gustaitis, Rasa, 1211
Guthman, Edwin, 1281

Hackett, Pat, 87
Hadley, Arthur T., 117
Halberstam, David, 802, 942
Haldeman, H.R., 297
Hale, Dennis, 725
Haley, J. Evetts, 240
Hall, Mitchell K., 894
Hallin, Daniel C., 1137
Halperin, Morton H., 120
Halpert, Stephen, 1282
Halstead, Fred, 895-96
Hamaliam, Leo, 733
Hamilton, Michael, 803
Hamm, Charles, 1067
Hammer, Richard, 848
Handel, Gerald, 330
Hanff, Helene, 508
Hansel, Robert R., 331
Hare, A. Paul, 439, 569
Harrington, Michael, 734
Harris, David, 35
Harroff, Peggy, 691
Hart, Richard L., 509
Haskins, James, 36
Hastings, Max, 943
Hayden, Tom, 440, 907, 944, 1283
Hayes, Harold, 37
Hayes, Thomas Lee, 897
Heath, Jim F., 38
Heath, Louis G., 510
Hedgepeth, William, 696
Hefferlin, J.B. Lon, 380
Heirich, Max, 511-12
Hemphill, Paul, 1247
Hendel, Samuel, 441

Title Index

About the Author

REBECCA JACKSON is coordinator for User Education at the Gelman Library, George Washington University, Washington, D.C. She has degrees in psychology, English, and library science, and has presented papers on topics ranging from Norman Mailer to the use of CD-ROM databases.